The Oceanic Feeling

The Origins of Religious Sentiment in Ancient India

Volume 3

The Oceanic Feeling

The Origins of Religious Sentiment in Ancient India

by

J. Moussaieff Masson

D. Reidel Publishing Company
Dordrecht : Holland / Boston : U.S.A. / London : England

Library of Congress Cataloging in Publication Data

CIP

Masson, Jeffrey Moussaieff, 1941-
The oceanic feeling.

(Studies of classical India; v. 3)
Bibliography: p.
Includes index.
1. Mysticism—India—Collected works. 2. Mysticism—Hinduism—Collected works. 3. Psychoanalysis and religion—Collected works. 4. Psychology, Religious—Collected works. 5. Mysticism—Psychology—Collected works. I. Title. II. Series.
BL2015.M9M36 294.5'01'9 80-11682

ISBN 90-277-1050-3

Published by D. Reidel Publishing Company,
P.O. Box 17, 3300 AA Dordrecht, Holland

Sold and distributed in the U.S.A. and Canada
by Kluwer Boston Inc., Lincoln Building,
160 Old Derby Street, Hingham, MA 02043, U.S.A.

In all other countries, sold and distributed
by Kluwer Academic Publishers Group,
P.O. Box 322, 3300 AH Dordrecht, Holland

D. Reidel Publishing Company is a member of the Kluwer Group

Printed in the Netherlands

Like everything else, for Terri and Simone

TABLE OF CONTENTS

FOREWORD

By way of a personal note, I can reveal to the reader that I was led to Sanskrit by an exposure to Indian philosophy while still a child. These early mystical interests gave way in the university to scholarly pursuits and, through reading the works of Franklin Edgerton, Louis Renou and Etienne Lamotte, I was introduced to the scientific study of the past, to philology and the academic study of an ancient literature. In this period I wrote a number of books on Sanskrit aesthetics, concentrating on the sophisticated Indian notions of suggestion. This work has culminated in a three-volume study of the *Dhvanyāloka* and the *Dhvanyālokalocana*, for the Harvard Oriental Series. Eventually I found that I wanted to broaden my concern with India, to learn what was at the universal core of my studies and what could be of interest to everyone. In reading Indian literature, I came across so many bizarre tales and ideas that seemed incomprehensible and removed from the concerns of everyday life that I became troubled. Vedantic ideas of the world as a dream, for example, to which I had been particularly partial, seemed grandiose and megalomanic. I turned away with increasing scepticism from what I felt to be the hysterical outpourings of mystical and religious fanaticism.

In order to get as far away as possible from the unintelligible, and impressed by the insights manifested in the works of Freud, Glover, Bernfeld, Fenichel and Fliess, I turned to the study of psychoanalysis. I did a full clinical training, a course of study that lasted eight years and included a personal analysis, three years of seminars on the psychoanalytic literature, and supervised control-analyses of three patients seen five days a week. After my training, I gradually became disillusioned with the parochialism and narrow interests of many analysts and, once again, I understood the value of learning a new language, a distant culture and a distant past. I now returned to Indian studies, my enthusiasm rekindled by a new perspective: my scepticism, fed by the absurdity of many of the unworldly assumptions upon which so much of Indian philosophy is based, had eroded my enthusiasm. Now, a new means of approach reawakened my interest and curiosity. Could these writings, these tales and legends, be understood as distorted expressions of ordinary human needs? Disguised pleas for love, affection and attention which we all need and seek in different, often bizarre ways? Was not a classical hysterical psychoneurosis, or an obsessional illness, at root a different expression for the same cravings? Perhaps the word I had used to dismiss what repelled me ('fanaticism') was simply a description in need of further explanation and having its own psychology. What, after all, lies behind the claim to omniscience and to omnipotence? Where do the claims of being able to fly and to walk on water and to speak with spirits stem from? Why would some people claim such powers for themselves, and still other people believe them? Asking these questions and attempting to answer them in a rigorous scientific manner produced the essays which make up this volume.

The essays which are the chapters of this book have not been published elsewhere. Written for a variety of occasions, they are tied together by a concern with the application to ancient India of psychoanalytic insights derived from a thorough study of the literature and gained from my clinical practice.

The introductory essay was written as a means of reviewing the literature on psychoanalysis and India and introducing the reader to those areas of ancient India that seem amenable to psychoanalytic scrutiny.

Chapters Two and Three, given as lectures at the University of California at Berkeley, and Oxford University contain my views on mysticism. I consider the states of feeling manifest in the practice of mysticism to be basically defenses against depression.

Chapter Four was delivered before the annual meeting of the American Psychoanalytic Association in Quebec City in 1977.

Chapter Five was given at the Annual *Rāmāyaṇa* Conference held in Berkeley in 1975.

Chapter Six was a lecture to the annual meeting of the Canadian Society for Asian Studies. As far as I know, nothing had been written on this curious encounter between Kṛṣṇa and a hunchback. I have gathered together the Sanskrit material, some of it little known, and I have brought out some of the psychological implications by reviewing the literature on sexual perversions. But a satisfying thesis uniting these two areas has yet to emerge.

Chapter Seven was first delivered as a lecture at Columbia University, then to the University of California at Berkeley, at the annual meeting of the American Oriental Society in Toronto in 1977, to the University of Vienna, and finally to Oxford University. Widely unpopular with audiences, it is nevertheless my favorite essay.

Dr. R. Lefeber, Mrs. M. Loring, Professor S. Sandahl-Forgue, Professor B.K. Matilal and Professor Phyllis Granoff offered many helpful suggestions. Professor Robert Goldman read through the manuscript and improved it noticeably. Ms. Pamela MacFarland read the final draft with great care and used her skill with the English language and her considerable knowledge of Sanskrit and psychoanalysis to improve the book. I am grateful to Dr. George Devereux, both for the inspiration I derived from reading his scholarly work and for writing a preface to this volume. My wife Terri improved my writing, my thinking and the whole book.

J. MOUSSAIEFF MASSON

München, 1980
Spring

GEORGE DEVEREUX

PREFACE

Some twenty years ago I asserted that an authentically inter-disciplinary paper must also be a contribution to each of the two constituent disciplines (Devereux, 1957). Professor Masson's book satisfies this requirement – which far too many books and papers on 'applied psychoanalysis' still fail to do – simply because the author, a leading specialist on India, is also a fully trained and practicing psychoanalyst. His Sanskritist reader will learn from his book something new pertaining directly to his profession: the psychoanalyst will derive from it illuminating theoretical and clinical insights. Both will gain a better understanding of the contributions psychoanalysis can make to all the sciences of Man.

The merits of this book are, thus, too obvious to require an endorsement. What is needed is an attempt to situate it – and what it represents – within the development of so-called 'applied psychoanalysis'. Though work in that field was initiated by Freud, few psychoanalysts seem to have realized that publications of this type played – and still play – a major role in the acceptance or rejection of psychoanalysis as a whole by the academic world. The psychoanalysts' failure to grasp this may, perhaps, be correlated with their long refusal to become involved with the academic community. It is hard to say whether, in so doing, they chose the splendid isolation of the ivory tower, or life in an intellectual ghetto. The tendency of many psychoanalysts to respond to incomprehension with the arrogant assertion that the unanalysed cannot possibly comprehend psychoanalysis also disregarded the crucial fact that antagonism to psychoanalysis was, in many instances, elicited not by theoretical and clinical publications, but by books and papers on applied psychoanalysis, whose scientific deficiencies shocked the specialists of the disciplines which 'applied' psychoanalysts 'invaded' without adequate preparation.

The 'public relations' role of writings on 'applied psychoanalysis' is glaringly highlighted by the influence of *Totem and Taboo* on the shaping of anthropological reactions to psychoanalysis as a whole. Kroeber's review of that work (1920) decisively influenced anthropological attitudes toward psychoanalysis *as a science*; Kroeber's subsequent reappraisal (1939) of his own review and of Freud's book was much less influential. In 1920, as in 1939, Kroeber highlighted the genuine methodological deficiencies of *Totem and Taboo* as a contribution to anthropology. In neither of his two papers did he 'refute' psychoanalysis as a whole, nor did he claim to have done so. Yet many anthropologists seemed to think that Kroeber had shown that psychoanalysis had nothing to contribute to anthropological research – some of them even held that he had proven psychoanalysis to be a fanciful pseudoscience. One result of this misunderstanding was that it left anthropology wide open for the pedestrian teachings of the so-called neo-Freudians.

It is a regrettable fact that many authors of works on 'applied psychoanalysis' have either been reputable psychoanalysts who did not take the trouble to familiarize themselves with the basic data and methods of the disciplines they 'invaded', or else scholars who knew their own discipline thoroughly, but had no real understanding of the theories, methods and data of scientific psychoanalysis. As a result, large segments of the field of 'applied psychoanalysis' present a rather dismaying spectacle. This has had a disastrous influence on the 'image' of psychoanalysis in academic circles.

Since it is evident that really sound work in applied psychoanalysis can only be done by persons possessing a dual competence, it is an encouraging development that experts in more and more disciplines are acquiring a complete training in psychoanalysis, in order to improve their insight into the facts and methods *of their own discipline.* The trail blazed by the anthropologist Géza Róheim, by the art historian Ernst Kris, etc., is broadened every day.

So far as I know, Professor Masson is the first Sanskritist to have acquired a complete psychoanalytic training and to engage in the practice of psychoanalysis. The earlier incursions of psychoanalysts into the field of ancient Indian studies have, as he indicates, been far from satisfactory. An immensely rich field of inquiry has been opened by him to psychoanalytic exploration. The present book is, thus, a landmark in the history of applied psychoanalysis.

The merits of this book should be obvious to anyone who knows the difference between scientific applied psychoanalysis and the pursuit of a mere hobby. Professor Masson's eminence as a Sanskritist is evident on every page.

Equally striking is the author's competence and originality in the field of psychoanalysis proper. There is no routine, unimaginative appeal to dictionaries of symbols, no music-boxlike, repetitive recourse to technical terms applied mechanically to anything and everything.

In the author's hands the world of ancient India comes to life. Living tissue is not dissected into complexes, defense mechanisms or whatever. The dead letter of tradition is resuscitated by a creative understanding, growing out of a complete grasp of psychoanalytic theory and out of indispensable clinical experience as well.

Actually, Professor's Masson's book does more than simply satisfy the criterion of dual competence, by making original contributions both to Sanskrit philology and to psychoanalysis. Most of his chapters are veritable models of what authentic applied psychoanalysis is, or should be. It is to the author's credit that where I do agree with him, which is most of the time, he does not simply confirm my pre-existing knowledge or views: he invariably broadens, deepens and refines them. As to the few details on which our views differ, the author's presentation of his point of view produces *creative* dissent.

In short, this fine book has much to offer to many. And not the least of its merits is a systematic avoidance of the kind of autistic, riddling rhetoric which is so fashionable in our day and age. The clarity of this brilliant book marks it as the work of an authentic scientist.

GEORGE DEVEREUX

References

Devereux, G.: 1957, 'The Criteria of Dual Competence in Psychiatric-Anthropological Studies', *Journal of the Hillside Hospital* **6**: 87-90.

Kroeber, A. L.: 1920, 'Totem and Taboo: An Ethnological Psychoanalysis', in *The Nature of Culture*, A. L. Kroeber, 1952 301-305.

Kroeber, A. L.: 1939, 'Totem and Taboo in Retrospect', ibid. 306-309

I: INTRODUCTORY ESSAY ON THE APPLICATION OF PSYCHOANALYSIS TO THE INDIAN TRADITION

A certain degree of interest in a psychoanalytic approach to India has been stirred by the recent appearance of a major work by Erikson (1969) on Gandhi.[1] Prior to that work, an unusually sensitive[2] but highly controversial, psychoanalytically-oriented book by Carstairs, a British psychiatrist raised in India, had been published (1957), followed by a chaotic volume by Spratt (1966) not entirely devoid of insight. Apart from scattered observations of a psychoanalytic nature about India,[3] almost everything else published would have to constitute a negative bibliography.[4] The most sustained psychoanalytic treatment of Indian material appears in the scholarly and sophisticated monographs of Goldman (1978 and forthcoming).

This paucity of literature is puzzling, since there is nothing inherent in Indian culture, past or present, that would make it refractory to psychological investigation.

As a historical science, that is, a science concerned with unveiling and understanding the past, psychoanalysis seems ideally qualified as a tool of investigation into India's psychological past. "The dead", as the historian Frank Manuel put it, "do not ask to be cured, only to be understood". Like the discipline of history, the science of psychoanalysis is not content with simple, formulaic, surface explanations for human behavior. I agree with Jacques Barzun (1972) when he writes:

> History is not linear but miscellaneous; hence it does not isolate causes: It does not say: The Roman Empire declined *because* of Christianity, or *because* of malaria. . . .If the facts are true and relevant they are conditions, not causes. The more conditions we can enumerate and organize truthfully and intelligibly, the stronger will be our divination of past reality (p. 60).

Some of the insights Freud derived from his clinical work are not, however, the peculiar idiosyncracies of one culture or even one epoch. They belong to the structure of the human mind, and are the property of mankind in general, exactly as are the insights derived from Darwin's observations. For example, genuine defense mechanisms[5] used to ward off inner pain are univeral (see the glossary of defenses in Bibring *et al.*, 1961). They were not, after all, 'discovered' by Freud, but merely explained by him, and are to be found in all cultures. No cultural artifact can alter the fact that such defenses as represssion, denial, reaction formation and so on will always be available to an individual. Societal conditioning can never obliterate them, but merely incline and encourage a person to overlook them. Certain societies, however, do place a greater emphasis on one defense or another and thus sanction their use by individuals whose behavior then appears to be perfectly 'normal'.

To learn about the tendency to flee the emotions in ancient Greece in Festugière's account (1954) and to see its manifestations in certain Chinese poets,[6] and to read Devereux's astute comments about the trend in modern culture towards the affectlessness that psychiatry terms the schizoid stance, is to learn something that is and has always been of immediate urgency: there exists a tendency, profoundly masochistic, in all of us, to detach ourselves from other people, and then to exalt that detachment into a philosophical principle of sublime proportions. The singular interest that Indian literature can have today for the psychologically-minded is that this stance was pushed to its ultimate limits in ancient Hinduism, Buddhism and Jainism; the enormous literature of these religions provide us with some of the most outstanding, far-pressed and interesting individual examples of a universal tendency. Modern psychoanalytic theory has connected this tendency with many other psychological phenomena, e.g., the inability to mourn,[7] but it should be stressed that, unlike psychiatric popularizations which speak superficially of the affectless character of our present age, psychoanalysis concerns itself with a universal and timeless tendency to blind oneself to emotional realities and to ignore, deny or obliterate affective ties. The heart of every clinical psychoanalysis is the unveiling of a hidden or unconscious emotional life. Granted that psychoanalysis often resorts to an appeal to 'latent' emtoions and that the issue of latency is certainly a difficult one. It is true that when an occasion calls for anger, the rejection or denial of anger immediately suggests to the clinician the unconscious existence of anger. A theory of universal and basic human emotions can no doubt be mechanically applied, but at least it provides a justification for reading as widely as possible and in as many different cultures as possible. Comparative studies are valuable precisely because they allow us, after a certain point, to scan a wider area than either our personal experience or our cultural experience will allow. This is the opposite of cultural relativism, for it permits us to form at least plausible notions of what are the universal and basic human emotions. The list is not that large, but it is surprising to note the relative absence of a given emotion in such a list from a given culture.[8] In this respect the scholar is better off than the writer, of whom Kenneth Grahame remarked (1892) "It is not given to know more than one land". Another source of removing the constrictions that have been placed upon our emotions is, at least in theory, psychoanalysis. The purpose of an analysis is to enlarge the range of our emotions, not by bringing in something new, but, as Freud put it in terms of Michelangelo's sculpture technique, *per via di levare*, by bringing out what is already there.

The impression I have gained from my reading of the classical literature is that the defense most frequently resorted to by those steeped in the culture of ancient India is a version of psychic fainting, a flight from the emotions and from emotional involvement.[9] Great value was placed on the ability to withdraw oneself from all but the most minimal entanglement with the external world of human relations. A specific historical event that involved three distinct cultures – Indian, Tibetan and Chinese – may serve to illustrate this point. The Council of Lhasa was a meeting between Indian Mahāyānist Buddhists and Chinese followers of Ch'an (Zen) in Tibet in the ninth century A.D. We are fortunate that many of the primary documents related to this complex incident have been preserved in the three relevant languages – Sanskrit, Chinese and Tibetan.[10] We can observe distinct and suggestive responses to the experience of the Council on the part of the three national delegations. For the Chinese, the trip to Tibet was filled with personal sorrow: they wrote nostalgic poems expressing their loneliness and homesickness. They observed much of what was of human interest on the long journey to Tibet and during the actual debate. They were sensitive to, and articulate about, various human details of psychological significance in their adversaries. In short, the Chinese delegation evinced a full human response, and to read their accounts, in Demiéville's masterful translation, is an experience to which anybody can respond. The Indian material presents quite a different picture. The texts preserved for us about the debate contain no personal expression of human emotions. They are doctrinal texts, concerned with technical details of theory. There is only the most indirect, remote hint that an actual historical event, involving real people, did in fact take place. What is the significance of such a difference in response between the two cultures? Kamalaśīla and the other members of the Indian delegation undoubtedly experienced the same feelings as their Chinese counterparts and were subject to the same nostalgia, loneliness and depression. But it would seem that the Indians, unlike the Chinese, could not allow themselves any expression of these inner feelings. Indeed, they *seemed* unable to recognize and acknowledge real feelings. The sadness of being removed from one's loved ones, far away from one's family, in a strange environment in a distant land, could not be publicly acknowledged no matter how poignantly felt. A deep and natural human need to express such feelings would have to be, by the dictates of Indian culture, rigorously suppressed. This culture sought to banish such feelings from consciousness totally. One is reminded of Freud's patients, in the 1895 *Studies on Hysteria*, who "suffered mainly from reminiscences" and "strangulated affects". I believe this retreat from the emotions, this dread fear of human feeling, is one of the fundamental disguised themes of almost all ancient Indian writing and stands in need of both exploration and, finally, explanation. Yet such a massive denial, wide as its force of operation on the suppression of descriptions of feelings in the literature might be, could never extend itself, with total success, to the inner life of the individual. For I believe that everybody desires to love and to be loved by another person. The intriguing question is why so many people, in so many cultures, and in so many different and disguised ways, run away from the possibility of such human love. Why such denial of our longing for it? The disappearance of love, or the gradual waning of love, is probably a universal experience. In addition, our childhood provides each of us with ample opportunity to feel the pains of unrequited oedipal love. And adolescence with its rich masturbatory activity, always accompanied by fantasies (even if unconscious ones), renews with a vengeance the fears and desires of earlier years. The increase in sexual capacity and the beginnings of the ability to have genital orgasms are powerful determinants in the great force of sexual desires and fears of this period. It is well known to child analysts how asceticism in its various forms (from fasting to general physical neglect) is often called upon as a reaction, a defense against this biologically determined upsurge of passions. The greater the physical and emotional needs, the more passionate the denial, the more absolute the renunciation. Fear is the anchor sheet of denial.

Does one ever succeed in obliterating such an ancient need? Is the struggle against the instincts ever won? Can human passions be entirely uprooted? Religious history asserts that success is possible and records traditions in every religion of ascetic monks who impress those around them with their ability to shed the normal passions of body and mind. The ascetic that the future Buddha meets tells him what every Indian has heard for centuries: "I look with equal mind on kinsman and stranger, and longing for and hatred of the objects of sense have passed from me" (*Buddhacarita*, Vol. 18. Johnston, 1936, p. 65). Undoubtedly such people exercise a considerable fascination upon ordinary mortals. A man who seems unmoved by human feelings is a figure of awe. But can anybody, even the man himself, ever know the price he has paid? If the rest of us know the awful calm that comes when the pain has been too great, can we envy him the still darker calm that comes from this form of deep emotional surgery?[11]

If this escape from the emotions is a genuine symptom, that is, if it represents an attempt to satisfy two conflicting desires, we can expect to find in the escape evidence, albeit in disguised form, of the original impulse which was so strong that it required this panicked flight. The literal flight into the forest, and the older, more pervasive tradition from which it stems, that of the wanderer, provides such evidence. The attraction of this compromise solution is evident in all Indian accounts of the wanderer: here is a man who renounces everything because, the texts tell us, of pain (*duḥkha*). The sadness of being abandoned, even if it looked as if one were acting by choice rather than being acted upon by forces one could neither understand nor master, became bound in a cultural tradition that sanctioned and rewarded such behavior. Hence the unbearable sadness became bearable, and the rich emotional life provided by family was replaced by intellectual and theological goals (mystic attainments) that could, in appearance, fill the affective void left by the uprooted family life. If we can only speculate on the deep loneliness and sadness that would surely overcome the *parivrājaka* periodically on his solitary travels,[12] we can nonetheless learn more about it through a comparative study of the psychiatric literature on fugue states.[13]

The Indian accounts (see those translated in Mitra, 1899) are often opaque in the revelation of the underlying human concerns, but not totally so. The verses of the *Theragāthā*, composed over a period of 300 years,[14] from the end of the sixth century B.C. to the middle of the third century B.C., show evidence of latent concerns diametrically opposed to those for the supposed demonstration of which they were written (cf. Lienhard, 1975). When, in Verse 528, a monk speaks of "delightful trees" that "hope for fruit" one catches a fleeting glimpse of his own lost hopes. We are moved by a recognition of buried yearnings, a totally secular love breaking through the pieties, when a monk writes, in Verse 1137: "When the sky has rained, when the grass is four-fingers high, when the grove is in full flower, like a cloud, I shall lie among the mountains like a tree. It will be soft for me, like cotton."[15]

In order to read this literature, rebus-like in its effaced and faded emotional content, we must become sensitive to chords struck well below conscious understanding. For example, a middle-aged female patient, described by Giovacchini (1967), feared that her body was beginning to disintegrate. Her dreams were filled with crumbling houses. That the crumbling houses symbolized the patient's body is an insight derived from the rather thin psychoanalytic literature on symbolism.[16] It is not startling, but it is true. Psychoanalysis allows us to hypothesize that the woman did not know about her concern with physical disintegration. Her active social life served to ward off this piece of self-knowledge, and it was only in the disguised form of the house, and even then only in a dream, that she could begin to face her own fears.[17] We have not yet gone very deep (the crumbling houses must also represent specific memories in the past of this woman), but even the short distance we have gone is possible only through the tool of psychoanalysis. Without this tool, the roots of psychologically relevant material will remain inaccessibly opaque.

I do not believe we can learn much about the inner meaning of various dietary restrictions, for example, and associated phenomena such as fasting and vegetarianism, unless we know something about eating disorders in childhood, about anorexia nervosa (the refusal to eat),[18] and an obsessive need to eat. The correlation cannot be automatic – we cannot indulge in wild analysis and claim that every case of vegetarianism is a reaction formation (that is, an overcompensating and ultimately ungenuine lurch in the opposite direction) against unacceptable cannibalistic urges, yet we will have to acknowledge that the problem with reaction-formations, as Fenichel informed us long ago in his important article on counterphobia (1939), is the leakages, the sudden, seemingly inexplicable eruptions of sadistic behavior that are in direct contrast with the manifest life style.[19]

In a later essay in this book, I have examined a traditional episode in the life of the Buddha, attempting to unearth its causal antecedents via the psychoanalytic method. Whether I was successful or not in this particular instance is irrelevant to the more basic issue of how an understanding into the life of the Buddha can be achieved. There seems to me one undeniable fact about the Buddha which all accounts stress: at some crucial point in his life he was severely depressed. He gave a kind of distorted recognition to this fact when he made *duḥkha* (sorrow, suffering, sadness, pain) the cornerstone of his ethical teaching. This is projection, the attribution of dimly perceived psychic states of feeling to the outer world,[20] but it is in an advance from other religions where supernatural revelations from god serve as the cornerstone of ethical teachings. The Buddha was able to perceive a basic fact of human experience correctly, even if he erred in seeking a direction for its provenance. Yet it is no diminution of the greatness of his achievement (nor even of our ultimate evaluation of this achievement in philosophical, ethical or historical terms) if we recognize that the Buddha suffered from a melancholia, and any attempt to gain some deeper, human understanding of him as a man must come to terms with his depression. It is true that before this task can be accomplished, we must acquaint ourselves as fully as possible with whatever is known about the life of the Buddha. This means reading through a vast, complex and often technical literature.[21] Doing this will make one sensitive to the more problematic area of mania.[22] It is then possible to recognize that much within Buddhism is a manic defense against depression. Mania need not be tied to its more agitated external manifestations; mania can betray its presence by a calm but unrealistic happiness, an emotional isolation from the only real source of happiness there is, other people, so that the Buddhist insistence on sealing off one's emotional and sexual responses to other people is a denial. The mania is then manifest in the calm and happiness this produces. It is therefore valuable to study in some detail the psychoanalytic literature on depression, which is no less large than that on the life of the Buddha.[23]

The retreat from the emotions presents only one side of the coin. An inevitable concomitant of this flight is an attempt at a re-creation.[24] This is, of course, true of all traditions which invest in fantasies of heavens and hells.[25] These places of the imagination extended to all natural boundaries: there were magic denizens of the forest, kingdoms beneath the sea, spirits of the mountains, pool sprites, and so on. These other kingdoms can range in any tradition all the way from the more or less rational thoughts about utopias[26] and the imaginary creation of other beings (Plank, 1968) similar to the imaginary companions of children, through to the creation of completely delusional worlds.

The legends of the life of the Buddha, so rich in mythological themes already operative in vedic and post-vedic Indian culture, raise the issue of a psychological approach to mythology in general. Psychological writing in mythology has been poor. The quality of research is poor, and the quality of psychological thinking is poor. Like the application of psychoanalysis to literature, it is too often done with a heavy hand. Freud had his genius to save his attempts; Abraham, in his purely mythological writing, in spite of an occasional brilliant psychological insight, is often absurd (cf. the acid comments of Krappe, 1929). Rank's suggestive work was marred by his own obsessions and eclectic scholarship. Biographical investigations[27] seem, in retrospect, too simple in even the better works.[28] The criticisms, however, are generally based on a superficial acquaintance with Freudian literature in general and with Freud's work in particular.[29] Folklorists, such as A. H. Krappe in his book *The Science of Folklore* (1929), have been particularly harsh on psychoanalysis, dismissing the whole of it in one or two sentences.[30]

While I would agree that the most satisfying form of understanding India can come only from the analysis of individuals, nonetheless the value of the ancient mythology is that it gives us direct access to the defense mechanisms prevalent in any culture: the stories hint at what lies uncomfortably close to the truth and tell us which truths are too painful to be permitted to acquire direct personal significance.[31] For ancient India, this study of the mythology replaces the direct study of the individual idiosyncracies of a single life. A careful, philologically-based and psychologically-oriented study of Indian mythology will nonetheless tell us much about the living of human lives which is, after all, what engages all of us most deeply and for which we reserve our most passionate interest.

A myth may act as a breakwater to a threatening loss of reality. Schreber's memoirs (Macalpine and Hunter, 1955), which contained a delusional religious world of great complexity, was the basis of the first case of an analysis of a psychosis, Freud's famous 1911 paper, "Psychoanalytic Notes on an Autobiographical Account of a Case of Paranoia (Dementia Paranoides)". Schreber himself, and the delusional world he created, are not totally dissimilar from the modern Hindu mystic Ramakrishna and his world (cf. Schreber's extraordinary biography translated in Macalpine and Hunter, 1955). Ramakrishna, the nineteeth-century saint from Calcutta, had delusions and hallucinations at least equal to, if not greater in severity than, those of Schreber. (In Chapter II, I say more about him). Among them was the idea that he was a woman, the beloved of Krishna, carried to the point where he "menstruated" and gave his disciples his own breast to suck (not for the first instance, by the way, for it seems that the fifteenth-century Bengali saint, Caitanya, the founder of the Hare Krishna movement of today, is described in the pious biography of him, the *Caitanyabhāgavata*, as doing the same, to the horror of his own mother). Far from being hospitalized, Ramakrishna was and is revered as a saint and the greatest religious leader of modern India. The society he founded, the Ramakrishna-Vivekananda (after his favorite disciple) Vedanta Society, is still the most important of its kind in India and the West. In fact, Ramakrishna can be said to be second in religious importance only to the ninth-century religious philosopher, Śaṅkarācārya, whose austere philosophical monism (Advaita) Ramakrishna claims to translate into personal terms. Hardly a religious movement in modern India does not either derive directly from Ramakrishna and his disciples or owe much of its doctrines and impetus to them. And yet, if one studies any of the biographies, one is struck by just how deeply disturbed Ramakrishna was:

> How can a man conquer passion? He should assume the attitude of a woman. I spent many days as the handmaid of God. I dressed myself in women's clothes, put on ornaments, and covered the upper part of my body with a scarf, just like a woman. . . .I cannot speak of myself as a man. One day I was in an ecstatic mood. My wife asked me, "How do you regard me?" "As the Blissful Mother", I said.[32]

Ramakrishna's world-view was not judged psychotic, because it was shared by his culture. Ramakrishna, in a profoundly regressed identification with the monkey Hanumān, claimed to have grown a tail. But it was other men (presumably not themselves psychotic) who "saw" this tail. In the recent critical edition of the *Vālmīkirāmāyaṇa*, Professor Bhatt writes: "Some anthropologists are of the opinion that some aboriginal tribes had a genuine tail."[33] The sober preservation of such and like tales does tell us something of significance about a cultural milieu. How far we can generalize on the basis of such cultural features is an old problem intimately tied to the problem of national character. Much has been written on this vexing question,[34] although most of it is of minimal value. Yet when all the objections have been weighed, there is still a certain inclination to make wide cultural generalizations.

It may be only the surface diversity of any given culture that invites such comments. There is nothing inherently more psychotic in nineteenth-century Bengali culture than in twentieth-century American culture. What we can say about the Hindu personality or the Arab personality (Patai, 1973) or the ancient Greek personality (Dodds, 1951)[35] is never more than the surface layer.[36] Beneath this it is as meaningful to speak of Ramakrishna as a homosexual as it is to do so of Schreber, regardless of how the culture viewed this sexual proclivity. It is meaningful precisely because it alerts us to certain etiological formulations at the root of homosexuality. Especially since the important work of Niederland,[37] we are more sensitive to the real traumata suffered by a paranoid psychotic like Schreber and we can assume, hypothetically but correctly I believe, that Ramakrishna too suffered such specific traumata in his childhood. His sexual choices were not dictated to him by his culture, but were the result of totally personal events in his own past. In this sense they were unique and humanly interesting in a way that an overlay of cultural artifacts can never be.[38]

This raises another much-debated topic on the role of child-rearing techniques in the formation of later character.[39] Influenced by the work of the early psychoanalysts (cf. the criticism by Orlans, 1949, and the response by Axelrad, 1962), many anthropologists (and educators) turned their attention in the 1930s, 1940s, and 1950s to the effect on character development of overt attitudes in the rearing of children (cf. Chombart de Lauwe, 1971). The subject of swaddling, for example, became of genuine concern, and we learned of the different cultural attitudes involved in this practice. We were told that for the Russian peasant swaddling was a means of protecting the baby against its own aggression: left to itself, went the fantasy, the baby would break its legs, or even tear its ears off. For the Polish peasant the body was divided into good and bad parts: the toes and genitals, for example, were bad; swaddling kept the bad in, as it were. For the Rumanian peasant, swaddling was primarily a means of preventing masturbation, and in later years the child's hands would be tied to its crib. For the Jewish mother, swaddling was intended to protect and defend the child against a harsh outer world.[40] Irrespective of their differences, it is quite clear that such early experiences were bound to have marked effects on the later personality of the child.[41]

Little Indian data are available[42] about the raising of children. In turning to this rather meager literature, however, we can learn things of interest, such as that in some strata of Hindu society, in some areas at some times, "Adult interaction with babies is generally aimed at producing a cessation of response rather than a stimulation of it."[43] We hear about a preference for male children, a fear of the evil eye, a lack of cuddling and play, a remoteness of the father during the first six years of life, and how children are punished primarily for asking for attention. We hear that, since a father is forced to deny having an active sexual life in front of his own father, it follows that he must show no affection to his wife or his child. The limitations of such information, even if factual, are evident. For surely all this and much more can be encountered in any household in any culture. We are told of the frequent exposure to the primal scene in Indian households. Can we be certain that it is any the less in Massachusetts? It may well be the practice in a culture for a father to be remote, but the 'remoteness', the psychological absence, is a deeply personal attitude. It cannot be merely imitated, or picked up, like dressing habits. To be real, it must correspond to inner needs. Some Indian fathers, today and in the past, were absent fathers. Others were not, no matter how much their society expected it of them or how much societal pressure was exerted. Can love be legislated? Its expression might: it is unthinkable for an Indian husband to kiss his wife in front of his father. But obedience to such external rules tells us nothing of underlying feelings. And children, especially,[44] know the difference between a mild, culturally determined reproof and a deep-lying hatred even if both are expressed, at the manifest level, in a similar manner.[45] This is why it is only through psychoanalysis that we learn of the true effects of the childhood environment.[46] In fact, we learn more in this manner about the true personality of the parents as reflected in the later life of the child than we do from direct statements from the parents, or even from direct observation.[47]

Yet the tool of psychoanalytic investigation is still most useful in the retrospective understanding of failure rather than success. Psychoanalysis was devised for the understanding of psychopathology, and whatever illumination it brings to the happier side of life is incidental. This means that we can apply psychoanalysis more successfully to phenomena in India which seem to require this particular kind of attention – Tantrism, for example.[48] To state as the Tantras do that ecstasy is reached when we learn to immobilize the *triratna*, mind, breath and semen, is to afford the psychoanalyst a glimpse into the world of unconscious fantasies, and to alert him to the existence of early parental preoccupations with the products of the body. In the immobilization of the mind is the fear of the emotions described earlier; to immobilize breath is a form of phobic preoccupation with the complete loss of breath – a form of a fear of dying; immobilizing semen is a barely disguised derivation of castration fears. I am not, of course, denying that more "primitive" fantasies might play a role.[49] For example, we can consider the following verse from the *Devīkālottarāgama: citte calati saṃsāro niścale mokṣa eva tu*, "When the mind moves, there is the phenomenal world – when it is motionless, liberation."[50] This urgent desire for stillness may well derive from early fears of sexual excitement.

Preventive medicine can only exist in the wake of a sophisticated pathology. The more we learn about a given disease, the greater our chances of counteracting it. What is valuable about the study of India is that we see certain developments almost in pure culture. Nowhere, for example, can we learn more about the vicissitudes of the psychology of the master/disciple relationship than in India, though I am certain that everything found in India is found elsewhere, and certainly the underlying mechanisms are the same, only more visible in India.[51] A thorough study of the guru/disciple relationship must be left to a future work, and I cannot pretend that I have uncovered the basic mechanisms. But certain things are evident immediately: the guru is always engaged in significant events. All his actions, all his words, are seemingly directed at earth-shattering happenings. Each and every guru either claims to be god directly, or is in some way close to god. This is not only in contrast to all his students, but is particularly in contrast to children. And indeed, this must be the source of this particular fantasy: every child imagines that the conversations he cannot understand (is this the genesis of the secret languages of mysticism?) by the adults around him are highly charged with significance. In a recent case history, particularly transparent, the black box a crazy inventor shows his young son (Berman, 1978) becomes the source of a later unshakable belief in the powers of certain parapsychological technology, because the son cannot believe that his father is crazy. Regression to intellectual and emotional childhood is the hallmark of every guru / śiṣya relationship. Not only does the guru use a language that the disciple cannot really understand (without ever stopping to consider that there is nothing to understand), but he also behaves in ways that are incomprehensible to the disciple. Whether the guru is described as irascible, testy, unpredictable and totally non-conformist, or as the most strict observer of orthodoxy and rules, he is engaged in something that the neophyte cannot do. The feeling of being excluded, even if it is unconscious, must be the universal experience of every disciple, just as it is of every child. At the same time, the illusion of having overcome this exclusion is provided by the brotherhood of the *āśrama* itself, and one notes with what regularity the older disciples mimic the gestures of the guru. The more persecuted a sect becomes (or the more ridiculed), the greater the sense of being noticed, of being singled out and the greater the illusion of the loss of insignificance. At the same time, chance events become magnified and treated as if they were expected, intended and willed (or directed from a higher power). Nothing ever happens to a guru, and, by extension, to his disciple, by chance. The pathos of the situation is that the disciple is invariably seeking the understanding, protection and love that he did not receive from his parents. He is under the sway of a noxious and wholly unsuspected repetition compulsion of tragic proportions: the love he was denied as a child will be denied him in the *āśrama* as well, and this strange urge towards the repetition of misery, this return again and again to the source of pain, remains the great mystery of masochism.

Similarly, one could examine in some detail beliefs about reincarnation (Stevenson, 1975). Why do so many of the stories involve young children? A closer examination of so-called "cases" would afford valuable material, as would much of the earlier Indian literature. Allied to this would be early Indian attitudes toward suicide (Thakur, 1963).[52] The Buddhist story of Māra, as a black cloud, searching for the poor monk who killed himself out of physical pain from an incurable disease, is an interesting example of the rational attitude of early Buddhism. At the other end of the spectrum are religious suicides – the *prāyopaveśa* of the Jains, and the *mahāprasthāna*, the long walk north of the *Mahābhārata* and allied texts.

An area of emotional intensity, in which the Indians and the Chinese have been more sensitive than Western writers, is the world in miniature, an imagined universe found in a small space. The idea already occurs in a series of Buddhist *Mahāyāna* texts. In the *Gaṇḍavyūhasūtra* (Suzuki and Idzumi, 1934-36), we are told of innumerable worlds, entire galaxies, found within a single grain of sand or pore of skin: *romamukheṣu ca paśyāmi tubhyaṃ tārakasanghasajyotiṣacandrān*, "I see in the pores of your skin the whole firmament, stars, moons and planets."[53] Similar verses are found in the *Vimalakīrtinirdeśasūtra* (Lamotte, 1962) and the *Samādhirājasūtra* (Régamey, 1938):

> On the point of a single hair there are as many Buddhas as there are grains of sand on the bank of the Ganges.... On the point of a hair there are beings of all the five regions: the damned of purgatory, the brute creation, inhabitants of the world of Yama, gods and men....In this space there are oceans, lakes, rivers, springs and ponds (19.16).

These themes become transformed in Chinese landscape painting, where the theme of illusion and reality is handled in a startling fashion. We hear there of painters who enter their own landscapes and get lost in their own bamboo forest (see Vandier-Nicolas, 1963, "Wen T'ong passe dans les bambou qu'il peint.") Sou Chei, speaking of a painting of Li Long-Mien, speculates about later travelers in these mountains who will be able to find their way, and will recognize, as if it were in a dream, paths they have known: "S'ils rencontrent, dans la montagne, quelque solitaire pêchant ou ramassant du bois, ils reconnaitront leur homme sans qu'on le leur ait nommé." The notion surfaces again in painted dragons whose eyeballs were left unpainted (Sirén, 1956-58) lest they come to life. What it represents, I believe, is a concretization of the moods that a landscape, or a painting of a landscape, or a poem about a landscape, conjure up. It is a means of recognizing the reality of the feelings and, at the same time, pointing to the difficulty in translating such strong feelings into concrete expression. Certainly one of the most peremptory urges given expression in Chinese landscape painting is the need for another world hidden behind the expression of a desire for solitariness, well portrayed in these lines:

> La lune [se reflète] dans l'eau, vide et paisible
> Les vapeurs les nuages passent, vagabonds.
> Je suis là simplement, sans haine ni amour
> Qu'elle est profonde, la blancheur lumineuse.[54]

The longing to enter another world need not, of course, be derived from Indian sources. The desire has a history in older Chinese poetry from before the Christian millenium. While I have translated this urge into psychological terms and while I see it ultimately as a flight from reality (which may well be the only solution available to a writer in his time), the sentiments can be interpreted very differently. Thus David Hawkes, in his fine translation of the *Ch'u Tz'u: Songs of the South* (1959), writes:

> In all of [the Sao-style poems] – or nearly all – the poet seeks escape in distant travel, either to an imaginary fairyland peopled by mythical beings, or into a mundane scenery of rivers and mountains. In all of them he reverts again and again to his grief and anguish; for before his journey he is wronged and embittered, and after he has embarked on it he is homesick and remorseful. And all of them end on the same note of embittered despair. . . .Yet this description is less than just because it omits the beauty of the language, the fascination of the supernatural world into which the poet introduces us, the profusion of symbols, the dreamlike movement of the narrative. . . .The Sao poet is no ordinary neurotic. He is, or aspires to be, a magician. He feels that he belongs to a supernatural environment more pure than his earthly one, in which he feeds on nothing less ethereal than the dews and vapours of heaven, in which he can summon gods and immortal spirits to do his bidding, and can roam at will to the uttermost ends of the universe.[55]

There are writers who claim that the fantasy world of the very young child is the source of these magic journeys, and that the ability to live in a world of magic, conceived as pure imagination, belongs *only* to the young child:

> . . .The most thrilling moments of happiness with a child are *secret and magical* and come from a level of reality which is completely different from the level of reality of grown-up people. Children do not play ordinary conventional games unless they are encouraged to do so by

> the older boys and girls. Children's 'games', strictly speaking, are not games at all. They are the child's inmost reality! They are the child's life illusion. They turn back to them with a sigh of relief from the impertinent intrusive activities of grown-up people. . . .It is always their old toys, however cheap, that children cling to. Why? Because they are no longer simply *toys*. They have become the mediums, the bridges, the ladders, the trap-doors, the magic carpets, by which they enter. . .the rainbow-land of their own imagination! (Powys, 1934).

All traditions have men who live at a peculiar angle to their culture, eccentric, insisting on the authenticity of their own emotional life, even if it is one that is officially proscribed. Hence in Japan, the Zen priest Ikkyū, who at seventy-eight fell in love with the blind woman poet Mori, could write:

> Ten years in the gay quarters, and still I
> couldn't exhaust the pleasures;
> But I broke away and am living here in empty
> mountains and dark valleys.
> In these favorable surroundings clouds blot
> out the world,
> But those winds over the roof from the tall
> pines grate on my ears (Keene, 1971).

Similarly, the Chinese poet Li Po (701-762) wrote:

> You ask me why I dwell in the green mountains
> I smile and make no reply for my heart is calm
> As the peach-blossom flows down stream and is
> gone into the unknown
> I have a world apart that is not among men.
>
> (From *The Penguin Book of Chinese Verse*, edited by A. R. Davis)

Finally, since so much of my earlier published research was devoted to aesthetics, I must wonder whether it would be possible to learn something of value from psychoanalysis for the study of what is not obviously a piece of psychopathology in ancient India.[56]

Many of the tenets of Sanskrit aesthetics bear a striking similarity to essential elements of psychoanalysis both as it is practiced and as a theory of human nature; perhaps psychoanalysis can, in turn, be enriched from such a remote and unlikely source as Sanskrit poetics.[57] I might merely mention in passing the sophisticated Indian notions about the advantages to be had from recognizing the unreality of a drama. Abhinavagupta, in the eleventh century, says: "Today I am going to a play – I don't have to *do* anything." In a similar vein, the analyst hopes his patient will eventually remember, rather than act,[58] and ultimately the patient must come to realize that his feelings for the analyst are, in some strange sense, unreal.[59] The finest Sanskrit poetry, I believe,[60] deals with loss, sadness, bereavement and separation. Similarly, people enter analysis because of sadness and loss, and develop a concern with their own personal past. Certainly all Indian literature is highly bound up with the past as well, even if projected on to mythological themes of a golden age and previous births. In contrast to the denial of emotion which pervades much of Indian culture, in Indian poetics we find a genuine concern for the life of the emotions. The literary critics were extraordinarily subtle in analyzing human moods and feelings, as we can see in the profound discussions on *rasadhvani* (the suggestion of an imaginative experience in literature) in two great monuments to the Indian genius, Ānandavardhana's *Dhvanyāloka* and Abhinavagupta's *Dhvanyālokalocana*.[61]

If someone were to ask me what of significance about India psychoanalysis had revealed to me, I think the answer would be that it has taught me how difficult it is for anyone to escape the pathogenic forces in his own culture; how pervasive and subtle are the directives toward various forms of hidden misery. The most deeply disturbing of these forces is that strand in Indian culture which leads a person away from other people, into the wilderness, either literally or in the form of a deep narcissistic concern with his own salvation. Perhaps the only other emotion, besides the kind of emotional isolation I have been speaking of, to which the Indians devote the same absorbed attention, is compassion. This is, I think, because it is somehow recognized, well below the threshold of consciousness, that compassion cannot exist in a private world of one's own making. It is the lifeline thrown up by ancient Indian civilization toward health and happiness in a world populated with real people, and as such it is the warning sign about the other darker and more destructive forces with which the culture has so long concerned itself.[62]

NOTES

[1] Cf. Masson (1974b).

[2] A view not shared by all. See Opler (1959): "A person who knows village India at first hand and who had read Carstairs' book came upon me as I was in the midst of it. His acid comment was: 'I see you are reading the Mother India of the intelligentsia.' "

[3] Bhandari (1960), Bharati (1971), G. Bose (1937, 1945), N. K. Bose (1952), Brill (1945), Bychowski (1968), Daly (1927), Devereux (1951d), Rao (1963), Ramana (1952, 1964), Sinha (1966), Vahia (1967).

[4] The number of works that purport to be psychoanalytic about India is large, and the works themselves unrewarding to read. A full list is unnecessary, but I have misused much of my time in reading through books that need not have been consulted. To preserve the reader from my mistakes, I am thinking of such books as that by Berkeley-Hill (1933), which is 'Freudian' but racist and without insight; Choissy's (1947) ignorant, superficial and pretentious book about Yoga and sublimation; Coster's (1934) foolish text; the Jungian nonsense of H. Jacobs (1961) on psychotherapy and *sādhanā*; Narain (1957) and Kakar (1968). I omit from consideration the purely psychiatric literature since it is rarely, if ever, rewarding.

[5] Anna Freud (1936), Gero (1951), S. Sperling (1953), Brenner (1957a), Marasse (1959). In my opinion, the concept of defense, which was initially very broad for Freud, should not be restricted to distinctly identifiable, specific mechanisms. For example, it seems to me that the so-called explanatory concept of a repetition compulsion, introduced by Freud in 1920 in *Beyond the Pleasure Principle*, is really a description of a clinical phenomenon whose defensive function is evident. But even as a pure description, the phenomenon is extremely helpful in looking at material from India. I recommend, in particular, Schur (1960, 1966a), Bibring (1943), Gifford (1964), Loewald (1971) and Kubie (1939, 1941). Similarly, masochism is a clinical reality, but it is not an explanatory concept that stands on its own. It requires dissolution because it is, I believe, a defensive gesture aimed at retaining love that is, in reality, scarcely available. See, in particular, Brenner (1959), Loewenstein (1957) and Brenman (1952). Even something as striking and as apparently autonomous as imposture reveals, upon careful analysis, its defensive structure (Deutsch, 1955) as does, even, a hysterical fate neurosis (Deutsch, 1930). Cf. Siegman (1954) on emotionality as a hysterical character defense, and see the symposium edited by Furst (1967). Trauma, no matter how difficult to observe from the outside, is certainly the agent responsible for this diverse clinical picture, from agoraphobia (Weiss, 1935) to alcoholism and addiction (Simmel, 1948), as I have tried to argue throughout this volume. This has also been my clinical experience and what I have learned from the study of remote civilizations. It is not, however, the standard view within psychoanalysis (cf. Khan, 1964), where less stress is laid upon real events (for the classical position, see the excellent work by Anna Freud, 1965). My use of 'trauma' is a shorthand for the investigation of early childhood experiences. I do not see how one can abandon such a search without removing oneself, to a greater or lesser degree, from the realm of psychological explanation and becoming dependent upon various forms of the constitutional argument. For example, Zilboorg, in his fine article on 'The Sense of Reality' (1941), has a good observation about the lives of certain scientists who "preoccupied themselves for most of their lives with concrete, seemingly 'realistic' subject-matter, but in the course of years began to behave as if they never had learned much from their investigations. . . .Oliver Lodge turned from physics to commune with the dead. Charles Richet, a physiologist of great repute, spent his later years with the same preoccupation. August Comte, the positivist and logician, became a mystic" (p. 199), and, one might argue somewhat maliciously, Gregory Zilboorg the psychoanalyst became a devout Catholic! But ultimately Zilboorg's only explanation for this fascinating observation is an over-intense "animistic drive".

[6] Cf. Waley (1946, 1956), Frodsham (1970).

[7] Deutsch (1937), Zilboorg (1933), Fleming and Altschul (1963), Pollock (1961, 1970, 1975) and Siggins (1966).

[8] The influence a culture has on the omission of emotions is an intriguing question. Can a given culture completely obliterate an emotion, or can it merely deny it access to verbal expression? I think it is indisputable that certain cultures do not provide the means for expressing certain emotional states. For example, I cannot think how one would express in Sanskrit, 'I am lonely'; 'I am disappointed'; 'I feel betrayed'. Even the concept of loss is restricted. True, Indian literature has an entire category, *viraha* ('absence') and its conventions, but among these conventions is the restriction of the depiction of *viraha* to lovers: I do not know how one would say 'I miss my child' in Sanskrit. Nonetheless, certain emotional states are universal. For example, everybody has felt at some point that he is being treated as if he were insignificant. This is inexpressible in Sanskrit and, in fact, as far as I am aware, descriptions of such a feeling, however paraphrased, do not occur in the literature. Nevertheless, the feeling must have existed in ancient India. Would a concept such as 'disappointment', inexpressible in language, surface in a dream, and if so, how would it attain representation within the dream? Indeed, even if one could postulate that the concept would translate itself into a plastic representation within the dream, one could still ask: translate itself for whom? How would it ever come to be recognized? The extent of later distortions of the original dream-experience when it is recounted, that is, the reworking of the material via secondary elaboration, can never be measured. The recognition of this problem is relevant to the telling and the preservation of mythology. Cf. Masson, 'Melancholia and the Buddha: Unconscious Love in the Lives of the Indian Mystics' (1979). Very different is the approach taken by Doi (1971) writing on such Japanese concepts as *amae*. Affect theory, particularly the notion of unconscious emotional states, see Knapp (1957); see Mullane (1965) for a philosophical treatment of this area; Schur (1969) for a clarification; and Pulver (1971, 1974) for a global treatment, is one of those crucial areas of psychoanalytic thought that has not been sufficiently developed. In an article with T. C. Masson (published in the *Bulletin of the Southern California Psychoanalytic Society*) on affect theory, I have tried to clarify some of the issues, with but limited success. Since emotional states, their description, their evocation and re-evocation, lie at the very heart of psychoanalysis, one would expect better work in this field. Besides the article by Jones on hate and guilt, mentioned earlier, I found most useful Zilboorg (1933), Kubie (1937), Weiss (1942b), Landauer (1938) and of course Freud's well-known theoretical work *Inhibitions, Symptoms and Anxiety* (1926; cf. Waelder, 1967). Deutsch's 1942 article on the 'as if' personality became very influential (cf. N. Ross, 1968a), as was Rosenberg's 1949 article on anxiety and the capacity to bear it. The affect most studied has remained anxiety, which is less of a specific emotion than a feeling tone pervading many other emotions (Schur, 1953; Greenacre, 1941; Brenner, 1953, 1957; Compton, 1972 gives a thorough historical treatment). Naturally, analysts have written more about the 'negative' emotions – besides the bibliography given earlier on depression, see Zetzel's article on 'Depression and the Incapacity to Bear It' (1965); the elaborate review article by Haynal, 'Le sens du désespoir' (1977); E. Weiss (1944), Mendelson's book on depression (1974); Mahler (1966); Ostow's book (1970) on *The Psychology of Melancholy* and Alexander's article (1929) on 'The Need for Punishment and the Death-Instinct'. Valenstein, in his 'On Attachment to Painful Feelings and the Negative Therapeutic

Reaction' (1973), deals with some of the theoretical issues (see his 1962 article as well). Much, of course, has been written about the influence of emotions on the body, but the field is so immense that I cannot even list the important articles in this now rarely-written-about area (though see Devereux, 1965 on 'Weeping, Urination and Grand Mal' and Kepecs *et al.* on the 'Relationship Between Certain Emotional States and Exudation into the Skin' (1951). Socarides (1971) has written 'On Disillusionment: The Desire to Remain Disappointed', and Balint (1963), 'On Being Empty of Oneself' (though it is not clear if this is painful or pleasurable). Greenson (1949) has written on apathy; Fenichel on boredom (1934) and jealousy (1935); Benedek on Morbid cravings (1934); Stephen on guilt and rage (1934). To the literature on mourning already quoted, I would add Loewald (1962) and Bowlby (1963) on 'Pathological Mourning and Childhood Mourning'. Schmideberg has written a well-known article, 'On Querulance' (1946), and most of the articles on emotions that are pleasant to the person (Slap, 1966 on sarcasm; Lewinsky, 1951 on 'pathological generosity'; Arlow, 1957, 'On Smugness'; Weiss, 1959 on 'Intensity as a Character Traint'; Horney, 1948 on 'The Value of Vindictiveness') stress their defensive and hostile character. Even nostalgia, which is often subjectively pleasurable, is primarily painful in its effects, one of which is withdrawal (see A. Freedman, 1956; Kleiner, 1970; Werman, 1977; and Starobinski, 1966). On affect theory in general, the best-known article is by Rapaport (1953) though I find it hardly intelligible. See, on the general theory of affects, Glover (1939), Glauber (1949), Novey (1959, 1961), Schafer (1964), Brenner, (1974, 1975), Blank (1975). For an article which deals with affect theory in relation to mystical states, see Ross (1975). That little progress is made in this difficult area can be observed by comparing the fine panel reported by Löfgren (1968b) with the one years later reported by Castelnuovo-Tedesco (1974). Socarides (1977) has edited a collection which contains some of the articles cited above. Relevant to the issues raised by emotions and their absences is the literature on sensory deprivation: Miller (1962), Freedman and Browns (1968) and D. Freedman (1975).

[9] Cf. Fine (1969), Geleerd (1965), Jacobson (1957b).

[10] Paul Demiéville (1952) has written a valuable book on the Chinese involvement; Tucci (1958) has written a learned history of the Tibetan side, and we have editions of the Sanskrit texts, written at the time by Kamalaśīla (Tucci, 1958, 1971). Doubts concerning the authenticity of the Council have been raised by Yoshirō (1975). See also Stein's 1971 article on sudden illumination, and Demiéville's articles collected in 1973. The emotional contribution of Tibet to this debate has not been discussed, though it must have been important. Although I speak from a superficial acquaintance with Tibetan culture (Bell, 1931; Ekvall, 1964; Haark, 1969; R. A. Stein, 1962) it seems to me that the Tibetans have been extremely interested in personal details about a man's life, and Tibetan biographies (Bacot, 1925, 1937; R. A. Stein, 1972) read very differently from Indian biographies. Even the accounts of the miracles of Milarespa have a personal ring to them, and at times totally human emotions break through. Thus Milarespa burns the books of his favourite disciple, Rechungpa, and then, in order to distract him,

> the Jetsun passed through rocks and other obstacles, flew by on a rock, walked and sat on water, poured fire and water from his body, flew through and sat in the sky and transformed his body from one to many and from many to one. . .as though spreading wings, Milarespa held out his robe and flew straight into the sky. . .he fluttered and hovered like a hawk, and then darted to the ground like a flash of lightning (Chang, 1962).

But Rechungpa responded with the laconic comment: "Perform the miracle of restoring my books." He stubbornly refuses interest in all further spectacles, demanding, instead, the return of his books, the only miracle, he says, that would impress him! Snellgrove and Richardson, 1968 (p. 207) speak of the sixth Dalai Lama, Tshang-yang Gyamtso, who could not forget the woman he loved, even when he became a Dalai Lama: "Though called to mind my Lama's face does not rise in my thoughts. Not called to mind, my loved one's face gently pervades my thoughts."

[11] The literature on wolf-children might prove an interesting direction from which to view this isolation. Much of the original literature is Indian (see Singh and Zingg, 1942; Mandelbaum, 1943; Bettelheim, 1959), but there are important European parallels (see especially the remarkable story of Caspar Hauser: Feuerbach, 1832; Malson, 1964; Shengold, 1978). In my opinion, these stories are fantasies (no less valuable or revealing for that), but as distinguished a child psychologist and pediatrician as Arnold Gesell felt otherwise (Gesell, *Wolf Child and Human Child*, 1940). The best comment on wolf-children is by Bettelheim (1959) on wolf-mothers (quoted by Fiedler, 1978):

> It seems to be the result of some persons' – usually their parents' – inhumanity and not the result, as it was assumed, of animals' – particularly, wolves' – humanity. To put it differently, feral children seem to be produced not when wolves behave like mothers but when mothers behave like non-humans. The conclusion tentatively forced on us is that, while there are no feral children, there are some very rare examples of feral mothers, of human beings who become feral to one of their children.

[12] It is an interesting exercise in the comparative analysis of cultures to speculate as to why the Japanese could so easily name this sadness and write about it so directly. It is called *sabi*, the style of loneliness, and some beautiful poems have been written on this theme (see Brower and Miner, 1966). The priest Ryōzen (fl. c. 1040-70) writes (ibid., p. 260).

> In my loneliness
> I step outside my hut and gaze
> In quiet reverie,
> But everywhere it is the same:
> The melancholy autumn dusk.

Or Shunzei says:

> As evening falls,
> From along the moors the autumn wind
> Blows chill into the heart,
> And the quails raise their plaintive cry
> In the deep grass of Fukakusa village.

The priest Jakuren (d. 1202) speaks of the loneliness when "over the dark evergreens, dusk gathers on far autumn hills".

[13] Fisher (1945, 1947, 1949), Geleerd (1956) Geleerd et al. (1945), Lagache (1947). Solomon's interesting article on fugue in a fouryear-old (1958) is relevant, as is Stanford's chapter on the wanderer (pp. 175-211) in his book on the Ulysses theme (1954).

[14] Norman (1969, p. 29).

[15] The Pali text (Oldenberg and Pischel, 1883) reads:

> vuṭṭhamhi deve caturaṅgule tiṇe
> sampupphite meghanibhaṃhi kānane
> nagantare viṭopisamo sayissam
> taṃ me mudu hohiti tūlasannibham

[16] Fliess (1973), Jones (1916), Kubie (1953), Segel (1961), Waldhorn and Fine (1974).

[17] Throughout this book I have made much use of dreams because I have found from my experience in working with patients that a dream is most often the quickest route to the recovery of an early, pathogenic and painful memory. The single greatest work on dreams is still Freud's *The Interpretation of Dreams*, and the only genuine advances in our understanding of the psychology of dreaming has come from the classical psychoanalytic literature (cf. Fliess, 1953b for an excellent critical review of contributions from 1900 to 1953; also besides those works by Kris, Lewin, and Isakower mentioned throughout this book, Fenichel, 1942; Kepecs, 1952, 1954; and Kanzer, 1955). Nevertheless, it is a striking and peculiar fact, one I find difficult to explain, that almost without exception the dreams reported in classical literature are invented dreams and not dreams dreamt by a dreamer. This is, of course, no more than an impression, since nobody has access to the actual dream-experience except the person who has dreamt, and even he is dependent upon the vagaries of his own memory. There is something paradoxical yet true in the statement, 'I know that I dreamt last night, but I don't know what I dreamt." If there is no content, what is the memory? In my opinion, this is a direct indication of unconscious knowledge. The dream is known, but unremembered. Similarly, the classical literature of a culture often points in the direction of a dream-experience without actually yielding the dream. Once in a great while, a real dream is reported, often with a transparent dream mechanism. What comes to mind is a dream reported in a ninth-century diary (*The Gossamer Years: The Diary of a Noblewoman in Heian Japan*, translated by Edward Seidensticker, Tōkyō: Charles Tuttle Company, 1964), possibly the very first true, detailed account of a bad marriage in the history of literature. The author writes:

> On about the twentieth day of the retreat I dreamed that my hair was cut and my forehead bared like a nun. Seven or eight days later I dreamed that a viper was crawling among my entrails and gnawing at my liver, and that the proper remedy for the difficulty was to pour water over my face. I do not know whether these dreams were good or bad, but I write them down so that those who hear of my fate will know what trust to put in dreams and signs from the Buddha (Op. cit., p. 98.).

Her life was in so many respects miserable, her marriage so beyond repair, her situation so totally without remedy, that this dream is a perfect symbol of internal denial: the viper crawling in her entrails is a correct endopsychic perception of her condition. The remedy is a plastic representation of the denial. The contrast between the horror of the first and the mildness of the second is the wish, "If only I could be cured by the simple device of pouring water over my face."

[18] See Kaufman and Heiman (1964), Bruch (1973).

[19] Thus Leonardo da Vinci was a vegetarian and bought birds only to secure their release, yet it took Freud (1910) to recognize the sadism involved in his dressing up lizards as dragons to frighten his friends, and his practical jokes involving the inflation of intestines. No amount of historical knowledge, important as it may be for the initial task of examining and gathering the evidence, can explain away these actions. Meyer Schapiro (1956; cf. Eissler, 1961) has a much more detailed and reliable knowledge of Leonardo's environment than did Freud. But for him to write that Leonardo was a vegetarian merely because it was the fashion is to abandon any attempt to understand, in any depth, the behavior of another human being. It was Freud's strength to have constructed an elegant and significant thesis with respect to Leonardo: he used his childhood and his unacknowledged sadism (seen in his fascination with the construction of war machines) to explain his inability to finish certain of his works of art and to account for his literal and frequent abandonments. This is neither trivial nor weak, and years later Freud (1920) was to recognize the universal validity of this need to repeat in reverse direction (as Leonardo was abandoned in his childhood and was a passive victim, so in later life would he actively be the one to abandon – including mature sexual love between a man and a woman) and to call it the repetition compulsion (see Kubie, 1939, 1941; Schur, 1960). It represents a genuine insight into the workings of the human mind, and cannot be ignored.

[20] Cf. Werman (1979):

> During an extended evaluation to determine whether a young woman, who had applied for analytic treatment, was actually capable of introspection, she reported several dreams whose manifest content disturbed her and whose latent content, relating to incestuous wishes, was close to awareness. The patient was dissatisfied because the doctor did not explain (away) the dreams. It become apparent that her mounting anxiety impelled her to seek explanations of her dreams that would repress the emerging material. When no 'explanations' were forthcoming, the patient supplied her own, characterizing her dreams as 'precognitive'. She related that she had had many such dreams in the past and described how they had foretold the future. In this way she effectively closed the door to the past (p. 111).

[21] I would select as most important the following books and articles: Burnouf (1844), Oldenberg (1882), Senart (1882), Rockhill (1884), Przyluski (1920), Eliot (1921), Clark (1930), Thomas (1927), Johnston (1936), Waldschmidt (1944-1948), Lamotte (1947-1948, 1955, 1958), Foucher (1949), Bareau (1963, 1965).

[22] Lewin (1950) and Abraham (1911, 1924); Klein (1934).

[23] I would recommend the following works: Feigenbaum (1926), Rado (1928), Blitzsten (1936), Deutsch (1937), Spitz (1945, 1946a, 1946b), Bibring (1953), Benedek (1956), Jacobson (1957a, 1971), Bowlby (1960), Beres (1966), Wolfenstein (1966, 1969).

[24] The idea of another world, another realm, is almost certainly modeled upon a current misery. The finest example of this is provided by the famous prose-poem of T'ao Chi'ien (see

Hightower, 1970) of a lost world, a peach-blossom forest where all live in harmony and peace. The story goes that a fisherman of Wu-ling

> Once rowed upstream, unmindful of the distance he had gone, when he suddenly came to a grove of peach trees in bloom. For several hundred paces on both banks of the stream there was no other kind of tree. The wild flowers growing under them were fresh and lovely, and fallen petals covered the ground – it made a great impression on the fisherman. He went on for a way with the idea of finding out how far the grove extended. It came to an end at the foot of a mountain whence issued the spring that supplied the stream. There was a small opening in the mountain and it seemed as though light was coming through it. The fisherman left his boat and entered the cave, which at first was extremely narrow, barely admitting his body; after a few dozen steps it suddenly opened out into a broad and level plain where well-built houses were surrounded by rich fields and pretty ponds. Mulberry, bamboo and other trees and plants grew there, and criss-cross paths skirted the fields.

Hightower points out (p. 254) that this land "differs in nearly every detail from the world of T'ao Chi'ien's own experience", and I think he has made an important observation which must be psychologically true for all such fantasy kingdoms. Of the poet himself, Robert Payne (1949) writes:

> He loved nature and wine, children and chrysanthemums; he loved walking desultorily through the countryside; he delighted in the seasons. He grimaced sometimes against the cold and against death, but he knew they were inevitable, and took comfort in birds. . . .He made no demands on fame, or even on life: he seems to have been contented with the world as he saw it – the world of valleys and plains, of a deliberate simplicity and an incurable nostalgia.

Chinese ideas about worlds within worlds – for example, of a man who falls asleep, finds himself entering his jade pillow, marries, has sons and a whole life, only to awaken and find his rice still cooking (Hsun, 1959, p. 52) – may well derive from Indian sources. Such worlds within worlds are mentioned, though only schematically, in the *Samādhirājasūtra* and other Buddhist texts. A similar idea is found in the famous story of the *māyā* of Viṣṇu, which I treat in Chapter II of this book, but I do not know of any early Indian fictional treatment of this interesting genre.

[25] We know a great deal about ancient Western ideas concerning the after-life, fantasies of paradise, return to an early home, etc. (see, in particular, the studies of Manuel 1971; Eliade, 1959; and the scholarly studies of Cumont, 1922 and Rohde, 1925). From a psychological point of view, our deepest knowledge about fantasies connected with death, dying and the after-life come from clinical studies, both of adults and of children (see Eissler, 1955; R. A. Furman, 1964; Knapp et al., 1966; Ries, 1945, particularly for the case history it contains; Zilboorg, 1943; and a review of the psychoanalytic literature in Miller and Menes, 1961). Images of an earthly paradise (see Giamatti, 1966; Spitzer, 1944; Poggioli, 1959; Trilling, 1964) are, of course, related. Panofsky (1936), in an influential article, pointed out that the phrase '*et in Arcadia ego*' has been frequently misunderstood, no doubt for purposes of defense: Death is the speaker, and he is telling the listener that he, too, is in paradise, a very Indian notion of death in life or even after-life. Cf. the Indian idea of a *punarmṛtyu*, an 'after-death' which seems to lie behind the often frantic desire for *mokṣa*, 'release' from the cycle.

Death, of course, exists in heaven according to the Indian theorists, and many an Indian philosopher has warned his students of the folly of expecting eternal peace as long as understanding (*jñānam*) had not been reached. But as far as I know, no study of this rich theme in Sanskrit literature exists. The topic of Indian ideas of heaven, hell and the after-life in general is well worth pursuing.

[26] See Elliott (1970), Levin (1969), Manuel (1965), Patch (1950), H. Ross (1938). Harry Levin (1969) points out, via Dante, how little imagination we have for the good life; how much more is written on the *Inferno* than the *Paradiso*: "Hell and purgatory are more closely linked to the circumstances of mundane existence."

[27] An interesting approach to the comparison of cultures could be made through a study of biography in the ancient world. Montaigne said: "There is no description so hard, so profitable as is the description of a man's own life." One can learn a great deal about a culture and its ideals by observing the omissions in the accounts of the lives of the great men of that culture. The most useful book I have found on the topic is Roy Pascal's *Design and Truth in Autobiography* (1960). On biography in general, I have profited from Nicolson (1928), Bates (1936), Misch (1907), Stauffer (1930), Edel (1957, 1961), Gusdorf (1956) and Cross (1924). On the psychological approach to biography, I have found the following worth reading: Axelrad (1960), Greenacre (1957a, 1958a, 1958b), Kohut (1960), Kris and Kurz (1934), Kris (1952) Mach (1971), Beres (1959) and Gedo (1972). For comparison with classical antiquity, I have profited from Fairweather (1974), Stuart (1931), Festugière (1961) and Delehaye (1907). Pascal (p. 24) speaks of Abelard's *Historia Calamitatum* in which

> we notice how anxiously he tries to avoid dwelling on the past which her [Héloise's] wonderful letters seductively and passionately evoke. But in the *Historia* one detects his need, beyond any immediate pastoral intention, in his banishment and spiritual loneliness, to recall all the circumstance of his raptures and torments. . . .

Seldom in any religious literature do we encounter such honesty as that expressed by Abelard when he says that "it was a feeling of shame, I confess, rather than a vocation, that drove me towards the shade of the cloister" (this after having been brutally castrated). Pascal writes that "the ostensible reason for this account is to demonstrate submission to God's will; the unconscious reasons are truly autobiographical – to recapture the past, to see his life as a whole, to find within its vagaries its one rapture and the one indivisible personality." Certainly in reading Abelard's *Historia*, one is aware of a miserable man, who at least in part is miserable because he cannot face the fact that he wants nothing of the Church – he wants his wife, the beautiful Héloise, who told him, over and over, that she entered the cloister for him and that she has no interest in God or the Church, but only in Abelard. This is an astonishing thing to have said in the twelfth century A.D. (and Etienne Gilson finds it painful and blasphemous), but we should be very clear: not an astonishing thing to have *felt*. (See the translation of Abelard's autobiography in Muckle (1964).

[28] The Sterbas (1954) on Beethoven and his nephew; Greenacre (1955b) on Swift and Carroll; Marie Bonaparte (1933) on Poe. An exception is the work of Eissler on Goethe (1963).

[29] Too often Freud's poorest work is quoted: *Totem and Taboo, Moses and Monotheism,*

Group Psychology and the Analysis of the Ego, The Psychopathology of Everyday Life. References to his greatest and enduring achievements, the work for which he is justly famous as the originator of a science (The Schreber case; On narcissism; The metapsychological papers: Repression, The unconscious, A metapsychological supplement to the theory of dreams; Mourning and melancholia; Inhibitions, symptoms and anxiety; Analysis terminable and interminable; Construction in analysis; An outline of psychoanalysis), are rare. There are seldom references to the better articles of Abraham, for example his fascinating 'The History of an Impostor in the Light of Psychoanalytical Knowledge' (1925) or 'Notes on the Psycho-Analytical Investigation and Treatment of Manic-Depressive Insanity and Allied Conditions' (1911), or 'Hysterical Dream-States' (1910). Nor are there references to such articles of Ferenczi as 'Confusion of Tongues Between Adults and the Child' (1933), 'Stages in the Development of the Sense of Reality' (1913), or 'The Ontogenesis of the Interest in Money' (1914). I have never seen a reference to Jones' great paper, 'Fear, Guilt and Hate' (1929) nor even to his well-known 'The Theory of Symbolism' (1916).

[30] Krappe, who has a virulent hatred of psychoanalysis, has written a cranky, cantankerous book, not without merit. William A. Lessa, in his scholarly book *Tales from Ulithi Atoll* (1961), is much more moderate and well-informed, but his final appeal to neo-Freudianism is an example of a scholar's refusal to acquaint himself with serious literature from another field. His falling back on Erich Fromm as a representative of the psychoanalytic position is irresponsible. Richard M. Dorson (1972), the dean of present-day folklorists, in his attack on psychoanalysis (Dundes, 1965), writes: "When applied to myths and tales, the language of the unconscious is as conjectual and inconclusive as Sanskrit." More sympathetic is Dundes (1975).

[31] See Devereux, 1957, p. 400:

> Myths frequently represent the projection of ego-dystonic insights, which are at once too powerful to be repressed and too painful to be applied to oneself. The 'mythopoeic position' appears to be the following: 'This is the truth, but it happened not to me, but to someone else; it applies not to me, but to someone else.' Such inventions are accepted by the listeners and are transmitted to future generations because the listener's unconscious echoes the latent content of the myth while the manifest content of the myth – the fact that it *is* a myth – enables the listener *not* to apply the insight to himself.

Cf. Wangh (1954) and Arlow (1961). I would define classical mythology as a screen set up against the real world. It hides, distorts and finally obliterates the real world. Some children, later as adults, no longer live in the world of the senses. They live in a world of mythology; a sad, barren world, where gods and demons rule, and hence the turn to miracles, and the comfort of miracles, rather than to a mother and father, and frail people with no special powers. The adult becomes a true ascetic. (See my article on the psychology of the ascetic; also Oman, 1903.)

I am intrigued by the increasingly impersonal tone of Indian philosophy: in the two great Upaniṣads (Senart, 1930, 1934), there are 'stories' (e.g., Raikva of the cart; Yājñavalkya and his love for one of his wives; Śvetaketu) that still resemble the world we all share. But by the time Śaṅkarācārya writes his systematized books, it is only a shadow world, with no people in it: Advaitavedānta, so brilliantly amplified by Śaṅkara, cannot permit the simple phrase, 'I miss my father', though one of the few facts about Saṅkara that we know with any degree of certitude is that he lost his father when he was very young. Did he erect his entire system in order to take him away from the pain of this loss? (cf. Altschul, 'Denial and Ego Arrest', 1968).

Of interest to the question of asceticism and its physical manifestations are the experiments in sensory deprivation. The article by Stuart Miller (1962) contains excellent coverage of an immense literature. This literature shows that while it is true that some people have a less-developed capacity for autonomy from the environment than others and even develop a 'psychological cyanosis', there are universal limits. Just as "the autonomy of the organism from environment in respect to oxygen concentration is only relative and limited to a narrow range" (Miller), so it is also true, I believe, that there is a limit to the degree of solitude that anyone can tolerate without falling into increasing solipsism or fulminating psychosis. Kanzer (1955) was the first to point out what should be obvious, namely that "sleep is not a phenomenon of primary but rather of secondary narcissism. . .and the sleeper shares his slumber with an introjected object", an insight that I believe applies to the fantasy world of the ascetic as well. It is possible that all ascetics live in a self-induced hypnotic trance? Miller quotes the jailed Paloczi-Horvath:

> In a self-hypnotized trance one could shut out the stench of the cellar, the brutal noises, the constant hunger, the various pains attacking our bruised, benumbed shivering bodies. In these good hallucinations one smelled the air of a Greek island in spring, sage and all; one's skin felt the soft warmth of sunshine. . .Hallucinations helped us to defeat our body, defeat our jailers, defeat reality.

[32] Nikhilananda (1952, p. 603; original publication date, 1897).

[33] Bhatt (1960, p. 447).

[34] Farber (1950), Gorer (1943, 1948), Klineberg (1944).

[35] There is a good psychological introduction to the life of a curious and deeply-disturbed medieval monk, with extraordinary sexual obsessions, who was nonetheless able to write openly about himself. See Benton (1970).

[36] The most sophisticated work I know on other cultures from a psychoanalytic point of view, both theoretically and clinically, is by Georges Devereux. See Devereux (1947, 1951a, 1951b, 1951c, 1953a, 1953b, 1954a, 1954b, 1955a, 1955b, 1956, 1958, 1961, 1967, 1968 [?], 1970, 1972 and 1973). Cf. Jackson's report (1968) on 'Aspects of Culture in Psychoanalytic Theory and Practice', and Spindler (1978), who edited a useful collection, *The Making of Psychological Anthropology*. See, too, Mead and Metraux (1949).

[37] Niederland (1951, 1959).

[38] I avoid the issue – on which, I believe, psychoanalysis has little to offer – of the relationship (if any) between mental disorders and creativity (see Eissler, 1963; Lidz, 1964; Trilling, 1945).

> Disciple: Why is there evil in the universe?
> Ramakrishna: To thicken the plot.

A man capable of saying this has a genuine talent. We know that Ramakrishna enriched the Bengali language, and was a master storyteller. Is there, however, any necessary connection between this and the pathology from which he suffered? Once we cease the age-old practice of attributing moral judgment to mental illness, is there any reason to abstain from speculations about psychopathology and its etiology even in the case of men of extraordinary talent?

However, I also believe that the deeper we penetrate into this problem, the more complex the issues, and I agree with Kubie (1958) that neurosis invades even the best work, not to its advantage as is popularly thought, but to its distinct disadvantage. Kubie has this moving passage about the tragedy of this invasion:

> That ancient tragedy of human nature, the success which brings no joy with it, occurs at least as frequently in the life of the scientific investigator as in art and business. A life of fruitful scientific exploration may end in a feeling of total defeat, precisely because in spite of scientific success the unconscious goals of the search have eluded the searcher. Sometimes at the end of a career this need to reach some still-undefined goal has led a successful scientist to turn to a pseudo-scientific investigation of the supernatural (1956, p. 255).

[39] While I would concede that much of the 'infant care and personality' literature is somewhat naive and simple (e.g., Gesell, Ribble, Bakwin), the theoretical issues that emerge are of great importance. The criticisms have been naive and simple in a different direction, sometimes of astounding psychological stupidity. The most influential of these criticisms, that by Orlans (1949), takes the position, for example, that the importance of good mothering has been grossly exaggerated. As proof, he reports with great satisfaction and scientific pride, a horror story:

> A crucial experiment conducted by Dennis [in the 1930s] throws some light on the question of how much and what kind of attention the infant requires if its physical and emotional development is to proceed unimpaired. He raised twin girls from birth in conditions of extreme isolation. The infants were separated from each other by a screen and received only the purely minimum attention required for feeding and bodily care, being kept supine on their backs and not spoken to or fondled or played with or exercised in any way until they were seven months old. Because of their restricted practice, visually-directed reaching and grasping, sitting alone and standing with help were retarded, but otherwise the children "yielded during most of the first year a record of development not distinguishable from comparison records of infants in normal environments" (p. 157). The children responded affectionately to the experimenter during his brief visits, so that Dennis remarks: "Fondling is not necessary for the development of interest in, and every sign of affection for, the adult" (p. 156). His over-all conclusions agree with the ones we have drawn:. . .normal behavioral development can occur in some infants when most of the first year is spent under conditions of minimum social stimulation and of very restricted practice. In other words, a large number of acts on the part of the adult which have been held by some people to be of importance may be dispensed with (p. 156) (Orlans, p. 154).

[40] On these topics see Benedict (1949), Mead and Wolfenstein, (1955).

[41] For the most elaborate argument in this direction, see Axelrad (1962) and Devereux (1961) for the anthropological and psychiatric method applied in its most sophisticated form.

[42] Carstairs (1957, 1976), Gorer (1938), Whiting (1963).

[43] Hitchcock and Minturn, 'The Rajputs of Kholapur', in Whiting (1963, p. 317).

[44] We should not underestimate the early age at which a child can become meaningfully sensitive to an unhappy environment. Helfer and Kempe (1968, p. 116) write: "We have seen babies respond accurately to rather unreasonable parental demands within the first six months and by the age of one. . .show exquisitely sensitive responses to parental needs." A very sad case is reported in the *New England Journal of Medicine* (Menking et al., 1969) of depression in a six-week-old child! He was admitted to the hospital at eight months, suffering from a deep depression that was not 'observed' for more than a month. The subject of childhood depression is an important one. But many authors claim (unjustly, I believe) that one cannot use the term 'depression' for infants. See Sandler and Joffee (1965), Rie (1966), Mahler (1961).

[45] In a series of important papers, Spitz (1945, 1946a, 1946b, 1949, 1951) has shown the dire results of emotional deprivation even in the face of adequate physical and nutritional care. The implications of these early studies have not, in my opinion, been entirely faced. In his article of 1949, he writes:

> We believe that in the coprophagic cases another of these syndromes will in due time become discernible, for, though these children may present many of the signs and symptoms of the anaclitic depression, a certain percentage of them show striking physiognomical differences. While the facial expression of children suffering from anaclitic depression is actually comparable to that of a grown-up suffering from severe reactive depression, more than half of the coprophagic children showed a facial expression which resembled far more that of a paranoiac suspicion or that of catatonic daze (p. 114, note 15).

Spitz shows that the mothers of coprophagic children are generally severely disturbed, borderline or psychotic mothers. They respond to their children with so-called 'love' periods lasting longer than two months (with suppression of the underlying hostility). This then swings to the opposite, overt hostility, again lasting for more than two months. Hence the suspiciousness of the child.

In a paper entitled 'The Navel of Neurosis: Trauma, Memory and Denial', written in collaboration with T. C. Massion, which was presented to the San Francisco Psychoanalytic Society on May 15, 1978, we have attempted to restore to psychoanalysis the early emphasis (and one never entirely forsaken by Freud) on the traumatic origin of the neuroses. See also our paper, 'Buried Memories on the Acropolis: Freud's Relation to Mysticism and Antisemitism' (Masson and Masson, 1978a), which contains basically the same argument. All of the essays in this volume are based on this hypothesis, but it is stated most clearly in the chapter on yogic powers and symptom-formation.

[46] See Spitz (1951a):

> The sample in question consists of 61 children from the age of three months to one year. These children were raised without their mothers in a nursery under the care of a very competent head nurse and a varying number of efficient assistant nurses. The hygienic precautions were adequate. Daily medical rounds took place. The food was varied, ample in quantity, hygienically prepared and distributed. Nevertheless the emotional climate was that of utter emotional starvation. Very few of the children had toys. The children were isolated each in a cubicle in such a manner that the child hardly had anything in its field of vision outside the ceiling. . .the decline of the quotient (DQ) is a progressive one; after the fifth month it falls well below 80. That this is not a transitory phenomenon is borne out by the fact that we followed these children up to and including their third year, at which time the developmental quotient had declined to 45. This is a quotient which corresponds to imbecility.

Granted the unsophisticated tables and the lack of eloquence in the presentation, what this article tells us is of startling and immense importance.

[47] Perhaps this is why the direct observation of infants, which at first seemed such a promising extension of psychoanalysis (see Spitz, 1950; A. Freud, 1953, 1958; and the discussion by Spitz, Hartmann and Waelder in A. Freud, 1953), has proved to be, to this observer at least (admittedly I am in the minority), so barren. The danger, I believe, is that the observation of the surface can replace the stubborn analytic scepticism that seems to me so characteristic of Freud. Appearances are deceiving. Even as acute an observer as Ernst Kris could err. For example, in his well-known article, 'Decline and Recovery in a Three-year-old' (published posthumously in the *Psychoanalytic Study of the Child* **7** (1956d), he says of the father: "He had come successfully through a hard life, as far as we know without psychological impairment" (p. 182). Yet on p. 203 he can also observe: "Later, when the child was disturbed and retarded in many functions, he [the father] was the one who refused to show concern, not out of lack of attachment to Anne, but according to his statements, the baby seemed to him to be at all times fully satisfactory." One of these statements, then, must be false. I suspect it is the former. I don't see how a four-year-old child can be analyzed as if he lived in a closed system, without reference to his parents. And the extent to which an analysis of a child can modify the parental environment is, of course, extremely limited (unless the parents are themselves in analysis), if indeed it can be altered at all. The Kleinian view that all pathogenesis is due to pathogenic fantasies from the earliest months (or even weeks, for some orthodox Kleinians) of the infant's life seems to me entirely 'fantastic' and utterly beyond scientific demonstration (see Bibring, 1947; Glover, 1945).

[48] Bagchi (1939), Bharati (1965), Chakravarti (1963), Dasgupta (1946), Shahidullah (1928).

[49] The eating of food, for obvious reasons (taking things into one's body), can be the occasion for hidden paranoid tendencies (cf. Schilder, 1935 on *The Image and Appearance of the Human Body*). A good example of this is found in the *Ādipurāṇa* (cited by Kane, 1941, Vol. 2, Part 2, p. 759), where we are told that a person should always eat alone, for *ko hi jānāti kiṃ kasya pracchannaṃ pātakam bhavet*, "Who can know what hidden sin another person has committed", with the obvious implication that this sin will be transmitted, physically, via

the food eaten. There should be no sounds, and if anyone is touched, water is placed on the eyes. Vegetarianism is not that old in India, for we find the famous passage from the *Śatapatha Brāhmaṇa* III. 1.2.21, where Yājñavalkya says: *aśnāmy evāham aṃsalaṃ ced bhavatīti*, "I eat it [meat] but only if it is tender!" Later, once again paranoid fantasies cluster about the idea of devouring flesh; for example, there is the common notion that one who eats meat will be eaten, in his next life, by the same animal he has eaten. The etymology often proposed by vegetarians for meat (*māṃsaḥ*) is: *māṃ saḥ*, 'he – me'. Manu (V. 56) is more sensible, even if ultimately taken by childhood fantasies: *na māṃsabhakṣaṇe doṣo na madye na ca maithune. pravṛttis eṣā bhūtānāṃ nivṛttis tu mahāphalā*, "There is nothing wrong with eating meat, or drinking wine, or engaging in sexual intercourse. It is normal for people to do so. However, to abstain leads to great rewards." An exhaustive study of vegetarianism has been made by Alsdorf (1961). See also Brown (1957). For a survey of the literature on feeding problems of psychogenic origins, see Lehman (1949). The best work on fasting is, of course, Kafka's 'The Hunger Artist'.

[50] Shukla (1970, p. 321).

[51] The great work of Scholem (1957) on Sabbatai Ṣevi is certainly a valuable source of information on this topic, even if Scholem did not intend it to be, as is the more avowedly psychological study of cults in Europe in Cohn's brilliant book, *The Pursuit of the Millenium* (1957).

[52] See Schmideberg (1936, p. 2):

> Fear of death and fear of life seem to constitute the strongest incentives to suicide. Certain patients make life and death alternately the subject of their paranoid anxiety – they do much the same with work and sleep, day and night. Suicide is an escape from the real and phantasied dangers of life to a greater happiness and safety – sleep and life after death. I do not believe that anyone kills himself who has not hope in a happier life after death.

See also Furman (1974), Haim (1974), Friedlander (1940), Murray (1967) and Kubie (1964), who writes:

> Suicidal efforts may be attempts to expiate death wishes. This seems more likely to occur in someone who throughout life has been a dedicated supporter of everyone in trouble. Such a man was in fact a compulsive do-gooder, whose benevolence effectively concealed a profound jealousy and hate, which had their roots in a secret sense of having been wronged. His strongest death wishes were directed against a mean, ungrateful, overtly paranoid and crippled sister. Only once did these death wishes break through in overt form, i.e., in a dream in which the sister had drowned in spite of the dreamer's heroic efforts to rescue her. After a day of brooding, his suicidal attempt occurred the following morning (p. 458).

Cf. Anthony and Chiland (1978), Anthony and Koupernik (1973) and Orgel (1974).

[53] Vaidya (1960, 34.24, p. 181), Suzuki and Idzumi (1934-1936, p. 236).

[54] Vandier-Nicolas (1963, p. 169). On Chinese landscape painting generally, see Fontein

(1970), Trevor (1969), Edwards (1962, 1967), Van Gulik (1958), Waley (1923), Lee (1954), Soper (1941), Sullivan (1955, 1962, 1974), Gray (1959), Bush (1971), Sirén (1956-1958), Demiéville (1972) and Cahill (1967). On painting and madness, see Wittkower (1967).

[55] For more on the shamanistic background to these poems, see Waley (1955); and for more translations, see the lively versions by Payne (1949) and Waley (1946).

[56] My answer to this question is largely negative. In general, psychoanalysis has not illuminated literature but has, on the contrary, taken from it. We have learned little from psychoanalysis about health. Freud gave a succinct definition of health: the capacity for enjoyment and for achievement. This statement, in its starkness, was not meant as an epigram but only as an indication of self-confessed ignorance. We know more about what makes a talented author grind to a halt than what enables him to work with pleasure.

My reading in psychoanalysis has not enriched my research on Indian poetics. The only work on creativity I can recommend is Kubie's *The Neurotic Distortion of the Creative Process* (1958).

[57] Masson and Patwardhan (1969, 1970).

[58] Freud (1914).

[59] Nunberg (1951). See Sachs (1941, p. 364):

> We meet our patient's real and ultimate wishes empty-handed. We may be able after a careful, painful and difficult study of his personality to show him when and where and why he has turned the wrong corner and point out to him the right direction for his search after happiness. . .

A fine example of the interplay of reality and transference is to be found in a moving case history by Peto (1960):

> I was thrown out into the world. When I was six, I once again lived with my aging and uneducated grandparents. On my sixth birthday I expected my father to visit me, as he had promised. Though my grandmother assured me that father would not come, I did not believe her, and was waiting for my father in front of the house sitting on a bench. Time passed and everybody went in for dinner; I did not leave the bench because I wanted to see him when he turned round the corner. Night fell, everybody went to bed, I was sitting and waiting there, until dawn came, and my grandmother forced me to go to bed. Never, ever did I trust anybody again.

This patient in his analysis must have experienced and re-experienced again and again in the transference relation to the analyst the sad myriad of feelings of loss, despair and mistrust contained and encapsulated in this symbolic memory.

[60] Masson and Merwin (1977).

[61] It will be clear to readers that I have, by choice, limited myself to those aspects of India which are less well-known, which do not represent the more obviously available attitudes of Indian culture. This has been done for reasons of personal preference, of course, because

these are the aspects of Indian literature that made a personal appeal to me. But I have also a certain theoretical justification: in analysis, it is often the disavowed, the minor, the whispered, the seeming irrelevancy, that channels the entire analysis into a new area. I think that something of this truth applies to Indian literature.

[62] I am actuely aware of the fact that I have touched on so many issues often only tangentially related to psychoanalysis that the omission of the relation between Marxism and psychoanalysis is bound to strike the reader. Such a glaring omission reflects neither a judgment (in my opinion, at present psychoanalysis stands to gain immensely from a rich infusion of classical Marxist theory, especially as found in the works of Marx and Engels, particularly their work on the origins of the family, their forceful rejection of religion and their early emphasis on alienation) nor a lack of interest, but is purely and simply a reflection of my own ignorance. I have read so little in this important field that I do not think what I have to say would be at all informative. However, I do want to mention one book in particular, since its title is deceptive, and that is the work by the Italian Marxist theorist, Sebastiano Timpanaro: *The Freudian Slip: Psychoanalysis and Textual Critism* (1974). Timpanaro subjects Freud's *The Psychopathology of Everyday Life* to a devastating critique, one which is entirely justified and done with great skill and a solid background in classical philology (his judgment of the works of others, especially those he singles out for praise, e.g., Roazen's slight *Brother Animal*, is less certain). Timpanaro points out that this early work of Freud does not take into account "the fear, which is sometimes general and sometimes related to a particular and imminent danger, of illness, senility, or death – of ourselves, our friends or our relatives" (0. 114). He also notes, in a withering footnote (p. 190, note 27), that late in his life (in *The New Introductory Lectures in Psychoanalysis*, S.E. 22, p. 180) Freud compares the writings of Marx to the Bible and the Koran as a source of revelation, but nowhere is there "in this last Lecture which surveys obscurantist or falsely-progressive 'world views', a single word against the Fascism that held sway in Italy and Hungary, against the clerical Fascism of Seipel and Dollfuss in Austria, or the Nazism which was about to triumph in Germany." I don't see how this charge can be answered. Finally, the work is rich in citations and in methodological sophistication. Commenting on "Negation" (S.E. 19, pp. 235-40), Timpanaro observes that

> the principle enunciated by Freud in this brief essay is, so to speak, a variant of the ancient *excusatio non petita, accusatio manifest* [an unsolicited excuse is a manifest (self-) accusation]. Every time, says Freud, that one of our patients for example declares: 'You ask who this person in the dream can have been. It was not my mother', we can be sure that it is his mother. . . . It is intriguing to imagine Freud's reaction if one of his patients – a neurotic, but a politically lucid one – in reply to the question which according to Freud was the best means of 'ensnaring' the patient: 'What would you consider was the most unlikely thing in the world in that situation? What do you think was furthest from your mind at the time?', had answered: "I consider the most unlikely thing in the world would be to see a capitalist renounce his own privileges without any use of force on the part of the workers he exploits." At this point, there would surely have been an exchange of roles: Freud would himself have succumbed to the behavior typical of a 'patient', he would have lost his temper or changed the subject – in short have revealed 'resistances' so strong that he would not even have been aware of their existence (op. cit., pp. 57-59.)

II: THE OCEANIC FEELING: ORIGIN OF THE TERM

In a paper on narcissism (Masson and Hanly, 1976), we indicated that the term 'oceanic feeling' or 'oceanic experience' (*ozeanisches Gefühl* or *Ewigkeitsgefühl*) used in *Civilization and its Discontents* (Freud, 1930) was taken from Romain Rolland and that it derived, ultimately, from Sanskrit sources. Further and more careful research has allowed me to be more precise in tracking this term back to its origins. An investigation of the surrounding imagery and related ideas suggested certain key features in such experiences (feelings of sadness, of the awareness of transience, feelings of world-weariness and of the dream-like nature of existence), and this in turn provided certain clues as to Freud's interest in these experiences. Following a hint of Kanzer (1969), I was able to link more closely than has hitherto been attempted the Acropolis experience and oceanic feelings. Finally, I was led to take a closer look both at the image of the sea and the experience to which it points in an effort to provide a psychoanalytic explanation for both the form and the content of the oceanic feeling.

My thesis in this and the following chapter is briefly that Freud took the term 'oceanic feeling' from Romain Rolland.[1] Rolland had been reading widely about Ramakrishna for his forthcoming biography of this nineteenth-century Bengali saint. In the description of his own mystic experiences in terms of the ocean, Ramakrishna was influenced not only by the larger Sanskrit tradition but, more specifically, by one text in that tradition to which he was particularly attached: the *Aṣṭāvakrasaṃhitā*, a medieval Sanskrit text. I will discuss the early legends about the supposed author of this text, *Aṣṭāvakra*, and then translate the relevant passages from his text. These are, I believe, the ultimate source of Freud's term the 'oceanic feeling'. My reading of the Indian texts has also alerted me to certain related experiences such as narcissistic fantasies of world-destruction, depersonalization, derealization and *déjà-vu*. This will allow me to indicate then, by an examination of Freud's relation to Rolland (pointing to similarities with the earlier and more tragic relation to Jung),[2] that Freud may also have felt that such experiences are related, although he never says so explicitly. It is my conclusion that Freud was led to investigate such experiences by personal and intellectual needs which were successfully met by his understanding both of the ultimate referent of the oceanic experience and his experience on the Acropolis.

Rolland, on the fifth of December 1927, wrote as follows to Freud:

> Votre analyse des religions est juste. Mais j'aurais aimé à vous voir faire l'analyse du sentiment religieux spontané, ou plus exactement de la *sensation* religieuse, qui est toute différente des religions proprement dites. . .Le fait simple et direct de *la sensation de l'Éternel* (qui peut très bien n'être pas éternel, mais simplement sans bornes perceptibles, et comme océanique) (Cornubert, 1966, p. 25).

Freud wrote to Rolland on June 14, 1929, as follows:

> My Dear Friend: Your letter of December 5, 1927, containing your remarks about a feeling you describe as 'oceanic', has left me no peace. It happens that in a new work which lies before me still uncompleted I am making a starting point of this remark. I mention this 'oceanic' feeling and am trying to interpret it from the point of view of our psychology (Freud, E., 1961, p. 388).

The reference is, of course, to *Civilization and its Discontents* (1929-30), in which the first chapter is devoted to a discussion of this theme in a manner known to all analysts.

It is a well-known fact, then, that Freud took this term from Rolland. From where did Rolland derive it?[3] From, I believe, the reading he did on Ramakrishna[4] in preparation for his work *Essai sur la mystique et l'action de l'Inde vivante*: I. *La Vie de Ramakrishna*; II. *La Vie de Vivekananda et l'évangile universel* (Rolland, 1929). I must pause.here to give the reader some idea of whom Rolland had chosen to write about.[5] Aldous Huxley, in a foreword to the main biography of Ramakrishna (Nikhilananda, 1942), notes that "of the day-to-day life of the great theocentric saints and contemplatives we know, in the great majority of cases, nothing whatever. Hence the special interest attaching to this enormously detailed account of the daily life and conversations of Sri Ramakrishna." But in reading through the mass of material available, one fact stands out: there is severe psychopathology in Ramakrishna. In a paper read to the American Psychoanalytic Association at its annual meeting in 1973 (Masson, 1973), I compared Ramakrishna to Schreber. In spite of his disturbances (which are not recognized as such by any of the authors who have written about him, including Rolland), his influence on the whole of Bengali culture has been enormous, and indeed, in reading the biography by 'M',[6] one is struck by the vigor of the language,[7] the intensity of the emotion and the power of folk expressions he revived. I cannot think of a single Indian author who so intensely lived through the experiences of Indian mythological characters in what is an often overt hallucinatory manner.[8] He identified with women in their role as the lovers of God to the point that "minute drops of blood oozed from his skin" (hysterical menstruation?); he cross-dressed frequently;[9] he identified himself with the great monkey-god Hanumān; he had visions of beautiful young women with flowing hair as he watched the Ganges at night from the balcony of the little temple where he was priest; he would faint in the middle of rituals, or would "stiffen into a statue". His most notable characteristic was his ability to pass into a trance-state, *samādhi*, with all its phobic entailments, upon the slightest provocation. "An insane woman came to him in the garden of Kashipore. Ramakrishna said that if she had touched him, his body would have dropped dead." "During the first days of his return from ecstasy. . .he howled with pain when he saw two boatmen quarrelling angrily." He had a series of encounters with odd men and women. For example, the mystic Totapuri tells Ramakrishna that he must pass beyond all "forms": "What! You say you cannot? You must! Looking about him, he found a piece of glass. He took it and stuck the point between my eyes. . . .Then I began to meditate with all my might, and as soon as the gracious form of the Divine Mother appeared, I used my discrimination as a sword and I clove her in two." Rolland, who had approached the life of Ramakrishna with no psychological curiosity, felt appalled by his odd behavior and wrote: "I will not deny the fact that when I had reached this point in my researches, I shut the book."[10]

The image of the ocean is very frequent in the carefully-recorded words of Ramakrishna. Here are two examples:

> Sometimes God effaces even that trace of 'I'. Then one experiences *jaḍa samādhi* or *nirvikalpa samādhi* (ecstasy without form). That experience cannot be described. A salt doll went to measure the depth of the ocean, but before it had gone far into the water it melted away. It became entirely one with the water of the ocean. Then who was to come back and tell the ocean's depth?[11]

This same image reappears in another passage even more directly suggestive of our theme:

> Weeping, I prayed to the Mother: 'O Mother, reveal to me what is contained in the Vedas and the Vedānta. Reveal to me what is in the

> Purana and the Tantra." One by one She has revealed all these to me. . . .Another day I was shown heaps of human heads, mountain high. Nothing else existed, and I was seated alone in their midst. Still another day she showed me an ocean. Taking the form of a salt doll, I was going to measure its depth. While doing this, through the grace of the guru I was turned to stone. Then I saw a ship and at once got into it. The helmsman was the guru. I. . .saw that 'I' and 'you' were not two different things. I found myself swimming joyfully in the ocean of *Sacchidānanda* (being, consciousness, bliss). These are all deep mysteries.[12]

But I believe that the actual passage[13] which inspired Romain Rolland to his use of the term the 'oceanic feeling', is the one he quotes at the beginning of his work. Ramakrishna was in anguish. He felt he was wrung like a damp cloth. Friends said his face and breast were "reddened by an afflux of blood, his eyes filled with tears, and his body shaken with spasms." In a frenzy he decided to end his life for he might never have a vision of the Mother of the Universe (*Kālī*).[14] He grabs a sword to kill himself, when suddenly. . .

> . . .The whole scene, doors, windows, the temple itself vanished. . . .It seemed as if nothing existed any more. Instead I saw an ocean. . . boundless, dazzling. In whatever direction I looked great luminous waves were rising. They bore down upon me with a loud roar, as if to swallow me up. In an instant they were upon me, they broke over me, they engulfed me. I was suffocated. I lost all natural consciousness and I fell. . . .How I passed that day and the next I know not. Round me rolled an ocean of ineffable joy. And in the depths of my being I was conscious of the presence of the Divine Mother.[15]

This, I submit, is the passage from which Romain Rolland took his term the 'oceanic feeling'. Our next task, then, is to discover the origins of this particular use of imagery in Ramakrishna himself.

It is difficult to gauge the extent of Ramakrishna's direct knowledge of the classical Indian tradition. For one thing, we have no reliable knowledge concerning his linguistic capacities. According to the great Sanskrit scholar F. Max Müller, "His knowledge of the *purāṇas*, the *Mahābhārata*, the *Rāmāyaṇa* and the *Bhāgavata* must have been in Bengali, as he never, according to Mazoomdar who was his friend, knew a word of Sanskrit."[16] This is certainly an exaggeration, for Ramakrishna was conversant with many Sanskrit technical and semitechnical words both from philosophy and mystical writings. This is not, however, equivalent to knowing Sanskrit, and it is not likely that Ramakrishna could read a text in Sanskrit without the aid of a translation into Bengali. However, there was hardly a major Sanskrit text that had not either been translated into Bengali, or that was not available with some form of a Bengali commentary, even, if need be, an oral one. I am particularly concerned with Ramakrishna's knowledge of a Sanskrit text called the *Aṣṭāvakrasaṃhitā*, or *Aṣṭāvakragītā*. This text, written in very simple Sanskrit, is an uncompromising example of *Advaitavedānta*, nondualistic Vedānta, which denies the reality[17] of all phenomena of the outer and inner world in favour of the one reality that is Brahman, and which is also the same as our innermost self, the Ātman. Here is a series of typical verses from that text:

15.4:
na tvaṃ deho na te deho
bhoktā kartā na vā bhavān
cidrūpo 'si sadā sākṣī
nirapekṣaḥ sukhaṃ cara

You are not the body. You do not have a body.
You do nothing and you experience nothing.
You are pure consciousness.
You are the eternal witness.
Free, wander [this earth] in happiness.

15.11:
tvayy anantamahāmbhodhau
viśvavīciḥ svabhāvataḥ
udetu vāstam āyātu
na te vṛddhir na vā kṣatiḥ

You are an infinite ocean.
The universe is a wave.
It can swell or subside.
What is the difference?
You neither gain nor lose thereby.

And so: 16.4:
vyāpāre khidyate yas tu nimeṣonmeṣayor api
tasyālasyadhurīṇasya sukhaṃ nānyasya kasyacit

Happiness belongs to the master idler
For whom it is too much effort to open and close
his eyelids.
And to nobody else.

As one of these verses shows, it is precisely in this text that I have found the most direct examples of sea imagery in terms of the mystic experience. When I first read these verses, it occurred to me that Ramakrishna might well have taken his imagery from this text. I knew that Ramakrishna had tremendous admiration for one of the great Sanskrit scholars of his period, the philanthropist Iśvaracandra Vidyāsāgara (1820-1891). He had heard about his fame and the relief measures he had taken in the great famine of 1864 and had visited him in 1882.[18] The visit to Vidyāsāgara was a memorable one, as is evident from 'M's description.[19]

Ramakrishna told this great scholar that "mere pandits are like diseased fruit that becomes hard and will not ripen at all." He punned a great deal on his name (Vidyāsāgara = 'ocean of learning') and spoke much of the ocean of bliss, the "ocean of immortality". In parting he told the sixty-two-year-old Sanskrit pandit:

> The words I have spoken are really superfluous. You know all this: you simply aren't conscious of it. There are many wealthy people who don't know the names of all their servants, and are even unaware of many of the precious things in their houses.

This scholar had published many accurate translations of Sanskrit texts, with fine commentaries of his own, both in Bengali and in Sanskrit.[20] His translation into Bengali of the *Aṣṭāvakrasaṃhitā*, with a commentary in Bengali, was posthumously published in 1901 (Vidyāsāgara, 1901), possibly Ramakrishna had seen the work previously. A Bengali translation already existed in 1854 (*Aṣṭāvakrasaṃhitā*, 1854), and this was almost certainly not the first printed. However, there is final proof that Ramakrishna knew the text in some version. In *Sri Ramakrishna the Great Master* (Saradananda, 1952), a work originally written in Bengali in five volumes by Swami Saradananda, a direct disciple of Ramakrishna, and printed as *Śri Rāmakṛṣṇa Līlā-prasaṅga* between 1911 and 1918, we find the following passage:

> Accustomed to the dualistic mode of worship in the Brahmo Samaj, the Swami [Vivekananda, the major disciple of Ramakrishna] regarded the nondualistic mode taught in the Vedānta as a blasphemy. But the Master (Ramakrishna) tried in various ways to make him practice it. The Swami said: "As soon as I went to Dakshineswar, the Master gave me those books which he forbade others to read. Among other books, a copy of the *Ashtavakra Samhita* was in his room. When the Master found anyone reading that book, he would forbid him and would give

him instead such books as 'Mukti and how to attain it', the Bhagavadgīta or some Purāṇa. But, scarcely had I gone to him when he took out the book and asked me to read it. . . .I said: 'What is the use of reading this book? It is a sin even to think "I am God". The book teaches the same blasphemy. It should be burnt.' The Master smiled and said: 'Do I ask you to read it to yourself? I ask you to read a little to me. Please do it. In that case, you will not have to think that you are God'."[21]

So it is clear that Ramakrishna knew the text of the *Aṣṭāvakrasaṃhitā,*[22] and that he valued it beyond most books that he knew. Before considering the verses from this book that were almost certainly the source of oceanic imagery, from Ramakrishna to Romain Rolland to Freud, it is worth pausing to inquire about the identity of Aṣṭāvakra, the supposed author of this text. What is known of him? The Indian tradition holds that the *Aṣṭāvakrasaṃhitā* was written by Aṣṭāvakra, a sage mentioned in the *Mahābhārata.* It is unfortunate that a text which has had such a profound influence on modern India should be almost totally ignored by Western Sanskrit scholars.[23] The translator, Nityaswarupananda (1953) writes that it may be put forward as an indisputable proposition that the work is older than Gaudapada's Karikas",[24] and this opinion is shared by Satkari Mookerjee, the Asutosh Professor of Sanskrit in Calcutta University: "The *Aṣṭāvakra Saṃhitā* bears close affinities to the *Bhagavad-Gītā* and seems to be the product of the same age."[25] "It is an ancient classic, which proves that Gauḍapāda or Śaṅkarācarya did not profound a newfangled philosophy under the influence of Buddhist idealistic thought, as facile scholarship seeks to establish nowadays on the basis of superficial and flimsy parallelisms. This system of thought, on the contrary, had its moorings in the Upaniṣads and received definite articulation in older works, including the present one."[26]

This seems to be the traditional opinion about the age of the text, evidencing an understandable but totally unscientific desire to put any admired text into hoary antiquity. The rather impolite reference in the last passage to the great work of a more sceptical-minded scholar of great eminence, Vidushekara Bhattacharya (1943), is not an argument, and in my opinion and that of most other scholars, I would place the *Aṣṭāvakra* as a late text, perhaps somewhere between the twelfth and sixteenth centuries.[27] This is also the opinion of Hauschild in his detailed study of the text.[28] This controversy over the date of the text is of interest because it shows that the Indian tradition was firm in maintaining an identity between Aṣṭāvakra, a character who appears in the *Mahābhārata*, in a passage that probably belongs to the second century B.C., and the author (in fact unknown) of a late medieval text.

The legends about this man are also significant, for we can be certain that Ramakrishna knew them, and it is unlikely that the legends he knew would not come to his mind, perhaps only preconsciously, when considering the later text. We shall probably never know what Ramakrishna actually knew about Aṣṭāvakra beyond the two legends which I shall presently recount, nor can we know to what extent he was intrigued by the character of Aṣṭāvakra. However, there is reason to suspect that his interest was considerable. Fortunately we do know one fact. 'M', the close disciple of Ramakrishna, knew and repeated a peculiar detail about the sexual life of Aṣṭāvakra, which he cites in his continuation of *The Gospel of Sri Ramakrishna*,[29] where he speaks of Aṣṭāvakra and other sages who "had seminal discharge at night due to the evil influence of nature. And they began to lament on waking up. On the other hand, perhaps throughout the day they were busy with *puga* (worship), *havan* (sacrifice) and *yajna* (another form of sacrifice)." No source is given, but it is possible or even probable that 'M' heard this from Ramakrishna himself. Where Ramakrishna heard it is a puzzle. Aṣṭāvakra is not mentioned in the Purāṇas (see Dikshitar, 1951) and indeed, the only two legends current about him are those found in the *Mahābhārata* that I shall presently relate. Did Ramakrishna apply his rich fantasy life to this question?

There seem to be only two legends concerning Aṣṭāvakra in the great epics of India (Sörensen, 1904). The first of these is found in *Vanaparvan*, the third book of the *Mahābhārata*, Chapter 132 (critical edition, Vol. 3, p. 430; vulgate, Vol. II). The legend is as follows: Uddālaka had a disciple called Kahoda, "restrained in his senses", "meek and obedient to his teachers", to whom he gave his daughter in marriage. Verse III. 132. 10 is the kernel of the legend, although it is rather ambiguous in meaning. I interpret it as follows: "A fetus grew inside her, similar to fire (i.e., it was a shining fetus). This fetus then said to his father as he was reading the sacred texts: 'Father, you have been reading the sacred texts the whole night, but it does not seem correct.' " The last line, *nedaṃ samyag ivopavartate*, I take to mean that his pronunciation of the text was incorrect, that is, in reading the Vedic texts he was not able to remember the proper accentuation. The father responds by cursing the fetus to be born deformed (*vakra*) in eight parts (*aṣṭa*), hence his name: Aṣṭāvakra. His mother, close to gestation, becomes "desirous of money", and asks her husband to obtain wealth somehow. He goes to King Janaka, debates with Bandin, loses the debate and is drowned in the ocean! Uddālaka hears of it, tells his daughter, and asks her not to tell her son Aṣṭāvakra. He believes his grandfather to be his father, and his uncle (who is his own age) Śvetaketu to be his brother. (Note that all these names, with the exception of Aṣṭāvakra, appear as important characters in the earlier Upaniṣads, presumably owing to the pervasive desire to keep alive the most inspiring characters from the theological tradition.) When they are twelve, Śvetaketu sees his nephew seated on his father's lap, pulls him off crying, saying, "This is not your father's lap." Aṣṭāvakra is pierced to the heart by these unkind words and runs home to ask his mother: *kva nu tāta mama*, "Where is my father?" He learns the truth and travels with his uncle to the court of Janaka in search of Bandin, "as he would look for a lone swan on the vast ocean." They enter a debate of riddles: naming things from one to thirteen in perfect verses.[30] When he reaches thirteen Bandin stops midway, unable to complete the verse. Aṣṭāvakra finishes the stanza and demands, as his reward, death by drowning for Bandin. Bandin then reveals that he is the son of the god of water (Varuṇa) and has sent his defeated contenders to his father's kingdom to witness his twelve-year sacrifice, whereupon he points to the sea and says: "Here they return." The father does indeed return, and blesses his son: "That which I could not do, my son has done for me." The father then has the son bathe in a river, and he emerges uncrooked. (Note, however, that this 'happy ending' is found only in the vulgate text; in the critical edition it has been omitted.) Bandin then *viveśa toyaṃ sāgarasyota*, "enters the waters of the ocean" to rejoin his father (3.134.37).[93]

I need not draw attention to the oedipal nature of this legend, a fact which will prove important later in this paper. The next legend is found in one of the last books of the great epic, the *Anuśāsanaparvan*. The critical edition (Dandekar, 1966) is particularly severe with this book, and omits some 6,000 lines found in the vulgate. Hardly anything, however, is omitted from our story, and so we can presume that it is ancient and common to all regional manuscript versions of the great epic. The legend is as follows: Aṣṭāvakra falls in love with a woman called Suprabhā, "whose face was like a whole forest at the beginning of spring." Her father, Vadānya, promises her hand in marriage if Aṣṭāvakra can take a perilous journey north in order to locate a beautiful woman ascetic. He agrees, and after a year's delay due to an entrancing dance he cannot stop watching, he reaches a beautiful forest and finds there a magnificent palace. Seven young women greet him and he, although an ascetic (*mahātapāḥ*), is captivated by the beauty of each one of them. He feels, for the first time, sexual desire. Inside the palace he is greeted by a very aged woman, heavily made up. He asks that the seven young women leave, with the exception of the one who is "wise and tranquil of heart." All seven walk out. That night, the old woman approaches Aṣṭāvakra and says that she is inflamed with sexual desire and that to refuse her would be sinful. He should make love to her, and all her wealth will be his. Aṣṭāvakra, repulsed by her age and the state of her body, refuses, but he does agree to stay in the palace for some time in the hope that he may someday come to love her. (The text is somewhat confused as to whose desire this is.) The next day, he finds it difficult to look at her, so decrepit is her condition. But that evening she comes to him, and "she massaged all parts of his body with warm water, and fragrant oil and her soft hands felt good on him." So pleasant was the sensation, that the whole night passed, and the sage did not even notice. The next night, she again comes to his bed and begs him to sleep with her. He says that he cannot sleep with the wife of another man. She answers that she is totally independent. Aṣṭāvakra replies with a speech about the impossibility of freedom for women, "who belong to their father in youth, their husband in womanhood, and their son in their dotage." She begs him to sleep with her, explaining that she is a virgin. She had already lectured him on the strongest power in the world, "sexual desire": "For women there is nothing greater than to have intercourse with a man they desire. This is the point of our whole existence. When a woman is under the sway of sexual desire she becomes independent indeed, and will walk over burning sand and feel nothing."[31]

The end of the story is rather obscure: Aṣṭāvakra confesses to her that he returns her desire. He then thinks to himself that it is a great mystery, how she is now so beautiful (to him?) and was yet formerly so ugly. He asks her how it is that she is able to change her appearance. She tells him that she is a goddess, and that "he has now seen that women are fickle, that even when they become old, the fever of desire inflames their body."[32] She was testing him; he has passed the test (?) and may now return to marry and bear children. It is a peculiar story, and the translator of the vulgate edition of the *Mahābhārata*, Volume 10, often disagrees with the commentary in his interpretations. A note in the critical edition of the *Mahābhārata* points out that the story seems to have no point, and this is also the view of an anonymous commentary cited in the critical edition.[33] Nonetheless, one thing is clear: the sage has hardly shown himself to be beyond desire. Indeed, this legend may well be the core of the story of Aṣṭāvakra's loss of semen, referred to earlier. It is not without psychoanalytic interest that the legendary creator of the most explicit passages on the oceanic experience is also a man deeply concerned and involved with instinctual temptations.

I will now give the text and translate five verses from the *Aṣṭāvakrasaṃhitā* which are, in my opinion, the source of the expression the 'oceanic feeling':

> *Aṣṭāvakrasaṃhitā* 11.23:
> *aho bhuvanakallolair vicitrair drāk samutthitam*
> *mayy anatamahāmbhodhau cittavāte samudyate*
>
> Oh! In me, the eternal ocean, marvellous waveworlds suddenly appear as the wind-mind rises.

The next half of this verse reads:

> *mayy anatamahāmbhodhau cittavāte praśāmyati*
> *abhāgyāj jīvanijo jagatpoto vaiśvaraḥ*
>
> When the wind-mind is in me the limitless ocean is calm, alas, the world-boat of the sea-faring Ego sinks.
>
> *mayy anantamahāmbodhāv āścāryaṃ jīvavīcayaḥ*
> *udyanti ghnanti khelanti praviśanti svabhāvataḥ*
>
> It is a marvel! In me the eternal ocean, the person-waves rise, strike one another, play together, and finally die, each according to its destiny.
>
> VII.3:
> *mayy anantamahāmbhodhau viśvaṃ nāma vikalpanā*
> *atiśānto nirākāra etad evāham āsthitaḥ*
>
> In me, the eternal ocean, is found the entire universe. It is nothing but a figment of my imagination. I remain, calm and beyond material form, this very thing (i.e., the truth itself).
>
> 14.18:
> *eka eva bhavāmbhodhāv āsīd asti bhaviṣyati*
> *na te bandho 'sti mokṣo vā kṛtakṛtyaḥ sukhaṃ cara*
>
> In this great ocean of existence, only One was, is and will be: You have nothing to do with being bound or with freedom. You have accomplished what must be accomplished. Wander happily.

Now the derivation of such typical expressions as the following by Ramakrishna:[35]

> There are hills and mountains, dales and valleys under the sea, but they are not visible from the surface. So in the state of *samādhi* when one

> floats upon the ocean of *saccidānanda* (being, consciousness, bliss), all human consciousness lies latent in him,

becomes clear.

Now, too, we can guess the source of the following quotation from *Vivekananda in America* (1896) which Romain Rolland uses as the frontispiece of his book:[36] "Never forget the glory of human nature! We are the greatest God. . . .Christs and Buddhas are but waves on the boundless ocean which *I AM*."

This historical investigation has revealed, I believe for the first time, the origin of the term 'oceanic feeling'. In addition, the investigation has had the incidental benefit of revealing a group of associated ideas clustered around the term that point to its complex and unsuspected history. It now remains to see whether in a similar manner we can lay bare the historical roots of Freud's concern with the experience itself and to discover whether this will enable us to trace the dense ramifications of this theme back to its deepest psychic roots. Such will be the subject matter of the next two chapters.

Notes

[1] I have to thank Dr. K. R. Eissler for drawing my attention to the thesis of Cornubert and for kindly arranging for me to see a copy of the relevant passages. The Freud/Romain Rolland relationship I find curious. When Freud sent Rolland a copy of *Civilization and its Discontents*, the dedication read: "From a Landtier to my Oceanic Friend" (Cornubert, p. 37; cf. Fisher, 1976.) Rolland for his part seems to have understood Freud's deep and humane pessimism, for he writes back (May 3, 1931) about Freud's intrepid work, motivated solely by his search for truth: "sans désir, sans espoir et sans peur!" Miss Anna Freud informs me that she does not believe that Freud read, in fact, the three volumes on Ramakrishna that Rolland sent him in July, 1929. Dr. I. B. Harrison is now engaged in a closer study of the relationship of the two men. See his two articles, "On the Maternal Origins of Awe" (1975) and most recently (1979), "On Freud's View of the Infant-Mother Relationship and of the Oceanic Feeling," which in many ways complements the present study.

[2] I have been struck with the obvious elements of anti-semitism in Romain Rolland to which Freud, as with Jung, seems to have turned a blind eye. In *Jean Christophe* (see Starr, 1971), Olivier, who is so often a voice for Rolland himself, says: "Les juifs sont comme les femmes: excellents, quand on les tient en bride. . . ." Lest I be accused of selecting a passage from a novel, here is an astonishing passage that Rolland wrote on September 14, 1930 (Rolland, 1960, p. 289). He is speaking of Sylvain Lévi, the well-known French Sanskrit scholar, a man of tremendous knowledge, warmth and charm, possibly the greatest scholar of India ever to have lived:

> Il hait d'ailleurs Vivekananda, comme il me hait. Pour lui, l'Inde doit rester un objet de

> musée et d'archives. Défense de revivre! Elle se passera de sa permission. . .Ces Juifs, qui se donnent le ridicule de poser en représentants (outrés) de l'Occident contre l'Asie!

Apparently Sylvain Lévi had written something on Rolland in the book by Henri Massis, *Les Appels de l'Orient* (Paris: Emile-Paul, 1925), but I have not been able to secure this article. One wonders just what was Rolland's attitude to Freud, "this god-forsaken Jew", as Freud once referred to himself. In a letter to Charles Baudoin March in 1930 (Cornubert, p. 36), Rolland quotes a passage from Freud about Jung, where Freud speaks of Jung's mysticism, and then says snidely, "Cela sent l'excommunication." Freud's great regard for Rolland (Jones, 1957) is puzzling. To be fair to Rolland, it should be noted that from 1932, on, he began to lose interest in India. (See the chapter on Rolland in Bies, 1974, and the excellent chapter in Robichez, 1961). There is an interesting unpublished letter of Stefan Zweig to Rolland of February 1939 where he writes: "Il avait raison le grand bon Freud, de se méfier de notre 'progrès' et de craindre la force implacable de mauvais instincts" (Nedeljković, 1970).

Rolland's interest in India seems to have originated with his beloved sister, who was involved in translations concerning India (see Barrèrre, 1966). She had translated an article of Tapanmohan Chatterji, "Les anciens chants mystiques du Bengale," in *Feuilles de l'Inde* (Chitra Publications, Boulogne-sur-Seine: C. A. Högman, 1928.)

[3] Is it possible that Romain Rolland was given an impetus to use this expression from his reading of an early Buddhist text, the *Saundarananda* of Aśvaghoṣa, the earliest example of classical Sanskrit poetry – after the multi-authored epic, the *Rāmāyaṇa* – to have survived (first or second century A.D.)? I am thinking of Verse 63 in Chapter 17 that reads (Johnston, 1932):

> Like one who has obtained safety after a great danger or deliverance from great oppression or light in a great darkness or, when without a boat, the further shore of the great ocean. . .even so have I come to supreme tranquillity.

The text (Haraprasad Shastri, 1910) plays effectively with *pāram*, 'other shore', and *parāmśāntim*, 'highest peace'. Romain Rolland was familiar with the Italian Sanskrit scholar Formichi (see *Rabindranath Tagore et Romain Rolland*, 1961), and Formichi was one of the early Italian editors of this text, who also wrote on Aśvaghoṣa (Formichi, 1912). This image, however, occurs frequently in the Buddhist *sūtras*. With reference to observations I will make later in this paper, it is interesting to take note of the fact that this text (Chapter 8) is one of the most vituperative documents ever written about women. The body of a woman is spoken of as "oozing and foul like a broken pot" (8.52). Such sentiments reach a crescendo when, in what appears to be a paranoid rage (of excitement and fear), the author claims that one Bṛhadrathā mated with a lion, for *agatir na vidyate*, "There is nothing [women] are not capable of" (8.44). But I have been unable to ascertain whether Rolland had in fact read a translation of this work. William James (1901), in his great work on mysticism, speaks several times of the ocean ("as the waters of the infinite ocean send their waves to break among the pebbles that lie upon our shores," p. 330) and knew the work of Max Müller on Ramakrishna (p. 286). Rolland quotes from James on p. 47. James wrote (Foster, 1945): ". . .there is a continuum of cosmic consciousness against which our individuality builds but accidental fences, and in to which our several minds plunge as into a mother-sea." It is interesting to note that in the 1890s James was enthused over the thesis "of a Viennese neurologist" (!) that a doctor must get in touch with his patients' *Binnenleben*, 'buried life'. Though James only met Freud once, at Clark University, he is reported to have told him that the future belonged to psychoanalysis.

[4] Romain Rolland (op. cit., p. 312) used a version of 'M' 's book published in Madras in 1922, *Gospel of Sri Ramakrishna (According to M, a Son of the Lord and Disciple) – Or, the Ideal Man for India and for the World* (2 vols., Madras: Ramakrishna Math, 1897). He also used (op. cit., p. 313) Max Müller's book (which was based on Müller's conversations with Vivekananda) as well as the book by Saradananda. In short, I am not using any source on the life of Ramakrishna that was not available to Rolland as well.

[5] For an account of Ramakrishna's life by the novelist Christopher Isherwood, see Isherwood (1959).

[6] The book translated by Nikhilananda is an abridged version of a five-volume Bengali work by Mahendranatha Gupta, with whom Romain Rolland corresponded (1929, p. 37) and who wrote the book under the name of 'M' and published it between 1897 and 1932, the year of his death. The work deals with four years of Ramakrishna's life, from March 1882 until April 24, 1886, a few months before his death.

[7] One of the terms that Ramakrishna introduced into Bengali is *kāminīkāñcana*, 'gold and women', to stand for the greatest obstacle to spiritual progress. Ghosh (op. cit., p. 438) notes that "this term has enriched the vocabulary of the Bengali language and it guards the intelligentsia against Freudian and Marxist ideas" (!).

[8] Gandhi did so as well, though in a more controlled fashion. See Masson (1974).

[9] It is astonishing that Romain Rolland could so overlook the blatant homosexual concerns of Ramakrishna. On the contrary, he seemed to perceive these elements as a sign of deep psychological penetration. Thus in his journal on India (Rolland, 1960) he writes (p. 206):

> Quand Ramakrishna voulait juger d'un homme ou d'une femme, il le faisait mettre nu devant ses yeux. Il en agissait ainsi, quand il apprenait qu'un de ses disciples voulait se marier. Il faisait venir la petite fille, et l'examinait, un instant, déshabillée. Alors, il disait: "Celle-ci sera ta compagne." Ou: "Cella-là ne pourra marcher avec toi sur la voie de Dieu."

Rolland goes on to tell how Ramakrishna would ask all young men who wanted to become disciples to show him their chests. He explains this by the necessity of doing breathing exercises in Yoga! In Saradananda (p. 150), we read:

> That was why, when they were recruited, they were subject to physical examination. . . . He was always careful to examine the tongue, the chest, the working of the organs. . . . He preferred them young, sometimes very young, hardly adolescent, and unmarried, "not yet caught in the net of desire". . . .

Since this is not a side of Ramakrishna that has ever been remarked on, I feel justified in quoting another passage (Nikhilananda, p. 952):

Haldar: Sir, when that boy (pointing to the younger Naren) came in, you said he had controlled his passions.
Master: Yes, it is true. He is totally unaffected by worldliness. He says he doesn't know what lust is. (To 'M') Just feel my body. All the hair is standing on end.
The Master's hair actually stood on end at the thought of a pure mind totally devoid of lust. . . .It was afternoon. M. and a few other devotees were seated near the Master. Narendra [Swami Vivekananda] came in. He looked, as the Master used to say, like an unsheathed sword. Narendra sat down near the Master and within his hearing expressed his utter annoyance with women. He told the devotees what an obstacle women were in the path of God-realization. Sri Ramakrishna looked at him intently without uttering a word.

[10] Rolland (1930, p. 21, note).

[11] Nikhilananda, op. cit., p. 197. Cf. *Chāndogya Upaniṣad*, VI.10.13.

[12] Nikhilananda, op. cit., pp. 376-377. What is odd about the first passage, and what makes Ramakrishna so interesting, is that one sees in this passage all the classical elements, but somehow transformed into a private world. Ramakrishna's pathology is entirely his own, though it is fashioned out of the elements given him by being steeped in the atmosphere of classical Indian mysticism. To a certain extent this also works in the opposite direction: it is hard to know when to judge a certain passage as entirely personal and not written with the effects of his background as the real motivating element. How much is privately his own, Ramakrishna's, and how much belongs to the tradition generally? How much does he simply take over, and how much does he transform? The 'transforming' element in Ramakrishna seems to me to outweigh the traditional. There is something peculiarly personal in the first passage that is missing from the classical texts. One wonders: was this a hallucination, or is the reporting deliberately metaphorical? Note the aggression in the image of the heap of heads. 'Taking the form of' is a standard Sanskrit phrase, but what personal significance did it have for Ramakrishna? Did he believe what he says? Was he psychotic?

[13] Romain Rolland tells us (op. cit., p. 47) that he was aware of similar experiences as described by Starbuck (1900), Flournoy (1915) and William James (1901). My reading of these authors leads me to conclude nonetheless that the specific image of the ocean in the oceanic experience was taken from Ramakrishna and not from these other sources, though no doubt they reinforced Rolland's belief in the universality of this phenomenon. Indeed, Rolland, in the letter to Freud cited earlier, says that he himself was familiar with this feeling, that in fact he had never been without it in his life ("je suis moi-même familier avec cette sensation. Tout du long de ma vie, elle ne m'a jamais manqué," op. cit., p. 26.), and this is the sense in which he considers himself 'religious'. He adds that this oceanic feeling does not entail a wish to live on after his death, that on the contrary he hopes for a "repos éternel". This feeling never left him, for in 1940 he writes: "Ma vie s'en va. Je m'en détache. . .Béni, soit l'au-delà du désir, dans la plénitude et le repos de l'infini" (Barrère, 1955, p. 119). It would be valuable to know more of the reading both in psychology and in mysticism that Rolland did in preparation for this book. (Freud, Cornubert, op. cit., p. 32, writes: "il ne serait pas concevable que je lise tout ce que, d'après les indications de votre lettre, vous avez étudié.") The standard studies of Rolland do not help much. Surprisingly, Rolland has no

reference to the work of Storch (1922), which was bound to have interested him. More serious is the omission of a work of remarkable psychological sophistication and subtlety, that by Ferdinand Morel (1918). I believe that the explanations that Morel gave of mysticism were too rich in psychological insight (while his understanding was not as deep as Freud's, his knowledge of the source material was better), and would not have appealed to Rolland. For example, Morel has this perceptive passage on mystics:

> Ils présentent pourtant quelques symptômes constants. Tendance très marquée à l'isolement social. Tendance générale à la continence, du moins au célibat. Partiques ascétiques, ou du moins austérites de vie. Tendance à 'fuir d'içi-bas' et nostalgie d'un autre monde ineffable, qui rappelle le 'non-être', 'l'increé', 'l'anéantissement total'. Déplacement d'intérêt qui, au lieu d'aller aux choses changeantes et passagères, se tourne vers une chose plus stable; qui, au lieu de garder le contact avec l'ambiance extérieure par le moyen des sens, les ferme, les répudie, et s'abandonne à une occlusion périphérique plus ou moins chronique, à un hermétisme plus ou moins complet (op. cit., p. 319).

Similarly, the work of Forel, while more sympathetic to mysticism, could not have been of very much solace to Rolland.

[14] It is worth observing that 'visions' of Kālī, the mother of the universe, were often extremely frightening to Ramakrishna. Nikhilananda, in his Introduction (p. 21), writes of a vision of Ramakrishna's:

> In this vision he saw a woman of exquisite beauty, about to become a mother, emerging from the Ganges and slowly approaching the Panchavati. Presently she gave birth to a child and began to nurse it tenderly. A moment later she assumed a terrible aspect, seized the child with her grim jaws, and crushed it. Swallowing it, she re-entered the waters of the Ganges.

[15] Romain Rolland introduces the passage with these words:

> Je le laisse parler. Sa voix rappellera à plus d'un parmi nous les accents de nos 'fous de Dieux', de nos grands voyants d'Europe (Op. cit., p. 45).

He has a footnote which reads:

> J'utilise trois récits qu'il a faits, semblables dans l'ensemble, s'enrichissant l'un l'autre, de quelques touches.

The passage he quotes reads:

> Un jour, j'étais en proie à une introlérable angoisse. Il me semblait qu'on me tordait le coeur comme un linge mouillé. . . .La souffrance me déchirait. A l'idée que je n'aurais pas dans ma vie la bénédiction de cette vision divine, une frénésie terrible me saisit. Je pensai: Si cela doit être ainsi, assez de cette vie! . . .La grande épée pendait; et j'eus le sanctuaire de Kâlî. Mon regard tomba sur elle; et j'eus le cerveau traversé d'un éclair. – Elle! . . ."Elle m'aidera à mettre fin. . ." Je me précipitai. Je l'empoigne, comme un fou. . . Et voici! . . .La pièce, avec toutes ses portes et ses fenêtres, le temple, tout s'évanouit. Il me sembla que plus rien n'existait. Et, à la place, je perçus un océan d'esprit, sans limites, éblouissant. De quelque part que je tournasse les yeux, aussi loin

que je regardais, je voyais arriver d'énormes vagues de cet ocean luisant. Elles se précipitaient furieusement sur moi, avec un bruit formidable, comme pour m'avaler. En un instant, elles fûrent sur moi, elles s'écroulèrent, elles m'engouffrèrent. Roulé par elles, je suffoquai. Je perdis conscience, et je tombai... Comment passèrent ce jour et le suivant, je ne le sais point. Au dedans de moi roulait un océan de joie ineffable. Et jusque' au fond, j'étais conscient de la présence de la Divine Mère...

Rolland gives as the source of this: *Sri Ramakrishna, The Great Master,* Vol. II, by Swami Saradananda (publié par la Ramakrishna Math de Mylapore, Madras, 1920) and says of Saradananda, "Mort l'an passé (1927), était un intime de Ramakrishna, une des hautes personnalités religieuses et philosophiques de l'Inde. Sa biographie, malheureusement inachevée, est la plus intéressante et la plus sûre." Note that Nikhilananda (op. cit., p. 13) quotes a passage, clearly this same one (though without any source):

> I felt as if my heart were being squeezed like a wet towel. I was overpowered with a great restlessness and a fear that it might not be my lot to realize Her in this life. I could not bear the separation from Her any longer. Life seemed to be not worth living. Suddenly my glance fell on the sword that was kept in the Mother's temple. I determined to put an end to my life. When I jumped up like a madman and seized it, suddenly the blessed Mother revealed Herself. The buildings with their different parts, the temple, and everything else vanished from my sight, leaving no trace whatsoever, and in their stead I saw a limitless, infinite, effulgent Ocean of Consciousness. As far as the eye could see, the shining billows were madly rushing at me from all sides with a terrific noise, to swallow me up! I was panting for breath. I was caught in the rush and collapsed, unconscious. What was happening in the outside world I did not know; but within me there was a steady flow of undiluted bliss, altogether new, and I felt the presence of the Divine Mother. On his lips when he regained consciousness of the world was the word 'Mother'. (I quote from the English translation, pp. 16-18, and give the French original earlier in this note).

[16] Müller (1923, p. 34).

[17] In the *Kārikās* of Gauḍapāda, we find (IV. 68) this doctrine at its most uncompromising, long before the *Aṣṭāvakra*:

> Just as the personality in a dream is born and dies in that very dream, so are the personalities that one encounters here in this life.
>
> IV.71:
> For no person (*jīva*) is ever born. There is no such thing as birth. This is the highest truth: nothing is ever born.
>
> (Bhattacharya, 1943)

According to this text:

> *andhavaj jaḍavac cāpi mūkavac ca mahīṃ caret*
> One should wander this earth like a blind man, like an idiot, like one who is mute.

I have traced this idea in my article on the psychology of the ascetic (Masson, 1976).

[18] Saradananda (1911, p. 188, note 33, p. 194, note 2).

[19] Nikhilananda, pp. 99-110.

[20] See also De (1919).

[21] Op. cit., p. 77.

[22] I wonder whether Romain Rolland himself knew the text of the *Aṣṭāvakrasaṃhitā*. There was an Italian translation published in 1868: *Asth.avakragita ossia le sentenze filosofiche di Asth.avakra.* Pubblicate et tradotte da Carlo Giussani. Florence: Tipografia Fodratti, 1868.

[23] It does not figure in either the two-volume *L'Inde Classique* by Renou and Filliozat (1947) nor in Winternitz's great work (1904), nor in Farquhar's useful volume (1920).

[24] Op. cit., p. 14.

[25] Mookerjee (1940, p. 23).

[26] Ibid., p. 11.

[27] It is clear that the *Aṣṭāvakrasaṃhitā* borrowed many passages from Gauḍapāda's much older *Kārikās*. See the passages cited in note 17, above.

[28] Hauschild (1967, p. 55).

[29] Nityatmananda (1967, p. 91).

[30] On these riddles and their significance compare Gonda (1950, p. 60).

[31] Cf. Sterba (1940) and Abraham (1922).

[32] 13.20.59-60, critical edition, Vol. 17, p. 165; vulgate, Vol. 6, p. 85, 13.19.87-88.

[33] The vulgate reads thus, at 13.21.4. The critical edition, 13.22.5, omits the first clause.

[34] Vol. 17, p. 1063.

[35] Müller (1928, p. 141).

[36] P. 229, English translation.

III: THE OCEANIC FEELING: THE SURROUNDING IMAGERY IN THE EARLIEST SANSKRIT TEXTS AND ITS PSYCHOLOGICAL IMPLICATIONS

In the preceding chapter, I traced the origin of the term 'oceanic feeling' through Freud to Romain Rolland, to Ramakrishna and finally to a medieval Sanskrit text, the *Aṣṭāvakrasaṃhitā*. The verses from this last text display an abstract quality and a degree of removal from the concerns of everyday life that are striking. I am reminded of a patient who reports that she has never known an affect: she is rarely aware of having dreamt, displays no symptoms, says she has no childhood memories and has never, so she insists, had a fantasy. Her entire emotional life lies submerged beneath an exterior of extreme calm and placidity, and it is only very occasionally that some subtle sign will signal the existence of a remote realm of feeling. In a similar fashion, the descriptions of oceanic-feeling states from the *Aṣṭāvakrasaṃhitā* take on a stark quality that nonetheless betray, by subtle signs, a different world lurking within the person who wrote them. Within these verses, and basic to all such Indian mystical texts, one can discern certain invariable themes occurring over and over again: feelings of sadness and of an awareness of transience; feelings of disgust with the world, or of world-weariness; the pull of the long sleep, of death; world-destruction fantasies; nostalgia. These are, I believe, some of the dominant themes of Indian philosophical writings. Furthermore, these themes seem to be related not only to one another, but also to the oceanic feeling.

One theme, best captured in an image that occurs over and over in Indian literature is the destruction of the world by a great flood. It is in this context that we find the very first recorded mention of Viṣṇu and his *māyā*, his 'power of illusion'. In the third book of the *Mahābhārata*, there is a short passage that has had a great influence on subsequent literature. The passage begins: "When everything in the world had been destroyed, and the whole cosmos was one enormous ocean...," *ekārṇave tathā loke naṣṭe sthāvarajaṅgame*. It was at this time that Viṣṇu went to sleep in these waters, sunk in his *yoga*, lying on the world-serpent Śeṣa (*susvāpa bhagavān viṣṇur apsu yogata eva saḥ*).[1]

This brief passage illustrates some of the dominant concerns of Indian literature: the importance given to the ocean and imagery connected with it; the power of sleep and the equation of sleep with death; Viṣṇu, the closing of whose eyes corresponds to the destruction of the universe; a pervasive feeling that all this is somehow not real, that it is all *māyā*, a trick of Viṣṇu; and that *yoga* is intimately connected to such practices. (Indeed, a name given to Viṣṇu in the later literature is Yogamāya – see Gonda, 1954.) The theme is continued in the *Āraṇyakaparvan* of the *Mahābhārata* at 3.186.81. The story is remarkable, and I give it here in the words of the editor of the critical edition of the *Mahābhārata*, V. S. Sukthankar, in his study of the flood myth:

> The man who could live through the dissolution of the world can only be a perfect Yogi; and a perfect Yogi is deathless. He requires neither food nor drink to live. He can walk on water as easily as on land. So when the world was overwhelmed with floods and the creation was gradually submerged, Mārkāṇḍeya found himself alone, walking on the waters of the ocean. After some time Mārkāndeya, being human after all, begins to feel a little tired and lonely, tramping about all by himself on the surface of the endless ocean. He also felt inexpressibly sad at that awful destruction. Then all of a sudden he noticed a little child resting on the extended branch of a huge banyan tree (*nyagrodha*). Mārkāṇḍeya could not at all imagine how that little helpless child could have survived all that cataclysmal devastation, and he kept pondering over that matter, standing near the child. Seeing his confusion, the child softly told him to go into his body and rest there, and the child opened its little mouth and drew him gently inside. And, lo and behold, inside the child he found the world whose destruction he had seen with his own eyes. The sun, the moon and the stars, all the oceans, seas and rivers of the world, all the men, women and children whom he had known, all animals, gods and demons – they were all there, inside the little stomach of that wonderful little child. He wandered about inside for hundreds of years and still he could not find the end of it all.[2]

In the critical edition of this marvellous text, at III.186.122, Mārkāṇḍeya, when he emerges, says to the little boy:

> *jñātum icchāmi deva tvāṃ māyāṃ cemāṃ tavottamām,*

"I want to know, O God, who you really are, and I want to know this deep *māyā* of yours." The little boy replies (III.186.1): *kāmaṃ devāpi māṃ vipra na vijānanti tattvataḥ*, "Brahmin, even the gods do not know about me as I really am."[3]

These themes occur again and again, undergoing many strange 'sea-changes' along the way. A later *Purāṇa*, the *Matsyapurāṇa*, recounts a legend similar to the *Mahābhārata* one, although its date must be much later. The legend warrants quoting:

> Then after some time coming out of Viṣṇu's mouth, the sage saw a boy sleeping on the branch of a banyan tree. He was seen playing all by himself without any anxiety in the universe bereft of creation. The sky was covered with mist and the down below was a vast expanse of water. There were no beings nor lives there. The sage was much surprised and tried, out of curiosity, to see the boy satisfactorily, but could not look at him on account of his dazzling brilliancy. Then he thought to himself while floating on the water, I undoubtedly saw him before, but am doubtful as I might be deluded by Devamāyā [heavenly delusion]. Then being amazed and struck with horror, the sage approached that boy swimming in the water. Then the Lord, in the form of the young boy, thunders to Mārkāṇḍeya "Son, Mārkāṇḍeya! Do not be afraid. Come near me."[4]

One intriguing aspect of this legend is its latent relation to the Kṛṣṇa theme. This is suggested by a single verse in the critical edition, 3.186.113,[5] where two adjectives are given to this little boy: *śrīvatsadhārī* and *pītavāsā*, 'bearing the Śrīvatsa mark', and 'dressed in yellow silk clothes', which are common epithets applied (though not exclusively so) to Kṛṣṇa.[6] Kṛṣṇa is, of course, an incarnation of Viṣṇu, and it is hardly astonishing to see this early myth connected with the later myths of this god-child. There is a great deal to say about this child-god and his childhood,[7] but for the present I would like only to point out that Kṛṣṇa as a child is the projection of all utopian bliss. He is a little god, 'his majesty the baby'. For example, in a medieval Sanskrit anthology of verses, the *Saduktikarṇāmṛta* (p. 69, Verse 253), we find the following charming verse given below in my translation:

> Kṛṣṇa was turned round and round.
> He shook all over.
> Yaśodā, laughing, kept time with her hands.
> She sang: "You are a little god, you are a little god."
> May he who was so addressed protect you.

The idea, of course, is that Kṛṣṇa is in fact god, but his foster mother

Yaśodā, a simple cowherd's wife, does not know this. A similar example, this time in Ingalls' translation, by the ninth-century poet Abhinanda, is:

> "My son, if entering the mountain caves
> in guarding of the cattle you should come upon
> wild beasts,
> then call to mind Nārāyaṇa the primal spirit."
> So spoke Yaśodā
> and I pray the smile which rose thereat
> but which Murāri [Kṛṣṇa] quickly hid by pressure
> of his lips
> may ever aid the world.[8]

Kṛṣṇa is, of course, Nārāyaṇa.

One must wonder as to the source for the rich legends that center around this charming child. Fenichel tells us:

> An extreme submissiveness is likewise found in some forms of hero worship which are based on the unconscious fantasy of being a part of the hero. It is characteristic for one type of religiosity, in which devotion to God is connected with the fantasy that God without oneself would be as incomplete as oneself without God.[9]

Indeed, this has been taken so far that in the *Padmapurāṇa,*[10] we find the following verse:

> All those great sages who long ago lived in the Daṇḍaka forest and saw the beautiful body of Rāmā, wanted to make love to him, and so they all became women and were reborn in Gokula. There they did make love to Kṛṣṇa [th incarnation of Rāmā] and were freed from the ocean of existence.[11]

It is interesting to observe that the most famous version of the Kṛṣṇa legend (from the *Viṣṇupurāṇa*, IV.24.123ff.) begins with a series of verses that are in themselves remarkable, but also deserve to be translated here because they alert us to yet another component in this complex nexus, which is the sense of the futility of strife, the theme of *où sont les neiges d'antan.*[12] The verses are meant to instil a sense of tranquillity (*śāntarasa*) in the reader, perhaps in preparation for what is to follow, which is almost the complete antithesis – for in the legend of Kṛṣṇa we find a noisy exuberance and *joie de vivre* unique in Sanskrit literature.

Here are the verses:

(*Viṣṇupurāṇa*, 1882)

(123) These and other kings, blinded by ignorance, have always sought to possess this whole earth, no better than a corpse fit to be abandoned.

(124) These kings thought: "How can this great earth become mine, my sons, my descendants?" Thus lost in preoccupation, they have all died.

(125) Other kings who came before them and others who come after, and those who will come in the future after them, will all die.

(126) In autumn the earth puts out white flowers and seems to laugh at them, seeing these kings so intent on military expeditions and observing their efforts at conquest [reading, with Hall, 1840, p. 238, the whole first line as a single compound].

(127) Maitreya, listen to these verses that had been sung by the earth, and which were repeated by the sage Asita to Janaka who had a banner of truth: The earth said:

(128) "How can men, otherwise intelligent, harbor such folly? For it allows them to feel completely confident even though they are hardly different from foam!

(129) "They subjugate themselves, then want to win over their ministers, their servants, their subjects, and then further want to conquer enemies.

(130) "In this order will we eventually conquer the whole earth, bounded by its oceans. Caught up in their plans, they are blind to death who hovers close by.

(131) "But what is it, after all, to conquer the whole earth covered by its oceans, for one who has really conquered his self? The reward of self-conquest is freedom.

(132) "Their ancestors had to leave me and died. Their fathers had to die and could not take me with them. And yet, out of the deepest ignorance, kings still want to conquer me.

(133) "It is on my account that father and son, brother and brother have turned against one another. This comes about through the deepest ignorance and through a desire for possession on the part of these proud men.

(134) "Every single king who lived had this insane (*kubuddhi*) thought: 'This whole earth is mine. Everything belongs to me. And it will stay in my family for eternity!' And he died.

(135) "When someone has seen his own father, engrossed in the

ambition of possession, having to give me up and make his way to another kingdom, that of death, how can he too entertain the very same ambition to possess me?

(136) "When I hear a king have his messengers say to his rivals: 'This earth is mine, quickly give up your pretension to her,' I roar with laughter. But later I feel only pity for such poor fools.

(141) "Who has heard of Ikṣvāku, Jahnu, Māndhātṛ, Sagara, and Avikṣita as well as the Raghus, Yayāti, Nahuṣa and many others, who have all died... ?

(142) "Great in strength, great warriors, who had amassed boundless wealth, all these kings have become, through the terrible force of Time, mere stories told to children.

(143) "When the wise man hears of them, he will no longer entertain a sense of 'mine' about sons and wives, houses, fields and wealth.

(144) "Brave men who performed great austerities, holding their arms in the air for many years, brave and strong men who made the right sacrifices over and over, are now, by time, reduced to a story!

(145) "Pṛthu, unconquered, marched over all the worlds, and conquered every one of his enemies; struck down by the wind of time he perished as quickly as a piece of silk-cotton tree in a fire.

(146) "The Kārtavīrya who killed all his enemies, overran all islands and enjoyed them, has now become a subject for debate when stories are told: 'Did he exist or did he not?', people ask.

(147) "Curse the kingdoms of Rāvaṇa, Avikṣit and Rāma which lit up all the quarters of the earth, for have they not all, in one instant, at the wrinkling of the brow of time, been reduced to ash?

(148) "Māndhātṛ was an emperor on this earth. Now he is embodied in a tale. When one hears this, who but a fool could harbor in his heart the thought of possession?

(149) "Bhagīratha, Sagara, Kukutstha, Rāvaṇa, Rāma and Lakṣmaṇa, Yudiṣṭhira and others – did they exist or is it all just a tale? Where are they now? We do not know."

Kṛṣṇa in later legend remains an eternal child, and the forest pasture ground that he inhabits here on earth, the Gokula, is transformed and identified with the Goloka heaven, the "heaven of cows", for Kṛṣṇa is the cowherd par excellence. For his later devotees, Vraja, the real place (on the legends concerning Mathurā see the excellent book by Grouse, 1874) takes on all the qualities of a fairyland (see Manuel, 1971 and Lovejoy and Boas, 1935), similar to Oblomov's dream and the legend of Atlantis (cf. Sprague de

Camp, 1954) where all is sunshine, warmth, abundance and green delight. His flute is magic, just like the *māyā* of Viṣṇu. Nanddās, the sixteenth century Hindi poet,[13] speaks of "that flute whose melody all human power transcends/Which cunningly transmutes/What never was, into reality."[14]

Kṛṣṇa, who is blue (possibly because he was originally a black aboriginal god, and the Sanskrit word for blue and black, *nīla*, is the same), is always associated with the ocean. Indeed, Professor Dimock of Chicago University, who is preparing a complete translation of the life of Caitanya, the fifteenth-century Bengali founder of the Kṛṣṇa cult in the Middle Ages (see Dimock, 1966), points out that a story is related in which Caitanya, who has totally identified himself with Kṛṣṇa, leaps into the ocean because the dark blue color reminds him of his beloved, and is later found washed up on the shore by fishermen. It is not surprising to learn that Ramakrishna also identified himself with Kṛṣṇa and was attracted to his dark blue color and its oceanic resonance. Here is a typical passage, recorded by 'M':

> Master (to 'M'): "Ah! How wonderful was the yearning of the Gopīs for Krishna! They were seized with divine madness at the very sight of the black tāmāla tree. Separation from Krishna created such a fire of anguish in Rādhā's heart that it dried up even the tears in her eyes! Her tears would disappear in steam. There were other times when nobody could notice the depth of her feeling. People do not notice the plunge of an elephant in a big lake."
> 'M': "Yes, sir, that is true. Chaitanya, too, experienced a similar feeling. He mistook a forest for the sacred grove of Vrindāvan, and the dark water of the ocean for the blue Jamunā." [That same day Ramakrishna speaks of telling Narendra that he need not fear going insane over god:] "But, my child, there is no such fear in the Ocean of *Satchidānanda*. It is the Ocean of Immortality. By plunging into It a man does not die; he becomes immortal."[15]

Moreover, the similarities to the original myth of the little boy on the banyan tree who was capable of such magic remained firm right up to Ramakrishna's time. Indeed, he was fond of recounting a legend which calls attention to the power of Viṣṇu's *māyā* in a very startling form. The story is told by Zimmer:

> Viṣṇu came to the hermitage of the sage Nārada and offered him a boon. Nārada asked to learn the secret of Māyā. Viṣṇu agreed and asked him to follow him. They left the hermitage and set out into the desert. After a while they became thirsty and Viṣṇu pointed to a small

> village on the horizon and asked Nārada if he would fetch some water for him while he waited in the shade of a cliff. Nārada agreed and set out for the village. When he arrived there he knocked at the first door he came to. A beautiful young woman greeted him and he felt, for the first time in his life, the stirrings of desire, mixed with a strange nostalgia, for he seemed to have seen her somewhere before. The father too he seemed to recognize out of some dim past. He was made so welcome that he forgot what he had come for and stayed there willingly. Eventually he asked permission to marry the daughter. In twelve years they had three children. In his twelfth year of marriage the monsoon was violent, the river from the hills swelled dangerously and the village was caught in a flood. He fled, his smallest son on his shoulders, holding his wife with one hand and the two older children by the other. But the torrent was too much for him, and the youngest child fell from his shoulder. With a desperate cry he let go of the others to save him when a wave hit him and all three children and his wife were carried away. He fell unconscious with grief into the water. When he awoke he found himself alone on a little cliff. The world was one vast sheet of water. He began to cry bitterly when a voice, strangely familiar, interrupted him: "Child! Where is the water you went to fetch for me? I have been waiting more than half an hour!" He looked around: sand stretched in front, and Viṣṇu stood next to him. He had revealed his Māyā.[16]

These, then, are the themes. What are the the psychological mechanisms that lie behind them? They are narcissism, depersonalization, derealization, *déjà vu*, sadness over transience; all of which are, in my opinion, related themes.

Narcissism

In the texts which I have quoted, we find particularly blatant examples of what Kohut has called "cosmic narcissism" (1971).[17] It seems to me that even the earliest legends of Narcissus[18] recognized the 'deadly' aspects of narcissism, for note that the narcissus flower is sterile, has a soporific perfume, grows in isolation by water, blooms late and withers after a short life, and finally, it is poisonous![19] It is not surprising that in the Indian texts, cosmic sleep is so often invoked in these narcissistic fantasies. I need hardly point out the aggression involved in being the only person alive – for these images are always of total destruction with the exception of two people, the great god and a great sage who usually unites himself with the god (the identity of the narrator constitutes something of a riddle[20]). Of course, this aggression is not wholly directed outwards, for as Spring pointed out, "To withdraw one's libido from the world does not seriously injure the world, but often severely impairs one's own ability to deal with the world. To destroy the world is therefore an act of self-injury",[21] which is very well observed. Indeed, it has become common to accuse Kohut, in his studies of narcissism (Kohut, 1971), of having ignored the role of aggression,[22] a criticism Kohut has attempted to answer (1972). My own criticisms went, I believe, much further (Masson and Hanly, 1976).

A term similar to Kohut's 'cosmic narcissism' is found in an early work by Morel (1918), where he writes of the *narcisme foncier* of the mystics, of their *narcisme absolu*, which "n'emprunte rien à la réalité extérieure et ne nous en apprend rien."[23] Cox, writing of Narcissus (1883, p. 95), notes that

> ...The geographer Pausanius...prefers the other but less known legend, that Narkissos loved his own twin sister, and that on her death he found a melancholy comfort in noting the likeness of his own face and countenance to those of his lost love. But in truth, as in the myth of Endymion...who sleeps in Latmos, so the name Narkissos denotes the numbness or deadness of profound sleep; and the sun, as he looks down upon his own face reflectd in a lake or sea, sinks or dies at last still gazing on it.

Kohut feels that the wisdom which comes of old age will be cosmic. Hanns Sachs, in his book *Memories of Life and Art,*[24] speaks charmingly of a wisdom that comes in old age as mellow, soft and friendly, in fact, the opposite of 'cosmic'. He reminds us that the old man who will soon take farewell of his surroundings does not rise above them in an isolated spiritual condition, but rather

> ...the foreknowledge of impending departure, if it means a removal for a long time, or, still better, forever, gives to old surroundings a new freshness, a revival of interest. What, for a long time past, has been stale and ordinary becomes meaningful, attractive, endowed with a new beauty, when the time draws near to say farewell to it.

We can contrast this with the ending of Christopher Isherwood's novel *A Singular Man*, which ends in an oceanic experience:

> But that long day ends at last; yields to the night-time of the flood. And, just as the waters of the ocean come flooding, darkening over the pools, so over George and the others in sleep came the waters of that other

ocean; that consciousness which is no one in particular but contains everyone, and everything, past, present and future, and extends unbroken beyond the uttermost stars. We may surely suppose that, in the darkness of the full flood, some of these creatures are lifted from their pools to drift far out over the deep waters. But do they ever bring back, when the daytime of the ebb returns, any kind of catch with them? Can they tell us, in any manner, about their journey? Is there, indeed, anything for them to tell – except that the waters of the ocean are not really other than the waters of the pool?[25]

Depersonalization, derealization and déjà vu

The Sanskrit material quoted in this chapter shows evidence of an obsessive concern with states of depersonalization[26] and closely-related moods and feelings that cluster around this entity: one is always someone else or wanting to become someone else. Although Freud refers to depersonalization only once, in the Acropolis paper, it appears that he was not unconcerned with the phenomenon *per se*. Nor would we expect him to be, if we agree with James B. Cattell[27] that depersonalization is the third most frequent symptom seen in patients at a mental hospital, exceeded in frequency only by anxiety and depression. In our texts we can identify the twin themes of aggression and sexuality in such states.[28] This aggression, as one might expect, is rarely confined to an outward expression. The externalization of the aggression "the whole world is unreal, only I exist" is often turned inward (in fact, invariably so, to judge from the material I have examined), so that depersonalization, as Oberndorf pointed out (1950), is like playing dead; it is a kind of psychic suicide. Walter (1968) says that a need to retain feelings of depersonalization can actually lead to suicide. The literature on depersonalization has stressed the negative aspects of this feeling; it is one of which patients generally complain. Stamm notes: "The feeling of pleasure in this condition is a most unusual feature and to the best of my knowledge, has not been recorded in the literature heretofore."[29] The whole of Vedānta philosophy, from the Upaniṣads forward, culminating in the extreme monism of Gauḍapāda quoted earlier, and made famous by his pupil's pupil, the great Śaṅkarācārya, can be said to be a paean of praise to the pleasures of depersonalization and derealization. We should look upon such claims to bliss with a sceptical eye. The psychoanalytical literature on this state rightly stresses its defensive aspects. Arlow captures the inner thoughts well: "I do not have to feel threatened or guilty. What is happening has nothing to do with me. I am only an observer."[30] In another article, Arlow translates the experience of derealization as "all of this isn't real. It's just a harmless dream, or make-believe."[31] The sexual aspect of depersonalization, already stressed by Nunberg in 1922, where the state acts as a screen against the frightening emergence of sexual, often incestuous fantasies, is well illustrated in Brian Bird's case history (Bird, 1957) of a fifteen-year-old boy who has his first experience of depersonalization after his first ejaculation. In his case the fear was that the wet feeling pointed to blood and the irreparable damage to his penis (cf. Woodbury, 1956). It is not uncommon to feel dissociated during masturbation (Roshco, 1967). I was very impressed with a fine reconstruction by Victor Rosen (1955), who pointed out that his patient "...had felt as if I had not restored a memory but had merely given him permission to talk about something he had known in some way all along."[32] The implication is that lack of permission can lead to derealization. This can be interpreted as the injunction: 'You must not remember your past', followed by the complete and perverse obedience that eventuates in: 'I don't even remember my present – do not fear – I see (hear, think, especially remember) nothing (sexual, aggressive) – in fact, nothing exists, so how can I be bad?" (a projection onto the outside that nothing had ever happened). 'You see, there's nothing outside', i.e., I have nothing inside for which you can hate me.

This prohibition on memory may have led Indians to cathect very early memories in a displaced fashion: the texts frequently tell us of men who can remember, with total recall, their births, and beyond that, their former lives. But the many accounts, especially in Buddhist and Jain texts, of this power of memory are always and invariably of the *past* life, not of the present early life. To the best of my knowledge *there are no descriptions of childhood memories in Sanskrit texts*. The forward drive of this suppressed past must account for the fact that *déjà vu* experiences appear so frequently in Indian literature. As Arlow puts it in his article on *déjà vu* phenomena: "...The memory, wish or fantasy which threatens to emerge is minimized as being unreal, dream-like or already past."[32] I would postulate that if scenes appear so familiar to Indians, and if they then explain this as being due to such experiences having occurred in a former life, I would, with Freud (1901) and other writers on *déjà vu*,[34] emend this to read that the scene is familiar because it exists on the borderlands of consciousness. Of course *déjà vu* phenomena also serve other purposes as well: the inevitable belief in reincarnation among Indians is certainly another rationalized use to which these experiences are put. Siegman puts it well:

There is a kernel of universal participation in the myth among the ancients, cited by Freud, that *déjà vu* is evidence of a former individual incarnation. What better reassurance could there be against the overwhelming realization of the ephemerality of narcissism and the painful inevitability of death?[35]

Sadness Over Transience

I have often puzzled over exactly what Freud meant when he said that the ego is a precipitate of abandoned object cathexes. It occurred to me that to cathect another person in early infancy depends, to a large extent, on the recognition that one is cathected by them. To take them over, when a loss occurs, also means to take over their cathexis, and to have one's sense of self enlarged. Pathological narcissism would result from an insufficiency in this two-way traffic. The narcissist is hungry for cathected memories, for an image of his own past that involved being the object of other people's love. If a person looks back on his past only to find an empty corridor, he is going to need emergency protection, and to believe that life is a dream is one such protective device. This is an ancient belief in India, dating back to the Upaniṣads, which is associated with early Indian ideas about sleep.[36] From India, it found its way into Buddhism, from which it penetrated Arabian sources. The Jews then came into contact with it and carried it into Spain. Calderón de la Barca gave his seventeenth-century play the title *La Vida es Sueño*, 'Life is a Dream' (Sloman, 1961). Rilke[37] was deeply moved by such ideas. In his famous walk with Freud and Lou Andreas Salomé (Lehman, 1966) in the mountains during the First World War, Rilke spoke of his feelings of sadness at the transience of all beautiful things (Freud, 1916). (Once again we see a connection from an ancient Sanskrit text to Freud[38]). If the Indian texts give evidence of some colossal need to have 'been there before', it is, I think, because the Indians have been denied access to their own childhood past. Nostalgia, I would postulate, must be very familiar to every narcissist: a longing to return somewhere he never seems to have been. Fodor (1949) speaks of fetal nostalgia, and indeed, the salt water we all knew before any other may well exercise a strange fascination that would account for the almost universal appeal of a sun-drenched beach on the ocean. But such explanations bypass the more obvious places where nostalgia and narcissism nest: early childhood. The seed-bed for all later unhappiness begins in the genuine miseries of childhood. The ocean imagery thus undergoes a change.

The tides of a bleaker memory wash out toward a darkened sea those very experiences we have sought to clothe in a fantasized ocean imagery of sheer sunshine. In the next chapter, I consider in greater detail these interior seascapes.

NOTES

[1] I have taken the description from Fausbøll (1903, pp. 108-110).

[2] Sukthankar, 1944, pp. 301-303; cf. Shastri, 1950. The *Yogavāsiṣṭhamahārāmāyaṇa* 6.77.49 (1937, p. 1235) speaks of the egg of Brahman, that is, the cosmos, which was, at the time of the deluge, *kubālalīlāvilolam iva bilvaphalaṃ viśuddham,* "Like a bilva fruit that had been playfully tossed about by very small boys until it was now totally empty." In the next chapter (p. 1237, Verse 28), it is described as follows: "There was no sky, no quarters, no up nor down, there was no living being, and no heaven – everywhere only one thing: water" (Mitra, 1899). (It is worth observing that Ramakrishna seems to have known this text. See Nikhilananda, 1952, p. 952.) This is similar to the verse in the *Subhāṣitaratnakoṣa* (Ingalls, op. cit., p. 309, Verse 1048) where we are told that if the ocean should transgress its bounds, then *na kṣonī nādrivargā na ca raviśaśinau sarvam ekārṇavam syāt*, "There would be no earth, no mountains, sun nor moon, but all would be an universal sea." As we have seen, Viṣṇu sleeps on this sea and when he falls asleep, or ends his lovemaking, the world is destroyed by fire and water (see Ingalls, p. 94). The universe then exists as part of Viṣṇu's dreams. But what kind of sea is it? It is not an ordinary sea, but a sea of milk! Surabhi (*Mahābhārata*, 12.173.3, vulgate edition) the goddess is grandmother of all cows, and it is her milk that becomes the milk-ocean from which the gods churned out jewels, liquor, and the drink of immortality (*Mahābhārata*, 5.110.11 – see Ingalls, op. cit., p. 71). In this churning of the ocean, the world-snake acted as the twirling string, the churning stick was Mount Mandara. After 1,000 years the snake spewed forth a dark, deadly poison. Then the moon emerged. The idea of the hidden, mysterious depths of the ocean is important to Sanskrit literature. In the *Rāmāyaṇa* (5.1.75-118, critical edition, pp. 17-24; see Jhala, 1966) (Bombay edition, 5.1.92-125), Hanumān the great monkey-god prepares to leap over this ocean: "He bristled his hairs and shook like a tree and then roared the great roar like a giant thundercloud" (*Rām.* 5.1.92). The ocean asks the crippled mountain (its wings cut off!) hidden in its depth to rise and offer Hanumān rest. But Hanumān is unable to stop in his urgent task of helping Rāma, and he but lightly rests his hand for a moment, out of sheer politeness, and then moves swiftly on.

[3] Sukthankar (1942, pp. 642-649).

[4] Akhtar (1972, p. 131, Chapter 167). Cf. Agrawala (1963). Note that on page 20 the great ocean is identified with the water in the womb: *garbhodakam samudraś ca.* Vāyu, IV.80. This is also the 'golden egg'.

[5] Op. cit., p. 648.

[6] The first, the Śrīvatsa, is a particular curl of hair – see Hopkins (1915, p. 184, 205).

[7] Cf. Masson (1974a). On the Kṛṣṇa theme more generally, see the studies by Masson (1974), Ingalls (1968), Vaudeville (1975), Singer (1966), Archer (1957) and Ṛuben (1943). A good, brief account of the Kṛṣṇa legend is Keith (1917). Burnouf's 1944 translation of the *Bhāgavata* remains unrivaled. Archer published in 1973 *Indian Paintings from the Punjab Hills: A Survey of Pahari Miniature Painting,* which is a careful and scholarly work with brief, useful discussions of all available paintings. Most of the paintings deal with the Kṛṣṇa theme. Some of them (e.g., pp. 207-208) depict explicit, nude love scenes not previously published. I have translated, from the *Harivaṃśa* the story of the childhood of Kṛṣṇa, from his birth to the point when he leaves his pastoral home. The translation will appear in two parts in the *Journal of the American Oriental Society* in 1980.

[8] Ingalls (1965, p. 106).

[9] Fenichel (1945, p. 353).

[10] Vol. IV, Book 6 (*Uttarakāṇḍa*), VI.272, 166-167 (*Padmapurāṇa*, 1894).

[11] The same story is recounted by Shashibhusan Dasgupta (1946, p. 150) who gives the identical interpretation that I have. Since this is such an unusual verse, and lest my *translation* be seen as a psychoanalytic *interpretation*, I include the original text:

purā maharṣayaḥ sarve daṇḍakāraṇyavāsinaḥ
dṛṣṭvā rāmaṃ hariṃ tatra bhoktum aicchan suvigraham
te sarve strītvam āpannāḥ samudbhūtās tu gokule
hariṃ samprāpya kāmena tato muktā bhavārṇavāt

[12] Indeed, the original lines from Villon's famous ballad are relevant:

Prince, n'enquerez de sepmaine
Ou elles sont, ne de cest an,
Que ce reffrain ne vous remaine:
Mais où sont les neiges d'antan?
Prince, do not ask in a week
Or yet in a year where they are;
I could only give this refrain:
But where are the snows of bygone years?

(Bonser, 1960).

[13] The verse, No. 28 of the *Rāsapam cādhyāyī* (Taṃḍana, 1960), reads:

taba līnī karakamala
jogamāyā sī muralī
aghiṭataghaṭanā catura
bahuri agharana sura jurate

The expression *aghiṭataghaṭanā* is an old Sanskrit phrase found in the texts on dramaturgy (see Masson and Patwardhan, 1970). In the fourth Uddyota of the *Dhvanyāloka* of Ānandavardhana, a ninth-century work on poetics (Paṭṭābhirāmaśāstrī, 1940, p. 527), we find a Prakrit stanza which translates: "The literary art of great poets is all-conquering. For it causes various ideas to enter the heart [of the reader] and appear [there] in a form which is different, as it were, from their real form." I have speculated (Masson and Patwardhan, 1974, p. 182) that this verse is from a lost work by Vākpatirāja.

[14] McGregor (1973, p. 66). Compare this fine verse by a sixteenth-century Indian mystic (Orr, 1947, p. 176):

I have seen the rain where there was no cloud
I have heard the thunder where there was no sound
I have seen the flash where there was no lightning
My bliss is supreme.

This same Dadu said: "Nothingness is the ocean. Within it is the Jewel. Plunge into the Self and behold Him."

[15] Nikhilananda (1952, p. 449; cf. p. 456).

[16] Zimmer, op. cit., pp. 32-34. Zimmer says that this story was taken from *The Sayings of Sri Ramakrishna*: Madras, Mylapore, 1938, Book 4, Chap. 22.

[17] Kohut is unaware of the fact that this term has already been used by Gaston Bachelard in his book *L'eau et les rêves* (1942, pp. 36-37).

[18] E.g., Ovid's *Metamorphoses, spem sine corpore amat, corpus putat esse, quod umbra est,* "He loves an unsubstantial hope and thinks that substance which is only shadow" (Vinge, 1967).

[19] There is a Chinese legend that a king of Kashmir caught a Simurgh and caged it, only to find it would not sing. His wife pointed out that Simurghs only sang when they saw their own kind, so he deceived the bird by putting a mirror in its cage. The bird then sang a mournful song and died (Frodsham, 1970, p. 221).

[20] In 'Analysis Terminable and Interminable' (Freud, 1937a, p. 245), Freud speaks with admiration of the pre-Socratic philosopher Empedocles. It is interesting that this same Empedocles was prone to having 'oceanic experiences' as we learn from Delatte (1934, p. 24), who speaks of him, in the language of the time, as being "possédé, inspiré, enthousiaste, il est saisi du délire sacré," classical terms for mania. Empedocles claimed "that he can teach his pupils to stay the winds and revive the dead, and that he is himself a god made flesh" (Dodds, 1951, p. 145).

[21] Spring (1939, p. 52).

[22] See, in particular, Kernberg (1974).

[23] Morel (1918, p. 336).

[24] Sachs (1948, pp. 294-297).

[25] Isherwood (1964, p. 155).

[26] See Bird (1958), Blank (1954), David (1971), Levitan (1969, 1970), Nunberg (1922), Oberndorf (1935, 1936, 1939, 1941a), Sarlin (1962), Stamm (1962).

[27] Stewart (1964, p. 171).

[28] In the early case cited by Feigenbaum (1937), we find a case of *déjà senti* connected both with happy memories of honeysuckle in childhood and with a lavatory stench and a dream of dying. Although Freud does not name it as such, one of the experiences of the Wolf Man, indeed his principal subject for complaint (*Hauptklage*), bears a resemblance to depersonalization: "...for him the world was hidden in a veil (*Schleier*)." Interestingly enough, "this veil was torn only at one moment – when, after an enema, the contents of the bowel left the intestinal canal; and then he felt well and normal again" (Freud, 1918, p. 75).

[29] Stamm (1962, p. 763).

[30] Stewart (1964, p. 182).

[31] Arlow (1966, p. 472).

[32] Op. cit., p. 216.

[33] Arlow (1959, p. 625).

[34] Oberndorf (1941b), Marcovitz (1952), Claparède (1911).

[35] Siegman (1956, p. 85). A particularly valuable and rich approach to the subject of depersonalization and its defensive aspects has been made by Isakower in a posthumous publication (Isakower, 1945) and in his earlier famous article describing what has become known since as the Isakower phenomenon (1936). See, too, the valuable articles by Lewy (1954) and Weiss (1942a), and the articles translated and annotated by Rapaport (1951).

[36] See Filliozat (1947). The theme of the unreality of life is not unknown to Chinese sources as well, as early as the famous butterfly passage from Chuang Tzu (see Arthur Waley's *Three Ways of Thought in Ancient China*, London, 1939). It is found again in the remarkable chapter on King Mu of Chou in A. C. Graham's translation of *The Book of Liehtzu* (London: John Murry, 1960, pp. 58-73). Such works may lie behind the exquisite fantasy of a lost world, where all live in harmony and peace, the famous prose piece and poem by the great T'ao Chi'ien (365-427 A.D.), the peach-blossom forest mentioned earlier. See Robert Payne, *The White Pony: An Anthology of Chinese Poetry from the Earliest Times to the Present Day.* (London: Allen and Unwin, 1949.) A charming eighth-century story, "A Lifetime in a Dream" by a Li Kung-Tso, may also be related to this ancient theme. See *The Golden Casket: Chinese Novellas of Two Millenia,* translated by C. Levenson (London: Penguin Books, 1967, pp. 102-117) from W. Bauer's and Herbert Franke's German version of the original Chinese (1964). For the general theme of utopias, see the literate *The Shape of Utopia: Studies in a Literary Genre*, Elliott (1970), and also the imaginative work by Patch

(1950), *The Other World According to Descriptions in Mediaeval Literature*, as well as the fine study by Bauer (1971), *China and the Search for Happiness.*

[37] That such sensitivity to unhappiness may have its roots in an isolated childhood and in an atmosphere of joyless, selfish love seems to me well indicated by a comment that Rilke made to Ellen Key in 1903: "I believe my mother played with me as with a doll" (see Groff, 1956). Rilke was fascinated, in adult life, with dolls. Dolls are preeminently 'unreal'.

[38] The history of this idea has been traced in the scholarly two-volume work of Farinelli (1916).

IV: THE OCEANIC FEELING: THE IMAGE OF THE SEA

Traditional studies of mysticism[1] have generally been written by men who were themselves aspiring toward the mystic experience. Two modern exceptions are the books by Danto (1972), a Western philosopher known for his earlier work in the philosophy of knowledge, and Staal (1975), a scholar who knows at first hand many of the texts about which he writes. However, it is not true that a close acquaintance with the original texts of mysticism inclines a scholar towards belief in them, in spite of the well-publicized views of R. C. Zaehner, who for many years occupied the Spalding Chair of Eastern Religions and Ethics at Oxford. Zaehner believed that no scholar who was acquainted in any depth with the original texts of mysticism could fail to be moved by the desire to experience the ecstatic states which these texts describe. However, we begin to understand his stance when we realize that he withdrew his sympathy in face of Sanskrit texts which were infused with monistic ideals (best summarized in the famous line ascribed to Śaṅkara: *brahma satyaṃ jagan mithyā jīvo brahmaiva nāparaḥ*, "Brahma is real, the world is unreal, the self is none other than Brahman"[2]) and attempted to persuade his readers of the superiority of the Indian dualist tradition, which was much closer to Zaehner's fervent Catholicism. To Zaehner, psychoanalysis meant Jung, for whom, of course, he had great sympathy. But such an attitude is not necessarily the result of scholarship. A very different view of mysticism has been espoused by Zaehner's successor to the Spalding chair, Professor B. K. Matilal,[3] whose acquaintance with the primary material, and indeed with the tradition most saturated with both forms of mysticism (the Bangali Vaiṣṇava tradition), is much deeper than Zaehner's.

This is not to say that there have never been psychological studies of mysticism. There have, and one or two of them have been perceptive and sensitive to psychological realities.[4] However, most psychological studies, including the most famous of them (James, *The Varieties of Religious Experience*), have not been psychological at all.[5] A few psychiatric studies[6] raise some pertinent questions, and there have been a few psychoanalytic articles as well.[7] But the most valuable study, even though not exclusively and directly related to mystic states, remains that of Lewin (1950), *The*

Psychoanalysis of Elation.[8] The same situation applies to the related study of Yoga. Traditional studies[9] tend to be sympathetic, with a few scholarly exceptions,[10] or even outright fanatical. Again, there are a large number of studies which claim to be psychological,[11] but which are far removed from genuine psychoanalysis. The early studies of Brosse, culminating in her 1963 book, encouraged a great deal of 'scientific' research that seems to have been a dead end. As Heonig accurately remarks, "On the whole physiological investigations of the claims of Hatha Yoga have not yielded much which can be of use to medicine and this at one stage so promising mine of information seems to have proved rather barren."[12] To my knowledge there is not a single study done with any psychoanalytic sophistication, with the one possible exception of an article by Jones which he mentions in his paper on auto-suggestion (1948), but which I have been unable to obtain. But, as in mysticism, there is nothing inherent in Yoga that repels analytic understanding (Masson, 1974d; 1976a).

It may well be that the best approach to mystic states will be via the study of mania, where the studies by Lewin[13] stand supreme, but where a number of other excellent studies exist.[14] Alerted by Lewin and these other studies, I have been struck by the deep depression[15] which I see as the central *unspoken* element of mystic states of elation. Although, for example, the legends of the life of the Buddha allow us little insight into the real life of a real man,[16] nevertheless a careful scrutiny of all available primary texts[17] definitely conveys the impression of a man struggling with a clinical depression. The singular solution he found to ward off this depression was to proclaim it universal: *sabbaṃ duḥkham*, he said, "All is sorrow." The defensive aspects of this are evident: '*I* am not depressed, everything is depressing.' Furthermore, like every symptom, this doctrine allows ample room for the repressed to return: it is now legitimate to be concerned with depressive states at the necessary philosophical distance that a doctrine provides. Hence one of the early Buddhist exercises is called the *aśubhabhāvanā*, the contemplation of what is horrible: somber and masochistic meditations, often in cemeteries, on decomposing corpses, for example. This reaches the point of 'borderline' macabreness in the extraordinarily terrifying 'exercises' of certain Tibetan Buddhists, described most vividly by Alexandra David Neel (1929) but more accurately by Tucci (1956) and Sierksma (1966). It seems that the more we search for the lost land of enchanting stillness, the more surely we reach down into the seething world of darker instincts. Whenever sixteenth-century cartographers plotted enchanted islands on their maps, they also drew opposite them the demons![18]

The longing for the ocean as an overt symbol of eternal peace is always a covert reference to the violence of suicide.[19] In Thomas Mann's *Death in Venice*, it is the destructive element in the homosexual relation that grows increasingly blatant towards the end of the novel. Kohut, in his article on this novel, writes: "In the engulfing passion for Tadzio there is also expressed a love for the sea which is paraphrased as a 'yearning to seek refuge. . .in the bosom of the simple and vast. . .for the unorganized, the immeasurable, the eternal – in short, for nothingness!"[20] Kohut, who expresses admiration for this feeling in his article on the psychology of music,[21] in his later writings[22] sees this feeling as underlying the 'cosmic narcissism' for which he evidently has a high regard.

The image of the ocean in the oceanic feeling does not seem to me to have been chosen at random. Rather, it points to the darker side of the mystic experience to which I wish to draw attention.[23] The somber seascapes that poets have written about often have a chilling effect, so devoid are they of the presence of human beings:

no hay nadie sino el viento, no hay nadie
sino la lluvia que cae sobre las aguas del mar

(Neruda, 1930), which I translate as, "There is nobody but the wind, nobody but the rain that falls on the waters of the sea." For the ancient Egyptians, Nur, the primeval ocean, is also the lake of the dead.[24] Fodor calls our attention to the reversal in astral projection: "I find it quite possible that people who are obsessed with the idea of astral projection are trying to satisfy an unconscious yearning to return to the womb."[25] But Fodor misses the evident self-destructive urge in both. The mystic desire for union is both an attempt to deny a deeper need for companionship, and a means of displaying totally-disguised annihilation fantasies. I am impressed with the anonymous commentator on an extraordinary case history presented by Pierre Janet at the annual meeting of the American Neurological Association in 1921. This patient told Janet, "Why do you want me to talk to you? You do not exist, neither do I. Good night. What I see is only a play, a Punch and Judy show; it is clumsy, vulgar, unpleasant, and, above all, false; it doesn't really exist."[26] Janet calls her a psychasthenic lacking will! But a discussant suggested that this patient was retreating from a dangerous world, like an ascetic to a marsh or desert. Relevant to this common feeling of Janet's patient is the astute observation of Fenichel in his classic paper, *The Economics of Pseudologia Phantastica*: "The fear which the patient had of the 'actuality' of her instinctual experiences finally led her, among other things, to regard everything as being not real, but only play-acting."[27] The emphasis here is on the raging denial: All *this* doesn't exist, so *that*, too, doesn't exist. However, the need for companionship, the hunger for a human affective response, is hard to obliterate. It breaks through, it seems to me, in varied disguises.

I would hazard the hypothesis that every depression contains embedded within it a mild form of depersonalization, and a feeling that one does not really belong. Jacobson writes of "...mild, fleeting experiences of depersonalization which may develop when persons are suddenly placed into a strange, unfamiliar environment. It is significant that such states may be caused by changes to fascinating new surroundings to which we can certainly relate and respond very vividly and pleasurably. But delightful as it may be, we feel that we do not belong to this lovely new world."[28] David (1971) in his obscure but thought-provoking piece on depersonalization speaks of the feeling that *quelqu'un manque*, and it may be that behind every depression is a memory of being alone, of being left.

Freud noted that for the Wolf Man "his principal subject of complaint was that for him the world was hidden in a veil, or that he was cut off from the world by a veil."[29] Similarly, Captain Ahab saw his life mission as to pierce the mask.[30] Many patients who come to analysis today speak of seeing things indistinctly, as if through a fog. Their feelings, too, they say, lack a certain sharpness. Many patients' strongest feelings are reserved for dreams, or for memories of early childhood. Feelings, of course, are always closely related to a particular time, and in this respect the sense of timelessness so common to mystic experiences may well be defensive.[31] Conrad, whose love for the ocean is well known, wrote (1906):

> Nowhere else than upon the sea do the days, weeks and months fall away quicker into the past. They seem to be left astern as easily as the light airbubbles in the swirls of the ship's wake, and vanish into a greater silence in which your ship moves on with a sort of magical effect. They pass away, the days, the weeks, the months.[32]

There is no doubt that the image of the sea lends itself particularly well to the great variety and great depth of emotions projected onto it.[33] Some of these can be seen in the novels of Virginia Woolf, in *To the Lighthouse*, for example, and *The Waves*. The sea is certainly silent, profound,[34] quiet and peaceful, yet children also think of the peopled sea, a place of fish swimming happily in shoals through the waves. A large literature, in such disparate traditions as that of ancient India and the ancient Celtic world, deals with kingdoms beneath the sea.[35] This is, in turn, linked to our fantasies about ponds (I think of the poems of Theodore Roethke), amniotic fluid and womb fantasies. The sexual aspects of ocean imagery are blatant: to merge with the most procreative womb of all time is to secure wider sexual horizons. The mystic almost always speaks of becoming both man and woman in his union with the universe, which surely contains a hidden fantasy of enjoying unlimited sexual experiences (Kubie, 1974). In French there is the actual pun on mother (*mère*) and sea (*mer*), which are homophonous.[36] Laforgue notes this in terms of the idea of castration: "The idea of castration as a punishment for having loved the sea so greatly."[37]

It is not surprising that the sea should almost always point directly to its counterpart, the sky, and that we find there the same defensive imagery. Thus Meyer Shapiro (1950, p. 34) writes about *The Crows*, one of van Gogh's last paintings:

> He is caught up across the yellow fields from the chaos of the paths and the dread of the approaching birds and carried to the deep blue sky. . .in which at last subject and object. . .can no longer be distinguished.[38]

We can remember Pascal's famous words in *Les Pensées*: "Le silence éternel des ces espaces infinis m'effraie." Glover, in an early article, noted the defensive and aggressive aspects of these experiences:

> . . .These patients tend to excessive idealization of their natural surroundings, the sun or sunshine, woods, flower gardens, cliffs, valleys, the sea. In their relations with adult objects, however, idealization is rare.[39]

Fenichel, too, in 1944, noted that

> . . .An object in nature may also represent other external objects, and the emotions seemingly aroused by it may be displaced from them. A mountain, for example, may represent father's penis, the endless ocean or desert, mother's womb. But even if that is the case, the narcissistic element is never entirely missing. The person, experiencing himself in a landscape, does not simply feel love or hatred for the father-mountain or the mother-ocean, but undergoes a kind of identification with them. He feels the *unio mystica* with the nature-parents.[40]

The child's preoccupation with small things and his fantasies about inhibiting another world may well be reversed here. Sir Kenneth Clark in his Romance Lecture at Oxford (1954) wrote, ". . .It is questionable if there is any central image in an artist's work which did not come to him as a moment of vision in childhood." He observes that Leonardo "secreted memories of the mountain streams at Vinci; of the lizards and other strange small creatures which haunt an Italian vineyard."[41] Of course, we must not press too far the idea of a model, for while it is true that Leonardo used rivers he actually knew intimately for his powerful paintings about the deluge, the model there was of trivial importance for the deep emotions expressed.[42]

The negative aspects of the oceanic feeling are also illustrated by a certain ambivalence about the maternal images frequently found in connection with these experiences. Karen Horney, in an early article (1932), notes certain poems, Schiller's "The Diver", "The Song of the Fisherboy", and "Wilhelm Tell", and Heine's poem of the legendary Lorelei, where water is the woman who swallows. There is an enchantment and mystery but an ever greater danger. In Byron's 'Childe Harod' (Canto 4, stanza 183), the sea is spoken of as "dread, fathomless, alone". The obviously aggressive character of the fantasy of having swallowed whole the entire universe is well brought out in some of the case histories that Storch quotes. He says of

> ...one gay catatonic that she says that she has the entire world in herself. I can go through walls. From the greatest to the least, everything is contained in me. How many persons are you then? Oh, many thousand. You can't understand it, because I have in me an entirely different outlook on life; you have an entirely different view of life.[43]

Lewin (1954) stressed a darker side of mania and noted that "the anxieties (of mania) are expressed in oral language: they are fears of being eaten, of starving, of being put to sleep (killed), of being separated...." Stern too observed of the Isakower phenomenon, "Why are the hallucinations...not only unpleasant and full of discomfort but often accompanied by the severest anxiety mounting to unbearable terror?"[44] It may well be, etiologically, that "the described phenomena do not reflect oral gratification but rather excessive traumatic oral frustration."

Conclusion

In the *Mahāsaccakasutta* of the *Majjhimanikāya*,[45] the Buddha relates his first experience of meditation: "I know that while my father, the Sakyan, was ploughing,[46] and I was sitting in the cool shade of a rose-apple tree..."

This short sentence has been the basis for a whole series of elaborations on this incident; it may be one of the few genuine memories of the Buddha. E. J. Thomas notes that it occurs in the *Lalitavistara*, where, he says, it is "an example of an old canonical passage embodied in the latter work."[47] But already in that text it is elaborated. I translate the passage from Lefmann's edition of the Sanskrit text:

> And so, Monks, the boy grew up. Now one day, as a youth, he went with some other boys, sons of the minister, to look at the "plowing village" (*kṛṣigrāma*). And having seen it, at the end of the plowing, he went to a garden. There, the Boddhisattva, lost in thought, alone, completely alone, wandering slowly, meandering, saw a charming, lovely Jambu tree. The Bodhisattva sat down cross-legged in the shade of that tree. And when he was seated, he concentrated his mind on a single point. And when he had done this, freed from sensual longings, freed from mean and sinful feelings, he reached the first delightful and happy stage of meditation, one with thought still attached to it, with mental effort, born of discrimination.[48]

The incident grows, sometimes retroactively thrown back to the first months of life of the Buddha and sometimes put just before his enlightenment.[49] The incident is found in the *Buddhacarita*, 5.4-10; in the *Divyāvadāna*, p. 391; in the *Mahāvastu*.[50] The fullest version, and the one best known to the tradition, is given in the *Nidānakathā*, the commentarial introduction to the *Jātakas*. Tradition ascribes it to Buddhaghosa, and "if not, however, by Buddhaghosa, the work must have been composed after his time; but probably not long after."[51] Here is the translation by Rhys Davids:

> Now one day the king held the so-called ploughing Festival. On that day they ornament the town like a palace of the gods. All the slaves and servants, in new garments and crowned with sweet-smelling garlands, assemble in the king's house. For the king's work a thousand ploughs are yoked. On this occasion one hundred and eight minus one were, with the oxen-reins and cross-bars, ornamented with silver. But the plough for the king to use was ornamented with red gold; and so also the horns and reins and goads of the oxen.
>
> The king leaving his house with a great retinue took his son and went to the spot. There there was a jambu-tree thick with leaves and giving a dense shade. Under it the raja had the child's couch laid out; and over the couch a canopy spread inlaid with stars of gold, and round it a curtain hung. Then leaving a guard there, the raja, clad in splendour and attended by his ministers, went away to plough.

> At such a time the king takes hold of a golden plough, the attendant ministers one hundred and eight minus one silver ploughs, and the peasants the rest of the ploughs. Holding them they plough this way and that way. The raja goes from one side to the other, and comes from the other back again. On this occasion the king had great success; and the nurses seated round the Bodisat, thinking: "Let us go to see the king's glory", came out from within the curtain, and went away. The future Buddha, looking all round, and seeing no one, got up quickly, seated himself cross-legged and holding his breath, sank into the first Jhana.[52]

(The text then recounts the miracle of the shadow of the tree; how the nurses return to find the shadow unmoved.)

In the previous chapters I have attempted to relate the origin of mystic experiences to the recovery of (or, more accurately, with the inability to recover) early affect-laden memories. In the various types of meditation and contemplation that all mystics employ, these are especially favorable conditions for the reinvigoration of old, deeply-charged memories. These memories are, I believe, almost inevitably of traumatic events. In these contemplative states, in place of the memory (whose reliving would be painful), the mystic substitutes a blissful, denying experience. No better example could be found than the experience related by the Buddha. It is, I believe, the one kernel of truth in his charmingly delusional system: something did happen to him when he was very young, and he has carried around this memory all his life. His final attempt at exorcism, interestingly, also took place beneath a tree. The Buddha's enlightenment under the Bodhi tree is a supremely successful attempt at denial. He is denying the memory of what was undoubtedly a real event: early in his life he was abandoned. He might have forgotten this abandonment if it were not followed by what I can only conjecture to have been a massive series of psychological abandonments by those closest to him. The reason I say that this was an *attempt* at denial is because the later depressions of the Buddha were only so many returns of the repressed. Each return necessitated a new denial, the results of which we can observe today in the doctrine of universal suffering. The reason for the almost universal appeal of Buddhism is the same as the reason for the success of the rose-apple tree incident. The story was taken up for elaboration in almost all later Buddhist texts. It is, I think, because we are all deeply engaged in a search for screens behind which we can hide the miseries of our 'past' lives.

With this background in the psychological antecedents of the mystical experience, we are better equipped to approach various derivatives in mythology which draw their strength from similar fears and wishes. The greatest storehouse of legends and myths is the epic literature. Both the *Mahābhārata* and the *Rāmāyaṇa* share much in common with the experience of dreaming – the realm of fantasy that we enter in reading these texts is reminiscent of old and dim memories of childhood and the compelling world of a dream shell. The *Mahābhārata*, vaster, more dense and disordered, yields less readily to psychological penetration than does the more accessible *Rāmāyaṇa*, whose influence over the whole of Southeast Asia can hardly be overestimated. The chapter which follows, then carries us further than the Indian subcontinent and beyond the Hindu mind.

NOTES

[1] Underhill (1911), Otto (1924, 1931), Zaehner (1957, 1960), Stace (1961), Bharati (1976).

[2] The most appealing literary expressions of this feeling are to be found in the earliest Upaniṣads, the *Bṛhadāraṇyaka* (see Senart's 1934 translation) and the *Chāndogya* (Senart, 1930) from the seventh or eighth century B.C. (cf. Keith, 1925). Nothing comparable was ever again to be written in India, a fact I have not been able to explain.

[3] See Masson and Matilal (1966), Matilal (1972, 1977).

[4] E. g., Flournoy (1900, 1915) or the massive case history in two volumes by Pierre Janet (1910-1919). The volume by Pratt (1920, especially pp. 337-480) is learned and judicious, though with a religious bias. Cf. Starbuck (1900).

[5] Leuba (1925), Marechal (1927), Boisen (1936), Naranjo (1971), Shafli (1973).

[6] Storch (1922), Deikman (1966).

[7] See the bibliography in Hanly and Masson (1976); also Schroeder (1922), Moloney (1954), Plank (1957, 1968), N. Ross (1958, 1968b), Ostow and Scharfstein (1954), Devereux (1959), Scharfstein (1973), Lubin (1958, 1959, 1969), Lubin et al. (1968, 1976), Werman (1979), Masson (1976a), Masson and Masson (1976).

[8] See, too, Gill and Brenman (1959).

[9] Woods (1914), Surendranath Dasgupta (1941), Filliozat (1953), Eliade (1962).

[10] Schmidt (1908), Poussin (1937), Senart (1900).

[11] E.g., Choissy (1947), Coster (1934), Jacobs (1961), Servadio (1966).

[12] Heonig (1968, p. 88). Cf. Wenger and Bagchi (1961), Mahotra (1963), and especially the judicious book of Barber (1970).

[13] Lewin (1932, 1937, 1941, 1949, 1959).

[14] E.g., Garma (1968), Levitan (1968), Blank (1954).

[15] Bonaparte (1948, p. 108) has a good explanation for the dark night of the soul:

> Dans ces alternances de dépression, le mystique retombé dans sa solitude en doit vouloir obscurément si puissament à l'Objet divin qui sembla ne s'offir que pour mieux se refuser. Et s'il n'ose retenue part la peur du blasphème, franchement alors nier Dieu, pourtant du fond de son âme il le supprime, et la 'grande négation' et la 'mort mystique' dont parle Madame Guyon sont au fond, bein que les mystiques n'osent se l'avouer franchement, la négation et la mort de Dieu lui-même.

[16] Lamotte (1947-1949), Oldenberg (1882), W. E. Clark (1930).

[17] See in particular the scholarly works of Bareau (1963, 1965, 1971).

[18] Carey (1969).

[19] A point of view also taken by Marie Bonaparte (1948, p. 108).

[20] Kohut (1957a, p. 213). Bonaparte (1948, p. 96):

> Certes, en dépit des promesses de paradis, la plupart des croyants, demeurés attachés à cette vie terrestre, mettent-ils en pratique la vulgaire maxime: Un tiens vaut mieux que deux tu l'auras! Ils ne se hâtent en général pas, tout orthodoxes qu'ils puissent être, d'aller dans l'au-delà fusionner avec Dieu et semblent tenacement préférer à cette union future leur présente misère... Tant le bon sens biologique peut primer sur les plus prometteurs délires de consolation (!).

[21] Kohut (1957b).

[22] Kohut (1966, 1971, 1972).

[23] In a recent novel by Bernard Malamud, the hero, in a state of depression, writes that "Life was a trace of dark light in a gaseous entity, a darkly flowing sail in an irradiated universal sea of loss" (1979, p. 318).

[24] Frankfort (1948, pp. 52, 115).

[25] Fodor (1950, p. 34).

[26] Janet (1921, p. 471).

[27] Fenichel (1939b, p. 137, note 9).

[28] Jacobson (1959, p. 605).

[29] Freud (1918, p. 605).

[30] But Auden (1951, p. 46), notes that Ahab "must beware of gazing too long at the sea or the fire, for even as he takes 'the mystic ocean at his feet for the visible image of that deep, blue, bottomless soul pervading mankind and nature', he is hovering over Descartian vortices 'and perhaps at midday, in the fairest weather, with one half-throttled shriek you drop through that transparent air into the summer sea, no more to rise for ever' – *Moby Dick*, Chapter 35."

[31] See Orgel (1965) and Zilboorg (1938).

[32] Cf. Bennet (1974).

[33] See Gerhardt (1967); and especially Niederland (1956, 1957). Cf. De La Mare (1930).

[34] Cf. Bonaparte (1946).

[35] Meyer (1909), Patch (1950), Daniels and Stevans (1903, Vol. 2, p. 1073).

[36] Cf. Bonaparte (1948, p. 371):

> La mer-réalité, à elle seule, ne suffisait pas à fasciner, comme elle le fait, les humains. . . .C'est le chant profond. . .qui a, de tout temps, attiré les hommes vers la mer. . . Ce n'est pas parce que 'la mer est bleue que nous l'aimons', c'est parce que quelque chose de nous, de nos souvenirs inconscients, en la mer bleue. . .trouve à se reincarner. Et ce quelque chose de nous, de nos souvenirs inconscients, est toujours et partout issu de nos amours d'enfance, de ces amours qui n'allaient d'abord *qu'*à la créature, en premier lieu à la créature-abu, à la crêature-nourriture que fut la mère. . .

[37] Laforgue (1932, p. 41).

[38] Shapiro (1950, p. 34).

[39] Glover (1938, p. 94).

[40] Fenichel (1944, p. 324).

[41] Op. cit., p. 23.

[42] See Eissler (1961).

[43] Storch (1922, p. 95).

[44] Stern (1961, p. 209).

[45] Horner (1954, Vol. 1, p. 301).

[46] Cf. Bareau (1963, p. 53): "Il semble bien alors que nous en possédions ici la forme la plus ancienne, présentée comme un souvenir qui met le Bodhisattva sur la voie de l'Éveil." Cf. also p. 70. Bareau (p. 52) places great emphasis, correctly I feel, on the fact that the earliest text we have on the life of the Buddha mentions the Buddha's father with so little of the idealization that is later necessary (*all* later texts change the description to that of a king). The Dharmaguptaka *Vinaya* version (T. 1428, p. 780c, I.26-p. 781a, I.11) as translated by Bareau (*op. cit.*, p. 48) reads: "Jadis, lorsque je demeurais chez le roi mon père, étant assis dans un champ, sous un jambosier. . ." In the Pali text we read (Bapat, 1958, p. 305): *abhijānāmi kho panāham pitu sakkassa kammante sītāya*, which I translate literally as, "I remember, indeed, as my father the Saka was working in the furrow [i.e., ploughing]." This is unquestionably evidence of the fact that the Buddha's father was not from a royal family, and in fact that he labored in the fields. Such an unornamented factual prose passage would lend strength to my belief that the rest of the passage is genuine as well, that in fact it represents a genuine reminiscence of the Buddha.

[47] Thomas (1927, p. 44).

[48] Lefmann (1902, p. 128).

> *iti hi bhikṣavo yāvad vivṛddhaḥ kumāraḥ. athāpareṇa samayena kumāras tadanyaiḥ kumārair amātyaputraiḥ sārdhaṃ kṛṣigrāmāvalokayituṃ gacchati sma. avalokya ca kṛṣikarmāntam anyata udyānabhūmiṃ praviśati sma. saṃvignamanās tatra bodhisattva ekākī advitīyo 'nucaṅkramyamāno 'nuvicaran jambuvṛkṣam apaśyat prāsādikaṃ darśanīyam. tatra bodhisattvaś chāyāyāṃ prayaṅkena niṣīdati sma, niṣaṇaś ca bodhisattavaś cittaikāgratām āsādayati sma. āsādya ca viviktaṃ kāmair viviktaṃ pāpakair akuśalair dharmaiḥ savitarkaṃ savicāraṃ vivekajaṃ prītim sukhaṃ prathamaṃ dhyānam upasampadya viharati sma.*

[49] See Bigandet (1888) and Kern (1901).

[50] For the Chinese versions, see Bareau (1963).

[51] Rhys Davids (1880, p. 60 of the introduction).

[52] Rhys Davids (1880, p. 163).

V: MONKEYS, CHILDREN'S LITERATURE AND SCREEN-MEMORIES: A PSYCHOLOGICAL APPROACH TO ENCHANTED FORESTS IN THE RĀMĀYAṆA

As one of the translators of the critical edition of the *Rāmāyaṇa*, I approach the text as a philologist.[1] However, just as it is difficult to determine what is genuine, in such a text, without the aid of philology, it is equally difficult to gauge the importance of specific passages without the aid of psychology. For example, one of the strangest passages in the *Rāmāyaṇa* occurs in the *Kiṣkhindhākāṇḍa*, when all the monkeys, led by Hanumān, enter a *bila*. What do they enter? The elegant French translation of Roussel says: *une cave, une caverne, un trou*. The English translations are equally indecisive. *Bila* can mean a hole or a cave or a cavern or any opening into the earth. Before we can decide on the possible symbolism we must decide, on philological grounds, what actually is being described. I am convinced (cf. Tilaka on IV.50.23: *adhomārga*), because of the large number of verbal prepositions (*ni, ut*, etc.) suggestive of ascending and descending, that it is a hole. Govindarāja in his commentary seems to agree, for he says that an analogy is intended with *pātāla* (IV.50.11: *kim idaṃ pātālam utānyan māyāmayam*). If it is a cave, we can turn to the relevant literature, for example the suggestive chapter of Bachelard (1948), on the psychology of caverns. If it is a hole, we can turn to the work of another French scholar, Francis Bas: *Les routes de l'autre monde* (1946). But at the same time, as we are deciding on this philological issue, we can also begin to think analytically about the possible meanings of entering the earth. We will resist any one-to-one identification, such as the early analysts were tempted to make: 'The earth represents the mother'; 'This is an intrauterine fantasy'. But we will not be surprised if an aged woman enters the story, nor will we be surprised to hear faint echoes of dying. And this is because we have been sensitized by the work of Freud[2] and others (Horney, 1932) to the ambivalent feelings men have about women and the terrors that lurk inside their bodies; for example, the sudden fear of a swimmer, in swimming into a grotto, that he might become entangled in the seaweed and drown. Is it, after all, so surprising that an early vision of our mother's public hair, forest-like to the young child, should later surface as a vague memory of dark dangers that lurk beneath surfaces we do not understand very well?

Although by and large I remain sceptical of Kleinian theory (Klein, 1932),[3] I find that some of her ideas can be particularly helpful in dealing with a work such as the *Rāmāyaṇa*. Sītā is too virtuous for us not to suspect a massive repression of fantasies of a very different sort. For if the author stresses the total goodness of Rāma and Sītā and the tranquillity of life in the forest, we can be fairly certain that his mind was unconsciously concerned with precisely the opposite set of feelings. Indeed, these feelings are displaced from their human bearers to the unremittingly evil *rākṣasas*.[4] For everybody *but* Rāma, the *rākṣasas* are phobic objects, great in their evil, and it is precisely their greatness that is feared, a fear that stems from a great, and greatly-threatening, forbidden craving in the child/adult. Rāma, on the other hand, adopts a counterphobic attitude[5] towards the demons and actively seeks them out. And, as in a bad dream, no matter how many he kills, there are always more: the numbers in the *Rāmāyaṇa* are taken from dream life. Moreover, since Rāma creates the demons in his own mind as fast as he kills them, there can be no end to his self-appointed task. Telling us that the gods imposed the task on him is a method of denying his own obsession. Similarly, the agoraphobic does not conquer his fear of the street by avoiding it, or the counterphobic his fear of mountains by climbing them.[6] All reading is accompanied by unconscious fantasies stimulated by the story, but these have a peculiar intensity in early childhood.[7] There is an interesting fable, that of the Lantern-Bearers by Stevenson. It is about small urchin boys who shelter in the cold sand on a bleak sea-shore on a dark autumn night, of whom Stevenson writes: "For no man lives in the external truth, among salts and acids, but in the warm phantasmagoric chamber of the brain, with the painted windows and the storied walls" (quoted in J. Buchan, 1931). Baudelaire said: "Tout l'univers n'est qu'un magasin d'images et de signes auxquels l'imagination donnera une place et une valeur relative; c'est une espèce de pâture que l'imagination doit digérer et transformer."[8]

In contrast to the tendency of most great literature to provide material upon which the imagination inevitably elaborates, the *Rāmāyaṇa* seems designed to frustrate such needs. The very fact that the *Rāmāyaṇa* is so bare of reality is analogous to the resistance manifested by a patient. Freeman Sharpe, in her book on dream analysis (1934, p. 155), writes: "Over and over again when phases of fatigue, listlessness, inability to remember ordinary things, inability to find things to say, appear during analysis I find them a prelude to struggling into dreams and consciousness of affective memories." I take the *Rāmāyaṇa* to be a cautionary tale. That is, at the same time as it is a story about a real world (no matter how fanciful that real world is), it is also telling us about the dangers of instinctual life, for we never totally disengage ourselves from our childhood, and that literature is most precious to us which awakens some dim memory of this past. I quote once again from Freeman Sharpe, this time from her article on cautionary tales:

> I have pointed out that these phantasies (cautionary tales, e.g., Christianity, a burning hell to which sinners are consigned – by mild or horrific example we are warned; the penalty is starvation, maiming, torture, death) whose function is to control unconscious impulses, utilise *those same injunctions* and warnings that once were implicitly or explicitly given to prevent bodily disaster and destruction.[9]

Children's literature and fairy tales

It is not surprising that in reading the *Rāmāyaṇa* we should think of fairy tales. Here is a prince and a princess banished to an enchanted forest. They meet wise men and demons and golden deer. The princess is carried away to a hidden island by the king of the ogres. The prince makes an alliance with a mourning monkey chief who can change his shape at will, and whose minister flies through the air and speaks elegant Sanskrit. Learned vultures who live for thousands of years give up their lives fighting the forces of evil. In fact, everything seems to take place in another world (Patch, 1950; Schuhl, 1969). While Vālmīki's text of the *Rāmāyaṇa* is of course never read to children, the story is told to them, and I suspect that we could learn a great deal about the significance of the literary Sanskrit version if we listened to a grandmother telling her grandchildren the story, and especially if we knew how the children responded to what they are told. Even more important, we could learn from their dreams, for they are certain to dream about precisely those parts of the story they do not remember (Fisher, 1954). This might help to explain why the *Rāmāyaṇa* has held such a grip on the imagination of so many people for so many years.[10] I think part of the answer lies in its having been told to them as children. The resultant utopian view of early life need not correspond to what was the reality. On the contrary, it is because childhood bliss[11] is an adult fantasy that nostalgia corresponds to adult needs.[12] And it is not that the *Rāmāyaṇa* manifestly portrays a world of enchantment; but, I believe, almost all people read it or listen to it with the specific unconscious fantasy of a personal utopian childhood of contentment in the hidden recesses of their minds.[13]

It was an article by a child analyst, Lilli Peller (1959), that made me aware of this possibility. In her discussion of Hans Christian Andersen's "Little Mermaid" she writes:

> *The Little Mermaid* also belongs to this group, and from this old favorite we get another glimpse of how a poet uses his materials: the little mermaid's older sisters too have taken good looks at 'the upper world', each one enjoying this privilege on her fifteenth birthday, but none fell hopelessly in love with a human as she does with the prince. The fairy tale does not give the reason for this infatuation at first sight – otherwise it would not be a fairy tale but a case history. But at the beginning, when we hear of the sisters' early childhood, there is an incidental comment about the flower beds which they owned and tended and how each one decorated her plot with shells and many strange objects, while the youngest had only one figure on hers – the statue of a little *boy*, a statue of white marble which had come down from a sunken ship. By chance or choice the image of a human was imprinted upon her in her sensitive childhood years. This part of the plot is crucial in understanding the heroine's later behavior, yet it quickly slips from the reader's awareness. The poet moves us, then provides other details superseding the one through which he drew us into the story and evoked our unconscious understanding.

I do not think it is trivial or irrelevant to claim that the creation of such a world acts as a defense against feelings of a very different kind. We see this in the world which Kenneth Grahame created in *The Wind in the Willows*, "sunny pre-war days of sun-drenched picnics, idleness, smooth lawns. . . ." A literalminded professor at London University asked Kenneth Grahame in 1919 how Mole's Goldfish had been looked after in his absence. Grahame wrote a revealing answer, which provides a clue to the price at which such a world was purchased: "The presence of certain characters may be indicated in or required by the story, but if the author has no immediate use for them he simply ignores their existence. . . .he doesn't say they are not there; he just leaves them alone."[14] Alas, Grahame extended such denial to his son, the tragic Alistair (Mouse), who could not live forever in the world that Grahame created for him and was totally unprepared, as was his father, for the real world that awaited him in Oxford: he committed suicide in 1920.

Grahame could never accept the fact. Peter Green in his perceptive biography sums it up well: "The overdrawn account with reality was squared at last; but it had been a grievous and insupportable price to pay for a lifetime of wistful illusion."[15]

The early analysts had an interest in fairy tales, children's literature and folklore because of the presumed primitiveness of children,[16] and the fact that the language of the unconscious could be more easily read in such works than in the more consciously-deliberated works of adult literature. But we should remember that Freud's interest was broader; he knew, as he demonstrated in his essay, 'Delusions and Dreams in Jensen's 'Gradiva'' (1907) that the experiences of our childhood enter both our later reading and our later writing.[17] Today, whenever one discusses fairy tales,[18] one inevitably comes up against the name of J. R. R. Tolkien and his Ring books. Perhaps a brief examination of Tolkien's work will help us to appreciate the more genuine creative abilities displayed in the *Rāmāyaṇa* (and indeed in Tolkien's unacknowledged predecessors, for example the charming fairy tales of George Macdonald, 1870, 1872, with their peculiar atmsophere, or the beautifully written and unpretentious *King of the Golden River* by Ruskin, or the haunting tale by Hudson, 1905).

So weighty a critic as Anthony Thwaite (cf. Wilson, 1956) has written of Tolkien as follows: "Professor Tolkien revealed. . .that he had a talent for songs, riddling rhymes, and a kind of balladry. In the *Adventures of Tom Bombadil* the talent can be seen to be something close to genius" (quoted in Raffel, 1968). The hobbits Frodo and Sam "stood as if enchanted" when they heard the following song of Tom Bombadil:

Hey! Come merry dol! derry dol! and merry-o,
Goldberry, Goldberry, merry yellow berry-o!
Tom's in a hurry now. Evening will follow day.
Tom's going home again water-lilies bringing.
Hey! Come derry dol! Can you hear me singing?

But in the book there is something much more sinister at work than the inability to write verse. There is a striking racism, and it is not inadvertent, as we can see in the 1936 Gollancz Memorial Lecture by Tolkien, 'Beowulf: The Monsters and the Critics': "It is the strength of the northern mythological imagination that. . .put the monsters in the centre, gave them victory but no honour, and found a potent but terrible solution in naked will and courage. . . .So potent is it, that while the older southern imagination has faded forever into literary ornament, the northern has power, as it were, to revive its spirit even in our own times."[19] This is Jungian nonsense (Jung, too, contrasted the Aryan psychological imagination with the Jewish one). R. J. Reilly, in his essay on Tolkien and the fairy story, writes: "Tolkien's theory, like this trilogy, seems anomalous. We should not be surprised if he tried to bring Coleridge up to date – to explain the creative imagination in partly Jungian terms, as Maritain and others have done; but we are surprised to see that he has done just the reverse, has instead taken it backwards and given it specifically Christian implications which it hardly had since Sidney's Defense."[20] In his famous essay on fairy tales (1947), Tolkien, speaking of the Gospels, makes the preposterous claim: "There is no tale ever told that men would rather find was true, and none which so many sceptical men have accepted as true on its own. To reject it leads either to sadness or to wrath."[21] This is as pathetic as it is untrue. It is interesting that Jung asserts, as part of his dream theory, that "Man is never helped by what he thinks for himself but by revelations of wisdom greater than his own." This seems to me the very essence of Jungian theory and the reason why so many people have felt repulsed by it. Tolkien too, in that same essay, shows a dislike of real dreams when he claims that "behind the fantasy, real will and power exist, independent of the minds and purposes of men."[22] Tolkien may believe this, and so does the author of the *Rāmāyaṇa*, but Freud certainly did not.

It was my feeling, when reading *The Lord of the Rings*, that it would not be long before somebody claimed that Tolkien had not exercised his imagination at all, but was only reporting what he saw: Middle Earth exists. Such a tendency is evident in Fracia Fey Ellwood's book *Good News from Middle Earth*. In the chapter entitled 'Everything is Alive: An Essay on Magic in Middle Earth and Elsewhere', she writes with great passion of "thoughtography", the ability to photograph the invisible by means of thoughts.[23] Tolkien might have been too shrewd to comment on such regressive thinking, but I cannot find anything in his writings which would be in any way at odds with it. Such thinking, in fact, amounts to an attempt to deny any responsibility for the content of our fantasy life, and stands in direct contrast to the attitude of Freud on the subject. When he first wrested dreams from the other world, Freud touched on responsibility and placed it squarely where it belonged, with the person. There is the well-known story of the patient who asked Freud: Surely you cannot hold a person responsible for his dreams? Whom else would you hold responsible? answered Freud. I believe that Freud did hold a man ultimately responsible for the content of his unconscious, and especially for the use he makes of it:

e.g., whether one would, in a blind rage, act out sadistic fantasies, or instead investigate them in oneself and others.

It is important, too, for psychoanalysis to face the issues raised implicitly in Tolkien's influential essay. These same criticisms have been explicitly voiced by Tolkien's friend, another don and writer of fiction for children, C. S. Lewis. He has written one of the most severe though least known criticisms of psychoanalysis in his essay 'Psychoanalysis and Literary Criticism' (Lewis, 1941). He makes three points in the essay. He refers to Freud who, in the Introductory Lectures, speaks of tunes we whistle and their psychological explanation. "I must however, make this reservation, that I do not maintain this in the case of really musical people." Lewis comments: "This is both honest and penetrating, and leads me to hope that the Professor would not have resisted the suggestion that a similar limiting clause would improve his theory of the imagination. 'It is true enough, if we do not apply it to imaginative people.'" In my opinion, Freudian psychoanalytic theory applies universally: musicians and imaginative writers are not different in their humanity from others, and they are subject to the same unconscious forces as anybody else.[24] Talent, an abstract thing, may not be analyzable, but the bearer of talent, a human being, is. The second criticism that Lewis makes is: "If the image of a garden is only a disguise for the female body, and if all the excitement with which I read *Paradise Lost: Book IV* is really erotic...." And finally: "In order to explain the symbols which they themselves insist on we must admit that humanity is interested in many other things besides sex, and that admission is the thin edge of the wedge. Once it is allowed that our enjoyment of *Paradise Lost: Book IV* is a compound of latent erotic interest and real though conscious interest in gardens, then it becomes impossible to say *a priori* in what proportion the two are mixed." My answer to this is that an obsessive and exclusive interest in gardens, to the exclusion of the normal interest in the female body, is a signal that parts of the mind have been sealed off, and the trouble with exclusion is atrophy, restrictions, and inhibitions. Lewis is less petulant than the majority of his Oxford colleagues in his objections to psychoanalysis, but in the end his criticism amounts to the same need to wish away the real existence of the human body.[25]

In Indian studies such learned essays as that by Bloomfield, 'On the Art of Entering Another's Body: A Hindu Fiction Motif' (1917), tell us little or nothing[26] about motivation or significance. Why would somebody want to enter another person's body? I have suggested, as one universal motive for wishing to make a strange voyage, whether into the interior or out into space, the desire to return to a fantasied world of childhood happiness. Kenneth Grahame expresses the sadness of recognizing that such a return is impossible in his essay at the beginning of *Golden Age* (1887): "Well! The Olympians are all past and gone. Somehow the sun does not seem to shine so brightly as it used; the trackless meadows of old time have shrunk and dwindled away to a few poor acres. A saddening doubt, a dull suspicion, creeps over me. *Et in arcadia ego* – I certainly did once inhabit Arcady. Can it be that I also have become an Olympian?"

Another intuitive conjecture is that no story can replace the story of our own past, and I would suggest that the universal motive for reading is a search for words for this past. There is no fairy tale that tells truths of the kind that a psychoanalyst discovers in his practice. The late Robert Fliess, son of Wilhem Fliess, the ear-, nose- and throat-specialist and friend of Freud, wrote a remarkable book, posthumously published, called *Symbol, Dream and Psychosis*, in which he makes the rather startling claim that all severely-neurotic patients he has had have been genitally-seduced by a psychotic parent. Fliess claims that such seductions, usually occurring before the age of five, are so deeply repressed that a patient cannot dispel his amnesia without a great deal of patient work on the part of the analyst who, Fliess observes, is himself resistant to such an appalling observation. Fliess was perhaps himself so molested, as he hints in the introduction to an earlier book, but when we make allowance for the natural tendency to soften the blow of one's personal experience by making it universal, there is too much in the case histories he reports which bears the watermark of truth for us to dismiss the theory out of hand. Is there any traditional tale, collectively accepted, that can do justice to this kind of a truth? Consider one of the most remarkable case histories ever recorded, that of the *Genain Quadruplets* (Rosenthal 1963).[27] It was written in an attempt to show the biological basis of schizophrenia; in fact, it shows something quite different. Never have four people been exposed to such a horrendous youth as these four deeply-disturbed sisters. The fairy-tale of Cinderella is literally child's play in the face of this kind of truth. Even the demons in mythology, while closer to a symbolization of reality, are still at one remove.

The *Rāmāyana* may well trigger unconscious fantasies of ante-diluvian joy, but it is also manifestly about deformed, misshapen, evil, pitiless demons. And indeed, children are often most attracted to a tale they fear: they want to hear about cannibals, witches, goblins, castration, amputation, death, disease and misery, an interest which is counterphobic. People have a need to hear, preferably in a somewhat disguised fashion, about what they fear, because our terror is less when we see and know. Possibly too (as in the explanation of a scopophilia by Fenichel: "I see, hence I did not destroy."): 'Look, it is in a book; I didn't invent castration – I am not the only one who fears being devoured.' Freud, in one of his late essays on humor (1927), puts this profound comment into the mouth of humor (cf. Schafer, 1960): "Look! Here is the world which seems so dangerous! It is nothing but a game for children – just worth making a jest about!" Fliess translates this into the analytic situation: "Look here, this is the (inner) world that seems so dangerous. A child's world – just a thing to be analyzed, i.e., to be re-experienced and to be understood." He notes that both speeches are soliloquies since, in both cases, it is narcissistic constellations which they are meant to depict (Fliess, 1942). What greater pleasure for a child than to be able to close the book on all his terrors and go to sleep. He drags the book over to his parents, he insists they read, he trembles, but he also puts the book back, and is tucked away to bed. Nothing really happened. Did Rāma exist, or is it just a fairy tale? Bedtime reading, a thing of long ago. 'Where did it happen, and when?' 'Over the hills and far away.'

> We may some time have a biochemistry of memory, but never of memories.
>
> Kety (1962)

SCREEN-MEMORIES[28]

In 1899 Freud wrote one of his first psychoanalytic papers, a brief essay entitled 'On Screen Memories' (Freud, 1899). He defines a screen-memory as follows: "A screen-memory is one which owes its value as a memory not to its own content but to the relation existing between that content and some other, that has been suppressed."[29] The screen-memory that Freud tells us about is as follows: Freud as a child of two or three is in a green meadow, thickly grown. The yellow dandelions growing in the grass stand out distinctly in his memory. Years later, Freud visits the same place – his birthplace by the way – and stays with friends of his family. He falls passionately in love, for the first time, with the fifteen-year-old daughter: "I can remember quite well for what a long time afterwards I was affected by the yellow color of the dress she was wearing when we first met, whenever I saw the same color anywhere else." As I understand it, Freud as an adolescent is not concerned with the color of the dress, but with what lies beneath it, understandably. Unable to acknowledge this, yet desiring to retain the image of it somewhere, he projects his interest in yellow backwards onto the flowers. These he can safely remember, over and over, but the pleasure in so doing came from its connection with a later event. Strachey notes: "It is a curious thing that the type of screen-memory mainly considered in the present paper – one in which an early memory is used as a screen for a later even – almost disappears from later literature."[30] This has been, as one may well imagine, a fertile area for psychoanalysts with their interest in memory and its distortions. In 1927 Fenichel spoke of a general "hunger for screen experiences", with the ego searching its storehouse of memories that it can offer up to consciousness. The ego, Fenichel writes, "has a 'free valence' for screen experiences and is economically eased when it finds them."[31] In other words, we are happy when we remember falsely but pleasantly. The opening paragraph of Freud's paper on the occurrence in dreams of material from fairy tales (1913) reads: "In a few people a recollection of their favourite fairy tales takes the place of memories of their own childhood; they have made the fairy tales into screen-memories." To provide an example of the complexity of a screen-memory, here is a classic case from Greenacre:

> A young man surprised a marauder as he opened the door of his home one night. He believed the man was armed but was not sure whether or not he actually saw a pistol. He was shocked by the experience, and was surprised to find his attention fixed on the door knob which shone in the light of the nearby street light rather than on the man and the question of whether or not he had a gun. The door knob was the vivid spot in his memory both immediately afterward and long after. Analysis showed that the deflection of focus to the door knob served to temper his anxiety at the time. Back of this, however, lay much earlier experiences of peeping through the nearly shut door of the bathroom to watch his parents at the toilet and of attemptinf to look through the keyhole to verify suspicions of their activities in the bedroom.[32]

Greenacre has also written about Lewis Carroll and has this perceptive observation about the author of the Alice books: "It is probable that within the cage of extreme reasonableness, intense self-criticism, control to the point of pedantic accuracy and infinite patience of the Christ Church lecturer on Mathematics that was the adult Charles Dodgson, there were old mad memories, like prehistoric monsters, Boojums, which he, like the Professor in Sylvia and Bruno, thought he had forgotten."[33]

A recent case was reported by Schreiber (1973) in his article in the *Psychoanalytic Study of the Child*. A patient was fascinated by the scene in the *Wizard of Oz* film where, after the tornado, Dorothy looks through the door of her house and sees a colorful world of fairyland. At that point in the film the sepia tone changes into color. What happened was that the patient did not want to remember a similar scene, when her mother was at the door, "leaving, with a bright light behind her – the moment that was associated with her feeling an irreplacable loss, an emptiness. When Mrs. R. was searching for screen experiences to help repress the painful percept. . .instead of feeling loss she recalled the discovery of a beautiful scene, where an object was found, not lost." The choice is determined by other associated links as well, of course. What is important for our purposes is that the patient had reported a six-month period in her life about which she had no memory. This period began when her mother left her in Boston when she was seven and ended at the moment of reunion with her mother in California, six months later. Calef, in his article on 'Color in Dreams' (1954), mentions the suggestion of Bernfeld that "perhaps color in dreams was connected with early childhood memories", an intriguing suggestion. This can be linked with Freud's yellow dandelions and Greenacre's explanation of the bright edge and vividness of screen-memory in terms of the severity of trauma and the subsequent overflow in the form of a secondary visual excitement (secondary because the real excitement lies with the trauma).[34] The bright orange in Calef's patient's dream might well refer to some lost colorful experience, where 'colorful' could well screen 'frightening'.

It remains to demonstrate the relevance of such material to the *Rāmāyaṇa*. The *Rāmāyaṇa* contains, in manifest form, none of the real concerns of life. For example, we never hear that Rāma had enuresis as a child. We never learn of the perpetual fears of parents that their children may fall ill. We hear nothing of the adolescent's momentous struggle with masturbation. Moreover, it is astonishing how totally Vālmīki manages to keep himself out of his work. One is reminded of Freud's visit to Weimar: when he saw the collected works of Goethe, he murmured, "He wrote all this in order not to show himself." Vālmīki wrote all this (32,000 verses) not only to hide himself, but to seal off from the vision of later centuries all the preoccupations of the population of Bhāratavarṣa, and thus the *Rāmāyaṇa* is filled with screen-memories. It is hardly surprising, then, that the opaque material he used for his screening process occasionally admits a little light from another, distant world, and allows us a transparent, fleeting vision of some deeper and darker reality belonging to our own lost childhood.

Dreams

Screen-memories are closely related to dreams, for they too often attempt to deflect our attention from a real event. Freud, in writing about a dream within a dream, said: "In other words, if a particular event is inserted into a dream as a dream by the dream-work itself, this implies the most decided confirmation of the reality of the event – the strongest *affirmation* of it."[35] A recurrent dream, I believe, signals a real event. Most of us forget the fact that we have recurrent dreams and that we have been deeply concerned with understanding their meaning. The affect in such dreams is often greater than in everyday life, a sure sign that the emotional significance of some early event has been denied access to consciousness. Some people seem capable of expressing, and indeed of experiencing, love only in dreams. Freud said in his chapter on affect in dreams, that "large numbers of dreams appear to be indifferent, whereas it is never possible to enter into the dream-thoughts without being deeply moved";[36] that is, it is not possible to understand a dream without having understood something profound about our inner lives. "Dreams are never occupied with minor details."[37] In the opinion of Sharpe, and I believe, of Freud, every dream contains a childhood memory – even if only in that dark and obscure place that Freud described as the navel of the dream,[38] the deep spot at which interpretation often fails us. Sharpe, in her fine book on dreams, speaks of the dream "as the key to the storehouse of memory and experience." Taking a hint from the title of one of Bachelard's chapters in his book *La terre et les rêveries du repos*, namely "La maison natale et la maison onirique", I might hazard the guess that we always dream in the house where we were born. And many people, as Novey has shown in his book *The Second Look* (1968), have a peculiar need to visit the house they were born in, which always produces a curious melancholy feeling. If the forgetting of dreams is as astonishing as the amnesia that seems to overcome our early childhood, so is their retention in memory. Arlow, in his paper on ego psychology and the study of mythology, has written that "perhaps society can exist only because the impossible burden of instinctual renunciation which communal living demands can be abrogated nightly in dreams. Personal dreams and daydreams are made to be forgotten."[39] But what of those dreams we never forget? Such dreams seem so important that one must wonder at the absence of dreams in the *Rāmāyaṇa*.

Suppose that Hanumān, the great monkey god, had the following two dreams: "One was a painting of a city that seemed dead – a 'ghost city'. It was painted in black and white and no human or animal figures appeared.

All at once the doors of the houses opened and gaily-dressed people came out [including my husband and me] including my monkey wife and me." The second dream of Hanumān was a horrible nightmare. In order to understand it, we must know that Hanumān in his childhood was terrified of dark corridors, and that his father was an embittered, irascible and pessimistic widower, highly critical and given to anger and violence. He saw threats, dangers and possible accidents everywhere. Nothing – not even his frightened child – found grace in his eyes, but for an unknown reason he loved frogs and toads. Hanumān, too, began to like frogs and toads. To tame them, he would feed them worms which they took from his hand, and in the garden they grew and multiplied. In the evenings he would play the *vīṇā* to them. Now Hanuman's dream: "I am on the terrace of our house lying on a sort of couch in a magnificent moonlight. Behind my head is a dark corridor instead of the living-room door. At the entrance of the corridor is a black frog, monstrous and horrible. I am seized with an inexpressible terror. Suddenly things change. Not the horrible frog, but my father emerges from the shadows of the corridor with a knife in his hand – like a common murderer. I feel paralyzed with fear! Awakening, I remained in the unpleasant atmosphere of my childhood and it was a long time before I could get out of it."

Of course, no such dreams have been reported of Hanumān or indeed in Sanskrit literature. (The first is a dream of nascent schizophrenia, reported by Mortimer Ostow in his book *Drugs in Psychoanalysis and Psychotherapy*;[40] the second is from a book by a Swiss psychoanalyst, *L'angoisse et la pensée magique*.[41]) I would go so far as to say that real dreams as we dream them every night are *never* reported in classical literature from any land.[42] All those nights in the forest, all those strange events impinging on Rāma's mind, and yet we are never allowed entry onto the royal road to the unconscious.[43] To read the *Rāmāyaṇa* without reading *The Interpretation of Dreams* is a deprivation.[44]

The monkeys

In order to ask pertinent questions about the monkeys in the *Rāmāyaṇa*, it is important to establish what the author *does not tell us* about them and what he is *not concerned* with. Consider the following tenth-century Chinese poem by We T'ung:

> Last year a Buddhist monk of Hua-p'ing, in the Min mountains,
> Obtained a gibbon for me and had it delivered from afar,

On arrival he was already tame and accustomed to captivity,
And his swift and nimble movements were a delight to watch.
He would come and go as told, as if he understood my speech,
And seemed to have lost all desire to return to his mountains.
Put on a leash he was not interesting to watch,
So I set him free and let him romp about as much as he liked.
On a moonlit night he would sing, swinging from a branch,
On hot days he would sit by the flowers and doze facing the sun.
When my children were around or my guests showed their interest,
He would hang upside down or jump about showing his tricks.
I had told a man to look after all his needs,
So that he never even once lacked his seasonal food and drink.
Yet the other day his keeper suddenly told me the gibbon was ill.
He stood on my steps, the gibbon in his arms and I went to look,
Offered him persimmons and chestnuts, but he didn't glance at them.
Legs drawn up, head between his knees, hunched up with folded arms,
His fur ruffled and dull, all at once his body seemed to have shrunk,
And I realized that this time he was really in great distress.
Formerly you were also subject to occasional slight indispositions,
But then, after I had fed you a few spiders as a remedy,
After having swallowed them, you would recover at once.
Why did the medicine fail now, though given several times?
This morning when a frosty wind was chilling me to the bone,
Very early I sent someone to inquire, and he reported you had died.
Although in this world it is hard to avoid grief and sadness,
I was tormented by repentance and bitter self-reproach.
You could be happy only when near your towering mountains,
You had been yearning for far plains and dense forests.
You must have suffered deeply being kept on leash or chain,
And that was why your allotted span of life was cut short.
I had his body wrapped up well and buried deep in a secluded corner,
So that at least the insects would leave his remains in peace.
Mr. Tzŭ-p'ing, my western neighbor, a man of very wide interests,
When he heard about this, slapped his thigh sighing without end.
He came to inquire several times, in deep sorrow over my loss,
Then, back home, he wrote a long poem of over a hundred words.
Reading those lines my lonely heart was filled with sadness,
Well he had expressed the grief caused by my gibbon's death!
He also tried to console me by referring to life's natural course,
That meetings result in partings, all subject to the whims of fate.

I took his poem out into the garden, read and re-read it –
Then, looking up at the bare branches, I burst out in tears.

This is quoted in a delightful book, *The Gibbon in China*, by van Gulick (1967), and there is nothing to parallel it in the *Rāmāyana*.[45] Consider the charming Chinese novel *Monkey*, translated in part by Arthur Waley (1942). Although it has been claimed, justly I believe, that the monkey derives much of his external traits from Hanumān (Dudbridge, 1970), his character is Chinese and very different from Hanumān.[46] In both the poem and the novel, for all the attempts at creating a fairy atmosphere, the feel is decidedly terrestrial and immediately recognizable to us. However, this is not so in the case of Hanumān. In order to appreciate the significance of the monkeys in the *Rāmāyaṇa*, I believe we have no choice but to draw on fairy tales and the insights of psychoanalysis. But before doing so, we must ask ourselves just who or what these monkeys are intended to represent.

Both Western and Indian scholarship (e.g., Ramadas, 1925) have insisted that these monkeys are tribals who *resemble* monkeys or who have monkey totems, though most have not gone as far as Bhatt, in his note to the first volume of the critical edition of the Baroda *Rāmāyana* (1966) in reference to *Rāmāyaṇa* I.16.6-7 (see above, p. 9). Research on the monkeys in the *Rāmāyaṇa* suggests that adults have some atavistic need to persecute or at least obliterate from sight what is strange, whereas children have a greater facility for accepting the unreal. The Chinese say that the dragon hibernates to survive. Children would never lure the Unicorn into a snare, whereas Odelle Shepard in her fine book on the Unicorn has shown how this poor beast has been the target of sexually-motivated murder.[47] Hanumān is a children's monkey. It was the happy child in Vālmīki who created Hanumān because of the affection he felt for him, and this affection has been passed on to two hundred generations of Indians.

To appreciate the significance of Hanumān we must also see the filmed versions of the *Rāmāyaṇa* in India, and see with what glee the arrival of Hanumān on the screen is greeted by the children in the audience. Hanumān and the monkeys are creatures of the imagination. Nonetheless, I believe we can still learn something about Hanumān by reading the works of the great naturalists.[48] Indeed, if Harry Harlow (1958, 1959)[49] had heeded the words of Kohler in his monograph *The Mind of the Ape* (1925), "A chimpanzee kept in solitude is not a real chimpanzee at all,"[50] he would not have needed to perform his cruel experiments on baby monkeys to establish scientifically what any child knows, namely that baby monkeys like their mothers and do not thrive without them. In his book *The Ape and the Child*, W. N. Kellog observes, "Sua was astonishingly sensitive even to the very weakest of stimuli. Faint noises, the sound of a raindrop, a distant automobile, a muffled foot-step would cause immediate changes in blood pressure, pulse and breathing rates....How responsive must these animals be to the extreme forms of punishment and deprivation employed in many of the ordinary types of experiments performed upon them."[51] Kohler has observed how "chimpanzees embrace each other, with all degrees of emphasis and fervour, partly as a reassurance of their social cohesion, and...'just because life is so jolly.' In moments of special cordiality they fall over each other to the ground."[52] And Kellog observed, in the female chimpanzee raised in his family, "her intense affection for those who care for her, at times amounting to an uncontrollable passion which nothing but physical contact, including embracing and kissing, would satisfy."[53]

Adults inevitably behave badly with regard to what they do not understand. Rāma, for example, kills the noble monkey chieftain Vālin in a most immoral and unwarriorlike fashion. Even though the commentators take great pains to establish the essential justice of his act, I have tried to show in my article 'Fratricide Among the Monkeys' (1976) that Vālmīki unconsciously knew the truth. I was pleased to learn subsequently that there is a verse in the Vulgate of the *Mahābhārata*, which the critical edition relegates to a footnote, that reads:

sthiraṃ sthāsyati cākīrtiḥ
trailokye sacarācare
rāme vālivadhād yadvat
evam droṇe nipātite

Long will stand the injustice of this act, in every corner of the universe. Droṇa was killed in the same inglorious fashion as Vālin (*Droṇaparvan*, 197:36-37, in the Kumbhakona edition; 196: 35-36, in Gorakh).

I understand from the book by Hooykaas on the Old-Javanese *Rāmāyaṇa* (1955) that a Dutch psychiatrist, van Welfften Paltke, treated a patient in 1938 (the case history was published in *Psychiatrie en Neurologie,* Amsterdam: Wenschappelijke Uitgeverij, 1948) who was convinced he was Vālin. My intuition tells me that this patient, too, knew the inner significance of Vālin's murder, and my guess is that he was a paranoid. Every paranoid who believes he is being persecuted *is* being persecuted in fact, only it is not always by whom or at the time he thinks.[54] If we wish to learn more about the psychological significance of Hanumān,[55] a delusional person who thinks he is Hanumān would be of immense help. Lacking such a patient, we could question very closely children who read about Hanumān in comic books, or make a careful study of legends current about him in the vernacular languages of India. The valuable book by Dineschandra Sen (1920) on the Bengali *Rāmāyaṇas* tells us that in the *Hanumāna Charita*, a work on astrology much loved by rural Bengalis, Hanumān is described as a great musician, a Brahmin, an incarnation of Śiva, or even as the head of a Buddhist monastery on an island east of Ceylon! He tells of the legend of Murāri Gupta, the celebrated poet and Sanskrit scholar and a contemporary of Caitanya who "is believed to have been an incarnation of Hanumān and we have it on the authority of the Bengali work, *Vaishṇava Vandanā*, written 350 years ago, that a Brahmin with all the members of his family actually saw that Murāri Gupta had a tail!"[56]

How will this psychologically-based knowledge shed light on difficult or obscure passages in the *Vālmīkirāmāyaṇa*? Let us consider one of the strangest episodes in the epic, which occurs in Canto 49 of the critical edition of the *Kiṣkhindhākāṇḍa*. Hanumān and his monkey companions have been searching the Vindhya mountains in vain for Sītā, and they are tired and thirsty, when:

> *avakīrnaṃ latāvṛkṣair dadṛśus te mahābilam*
> They saw a great hole covered with vines and trees.

Out of the hole they see issuing forth (*niṣkraman*) water birds, their wings still wet. Led by Hanumān, the monkeys enter that *timirāvṛtaṃ bilam*:

> *tatas tasmin bile bhīme nānāpādapasamkūle*
> *anyonyaṃ samparisvajya jagmur yojanam antaram*
> Then into the terrifying hole filled with many trees, hugging one another, they went deep inside for one mile.

Finally they come to a forest filled with light, where they see trees made of gold, vines as bright as the morning sun, and flowers made of lapis lazuli, emeralds, rubies and sapphires. Silver and gold palaces rise high into the sky and there are magic lotus ponds of pellucid water. The trees are laden with coral-like fruit, and everywhere they see wine and jewelled benches, colorful blankets and the choicest of foods. Finally they meet a female ascetic, dressed in a black antelope skin and restrained in her eating habits, who is shining like a light (*tāpasīṃ niyatāhārāṃ jvalantīm iva tejasā*). Hanumān asks her who she is, and she tells him that a demon magician (*māyāvin*) by the name of Maya built the golden forest by magic (*māyayā*) for a woman, an Apsaras by the name of Hemā ("gold"; hence his obsession with gold). Indra killed him, and Brahmā gave Indra both the forest and the woman. "I am *svayaṃprabhā* (the selflighting one?), a close friend of Hema, and I am guarding the place while she is away dancing and singing." The monkeys then feast, and there is an obscure implication that they spend quite some time doing so (cf. 52.2: *sa tu kālo vyatikrānto bile ca parivartatām*; Govindarāja on IV.50.3 says the monkeys spent one month inside the hole). Hanumān then asks her to take them out of the terrible *bila* (*bilād ghorād uttārayitum arhasi*). She replies cryptically:

> *jīvatā duṣkaraṃ manye praviṣṭena nivartitum*
> *tapasaḥ tu prabhāvena niyamopārjitena ca*
> *sarvān eva bilād asmad uddhariṣyāmi vānarān*
> *nimīlayata cakṣūṃṣi sarve vānarapuṃgavāḥ*
>
> I think it is difficult to leave this place alive. But through my ascetic powers which I have earned through my restraint, I will take all of you monkeys out of this hole. Close your eyes.
>
> *na hi niṣkramituṃ śakyam animīlitalocanaiḥ*
> *tato nimilitāḥ sarve sukumārāṅgulaiḥ karaiḥ*
>
> For it is not possible to leave here without closing your eyes. So all the monkeys closed their eyes with their delicate little fingers.

And she takes them out of the hole and shows them, shining before them, the great ocean. They emerge into spring in full bloom and look with awe at the *ghoraṃ sāgaram,* the terrible ocean. Frightened at the passing of the time set for their return, Tāra suggests to the monkeys that they re-enter the hole and live in it for the rest of their lives, free from worry, and from Rāma or Sugrīva.[57]

This is a strange story. It seems to have no purpose in the *Rāmāyaṇa* itself: it is not referred to again, nor is it a *deus ex machina*. So what is it doing here, and what does it mean? It seems to partake of the elements examined earlier. It has the earmarks both of a screen-memory and a dream, and seems to be related to the early life of somebody, and it is certainly a fairy tale. Furthermore, it has certain obscure resonances.[58] This *bila* seems to be the same one that Vālin entered in his pursuit of the demon Māyāvin with whom he had a quarrel "over a woman". Blood and foam gushed forth then; now, as in a reversal (almost always a form of denial), beautiful birds emerge. This place is life-giving, containing as it does the pure water that the monkeys thirst for, and yet it is also a terrifying place that in legend belonged to an uncanny demon and his goddess wife. Since we are dealing with denial and reversals, and the rather suspect insistence on gold, can we not see buried there a reference to feces, a common piece of symbolism?[59] Again, we are told that nobody comes out of his hole alive, unless the old woman, who lives there in sexual abstinence, allows him. And who is this old woman? A friend of the real owner, the tempting, dancing and singing Apsaras Hemā, who accepts without protest first a demon lover, then the god of the gods. Yet in the hole, amid all this sensuous splendor, lives an old, withered *tāpasī*, a chaste ascetic. Why chaste? Because, says the dreamer, she is really an alluring temptress. Melanie Klein would seem to be right: what place can possibly be more fascinating, more mysterious, more terrifying, more forbidden, unknown and unknowable than the inside of our mother's body? However, we can go further than this. This seemingly innocuous and irrelevant journey into the interior now takes on a rather startling significance. I said earlier that the episode plays no role in the subsequent story, but that is not strictly true, for it is only when the monkeys emerge intact at the other end of the hole that they see the ocean, meet Sampāti (Jaṭāyu's elder brother) and take the first step towards the recovery of Sītā. It is as if some oedipal struggle had been successfully overcome and the contestant emerges a new man, able at last to act in a purposeful way. Nevertheless, I believe that all great literature concerns itself primarily with tragedy and conflict, rather than with resolution, just as I claim analysis deals with suffering rather than achievements. So the heart of the *Rāmāyaṇa* lies in loss and bereavement (*karuṇarasa*), not in reconciliation.[60]

If Rāmā, while also a god, is yet considered the ideal man, Kṛṣṇa is the perfect playful god, whose childhood and youth was given over to the full expression of instinctual gratification. The story in which this adolescent freedom is brought to an end is not as well-known as it deserves to be. The passages themselves are seldom quoted and the incident with which they deal, Kṛṣṇa's strange sexual encounter with a deformed woman of great beauty, remain unplumbed. In the next chapter, I make an initial attempt at throwing some light on certain features of this tale that have intrigued me; they reveal a peculiarly Indian solution to the universal need for sexual autonomy and emotional distance from the parental home.

NOTES

[1] It is difficult to unlearn the rigidity of our philological training, which has us look for the oldest, purest version, and to regard with some contempt the vulgate. But to derive the richest

possible benefit from a wide reading pertaining to the *Rāmāyaṇa* we must undo this rigidity. The vulgate of the *Rāmāyaṇa*, is, in many ways, more important than the critical edition, and not just because this particular critical edition is a poor one, and not only because the vulgate contains the commentaries (though this, too, is weighty). But it is sometimes the very passages omitted from the critical edition which are the most important from a psychological point of view. Thus a work like D. C. Sen's on the Bengali *Rāmāyaṇa* is invaluable. Legends about Laksmana and Hanumān are legion in the vernacular literature and in the oral tradition and merit a study as diligent as Schwarzbaum's book on Jewish legends (1968). But we should not imitate this scholar nor his folklorist colleagues in their zeal for collecting while refusing at the same time to consider any possible significance in the material they assemble. Folklore studies on the whole seem bereft of human insight (an exception, one of the few I know, is the fine work by André Lévy on the Chinese folktale, 1971). Surely the Brothers Grimn collection must tell us *something* about children. So must the themes of the *Arabian Nights* (Gerhardt, 1963) and the *Kathāsaritsāgara*. Penzer's learned essays are a delight to read but do not take us very far into the psychology of the stories concerned.

[2] Cf. the concluding comments in Freud's paper on the three caskets (1913b, p. 301):

> ...three forms taken by the figure of the mother in the course of a man's life – the mother herself, the beloved one who is chosen after her pattern, and lastly the Mother Earth who receives him once more. But it is in vain that an old man yearns for the love of woman as he had it first from his mother; the third of the Fates alone, the silent Goddess of Death, will take him into her arms.

[3] Klein (1932). My objection to the Kleinian theory is that what makes an analyst good is exactly what makes a novelist good. It is a major defect in a writer, even a scientific writer, when you cannot tell whether the analysis took place in England or Germany except by noting whether the patient is called Hans or John. Though it is true that there may be a limited number of universal early fantasies, yet as Freeman Sharpe puts it: "In dealing with the emotions common to all mankind the perennial interest lies in their endless manifestation in individual settings."

E. R. Hilgard (in Szasz, 1958) reported on the work done in the 1920s by Zeigarnik. She showed that a person's ability to recall tasks which have been successfully completed is much less than his ability to recall unfinished tasks. Hilgard comments that "the practical implications of Mrs. Zeigarnik's findings are somewhat obscure." However, Thomas Szasz, in a 1958 article entitled 'The Role of the Counterphobic Mechanism in Addiction' takes issue with Hilgard and makes the pertinent observation that "in psychoanalytic work really first-hand observations are gathered only about unmastered ('traumatic') situations. Observations about the past 'positive' influences on the analysand's personality are, by necessity, most indirect and inferential."

[4] This mechanism of smuggling in the opposite of what one is consciously interested in is illustrated in a case history by Melitta Sperling (1970, p. 559):

> ...The mother of a young boy who suffered from ulcerative colitis expressed her feelings by saying: "I'm such a clean woman and he has such a messy disease!" In this case, the forbidden and deeply repressed anal pleasures could be indulged in only under the guise of illness. This boy showed very early reaction formations and signs of a

compulsion neurosis. Already, at less than the age of two, he was anxious and concerned when a drop of food dirtied his bib. At the age of four and a half, when he entered treatment, he was afraid to touch clay in the playroom and had a hand-washing compulsion. But due to his 'illness' he soiled himself often fifteen times daily.

[5] Fenichel (1939a), Weissman (1966).

[6] The Kleinians claim, perhaps correctly, that all art is the drive to overcome an unusually strong depression. Rilke said that beauty is nothing but the beginning of terror that we are still just able to bear. Hanna Segal, in her article "A Psychoanalytical Approach to Aesthetics" (1955), wrote that "the audience unconsciously re-lives the artist's depression and shares his triumph of achievement and his final detachment."

[7] The reading, or listening, of the child, the adolescent and the adult differ. It seems to me that the earlier the reading, the greater the power of the text to enchant. The greater appeal of one element of a story over another will have to do with the personal history of the reader. In one case where a two-year-old boy's mother committed suicide by jumping off the roof of her house, the boy showed a curious obsession with games that involved jumping off pieces of furniture. Certainly, he is bound to show an equally unconscious desire to read about events that involve falling, but one cannot say exactly in what way this interest will surface. He could become a parachute jumper, but then again he might reverse this interest by becoming a miner. Psychoanalysis is a postdictive rather than a predictive science. It cannot say for certain just how a story will reflect an event, but once it knows the stories, it can show how one event was grafted onto the other. And this is by no means a trivial achievement, as anybody knows who has been enslaved to a totally-opaque activity for its resemblance, on a primary process level, to unconscious needs.

[8] Cf. Gilbert Murray (1922, p. 117) on the Roman poet Ovid's *Mythology*:

> A world of wonderful children where nobody is really cross or wicked except the grownups: Juno, for instance, and people's parents and, of course, a certain number of fairies and witches. I think among all the poets who take rank merely as storytellers and creators of mimic worlds, Ovid still stands supreme. His criticism of life is very slight; it is the criticism passed by a child, playing alone and peopling the summer evening with the delightful shapes, upon the stupid nurse who drags it off to bed.

[9] Freeman Sharpe (1943, p. 180).

[10] We can see from Mary Frere's book what master storytellers the Indians can be. Why then, is the *Rāmāyaṇa* such a boring story? It has style, and beauty, and dignity, but no humor, no suspense and no characters. The story itself can be told quickly; indeed, it has been, and *saṃkṣiptarāmāyaṇa*s of 100 verses, 10 verses and even one verse are very popular. Is this an obscure recognition that the story isn't worth all that much? What, then, impels people to listen to the *Rāmāyaṇa* in all its many variations with such utter and almost trance-like absorption?

[11] Myths of the good life are not restricted to ancient fables, or to the distorted memories of our own childhood. Even as sophisticated an observer as Verrier Elwin (1947) is capable

of this astonishing comment (p. 325): "On the whole the relationship of children and parents is a happy one. This may be at least one reason why there is so little conflict and jealousy, so little strain, among the Muria." More to the point, in my view, is this observation of Oscar Wilde: "Children begin by loving their parents. After a time they judge them. Rarely, if ever, do they forgive them."

[12] All adults live on the fringe of nostalgia – looking back to happier times. One of the joys of having children is to return to fairy tales, and to at least attempt to recover some of the actual feelings we had at the time. But when such a need is unconscious, it can soon pass beyond our own control, and then it produces such outlandish things as the current interest in dragons. The so-called scientific research on the Loch Ness monster is, in my opinion, not worth the single story by Kenneth Grahame, *The Reluctant Dragon* (Grahame, 1898).

[13] It would be a mistake, however, to assume that all great children's literature must deal with a fairy world. A book totally devoid of any reference to the supernatural, and yet in my opinion one of the greatest books ever written for children (and the finest example I have ever seen of a spontaneous cure) is Burnett's *The Secret Garden* (1911). The balance seems fairly even between great works of fancy and the work of everyday life. To balance *Le Petit Prince* we have *Les Lettres de Mon Moulin*; for *Le Grand Meaulnes, Platero y Yo*; for *At the Back of the North Wind* we have Korczak's political book on *Mathew the Young King* (1925). But I think it is safe to say that the topic of any good children's book will always be one that has links to the great themes of the past and to the basic preoccupations of adult literature as well. If one looks at so simple a book as Maurice Sendak's *Where the Wild Things Are,* one can see that its theme is an important one: it is that of many events taking place in a special dream-time, so that everything has stood still at home in one's absence. This is an old theme, well-known in Chinese (Hsun, 1959) and Indian literature, and used in much medieval European literature. I refer the reader to Farinelli's neglected classic. *La Vita e un Sogno* (1916). Note Bas (1946) on Ossian: "Ailleurs, c'est une vision du pays natal qui apparut a l'heureux exile et qui provoque en lui la nostalgie."

[14] P. Green (1957, p. 324).

[15] P. Green (1957, p. 330).

[16] For a criticism, see Bartlett (1920) and a good rejoinder by Roheim (1923).

[17] For a review of the literature on folktales and psychology, see Fischer (1963).

[18] The actual psychoanalytic literature on children's literature and fairy tales, besides the works mentioned in this essay and older works, is not very large. See Friedlander (1942), Grotjahn (1939-1940), Huckel (1957), Lorand (1935), Peller (1958), Rubinstein (1955), Skinner (1957), Desmonde (1951), Fraiberg (1954), Rowley (1951), Petty (1953), Buxbaum (1941), Bettleheim (1975).

[19] Quoted in Reilly (1968, p. 77).

[20] Isaacs and Zimbardo (1968, p. 129).

[21] Tolkien (1937, pp. 83-84).

[22] Tolkien, op. cit., p. 45.

[23] We may profitably compare this with the story of the Cottingly photographs. "Surely one of the oddest events in the history of human dealings with fairies is the case of the Cottingly photographs taken in 1917 by a ten-year-old girl and her thirteen-year-old cousin in a 'wooded glen'." These show the girl in deep communion with tiny little fairies, very white, very English indeed, and very Edwardian, with little ballerina dresses and pointed shoes. What is astonishing is not that such evident and good-natured hoaxes by members of the Theosophical Society should exist, but that intellectuals of the eminence of Leslie Fiedler, half a century later, should take them seriously: "The plates on which the demure and diminutive creatures seems to hover in the air in filmy pantomime garb have been examined and re-examined by experts who assure us that there is no evidence of tampering or even double exposure" (Fiedler, 1974, p. 20). See the judicious review by Sanderson (1973). I am not saying that fairies are not important in literature, or that their role cannot be responsibly studied. On the contrary, as K. M. Brigg's book, *The Anatomy of Puck: An Examination of Fairy Beliefs Among Shakespeare's Contemporaries and Successors* (1959) and others similar to it (Brigg, 1967; Latham, 1930; Rathborne, 1937) show, serious research on fairies is possible. But when people begin to believe in the literal existence of fairies, it is time to ask pertinent questions about the psychopathology of the need to believe in fairies. "I have known many young people, who particularly in late adolescence come to a belief in magic, to compensate for their having been deprived of it prematurely in childhood" (Bettelheim, 1975, p. 61). As an example, one may look to the current interest in parapsychology. The best article on the subject that I have seen is by a Swedish psychoanalyst. He writes (Löfgren, 1968a, p. 177):

> I myself have never performed such an unpleasant task as this review and I have deeply regretted many times that I ever got into the field. After a while the feeling of being in bad company is really quite overwhelming. The primitive thinking, the atmosphere of cheap magic, the emotional poverty, and the constrictive thinking finally impart a feeling of being exposed to decaying minds. . .

[24] Periodically, a related issue, the question of 'human progress' comes up, and sometimes chess is used as a paradigm. It is held that since, in India in the tenth century, there was a form of chess that was played by using dice to determine the moves of the pieces, 'real', or 'classical' chess must be a later development, for it represents a stage of human thinking (where there is no dependence on chance) that is 'later' than that represented by a passive dependence on fate. But it should be pointed out, as Thieme has, that this argument is *at least* historically fictitious. For, according to Thieme (in Bender, 1962), 'real' chess existed in India as early as Pāṇini (in the fifth century B.C.) and Patañjali (in the second century B.C.), whereas the use of dice seems to be a corruption at a later date. And, as Thieme justly points out, a civilization which was capable of inventing the abstract principles of Pāṇinian grammar was certainly capable of inventing chess (which it seems the Indians did; see Macdonnell, 1899). While there may well be an accumulation of knowledge, I do not think that any case can be made for anything like ethical advances, or even 'cultural' advances, whatever that might mean: psychologically, we are the same as we have always been.

[25] It is unfortunate that the best-known writing on children's literature, Jan (1969), *On Children's Literature*; Thwaite's *From Primer to Pleasure: An Introduction to the History of Children's Books in England* (1963); Lüthi's *Once Upon a Time: On the Nature of Fairy Tales* (1962); Green's *The Teller of Tales* (1965); Hazard's *Books, Children and Man* (1933); Smith's *The Unreluctant Years* (cf. Avery, 1975) never mentions Freud at all. An exception is the fine book by Soriano (1968). For it is not enough merely to collect tales or versions of tales. Beauty and the Beast, or Cinderella, may well have 700 variants (see the collection with good introductions and notes by Iona and Peter Opie, *The Classic Fairy Tales*, 1974), but unless we learn something about the deeper needs to which this tale speaks, we will not have furthered human understanding. India is, after all, one of the great storehouses of tales. (For a charming collection, see the very first one: Mary Frere's *Old Deccan Days, or Hindoo Fairy Legends Current in Southern India*, 1881; the autobiography by "the narrator", Anna Liberata de Souza, is moving; see too J. Jacobs' fine collection (1892); Thompson and Balys (1958), Thompson and Roberts (1960) and Bødker (1957) are useful. Buddhism, of course, provided one of the richest sources of Indian story-literature (see Warren, 1922), in particular the *Jātakas* (Cowell, 1957). For an excellent discussion see Foucher (1955). For the Jain stories, see Brown (1933). Another good collection is in Edgerton (1926) and Meyer (1909). The greatest single collection of old tales is to be found in one of the great works of Indology, Tawney's ten-volume translation of the *Kathāsaritsāgara*, edited by N. M. Penzer (1924-1928). Perhaps even greater than this work, however, is the older *Bṛhatkathāślokasaṅgraha* by Buddhasvāmin, of which there is a fine French translation by Félix Lacôte (1908). See, too, Sylvain Lévi's edition and partial translation of the *Bṛhatkathāmañjarī* of Kṣemendra. Of the Buddhist *avadānas*, certainly one of the most moving is the *Aśokāvadāna*, of which a useful edition was published by Mukhopadhyaya in 1963. This is the story of a handsome son blinded through the lust of his stepmother. He is found many years later, a blind begging minstrel, by his own royal father. The story, in Buddhist Hybrid Sanskrit, deserves to be placed next to the Oedipus legend. Though it has exercised a fascination on the Indian mind for two millenia, it has, surprisingly, never been fully translated.

Collecting tales without attempting to understand them has a venerable history. Kirkland in his bibliography of South Asian folklore lists 7,000 entries (without annotation), among them such fascinating titles as: hailstorms-virgins-charms; shoes-brooms-dreams; milk, dying-serpents; the lizard and medicine; bathing-mothers-in-law and Bombay; on the use of swallow-worts in the ritual, sorcery and leechcraft of the Hindus and the pre-Islamic Arabs (Kirkland, 1966). I can only urge the reader to contrast these articles with one by the psychoanalyst Norman Reider, with an equally intriguing title: *Chess, Oedipus and the Mater Dolorosa* (Reider, 1959) to see just how much can be discovered about such seemingly innocuous topics, given the right questions.

[26] An exception must be made for the scholarly and valuable article by E. Washburn Hopkins on "The Fountain of Youth" (1905), which does make an attempt to understand the legend, even if only cursorily.

[27] Rosenthal's theory of the origin of schizophrenia seems to have become the dominant one. He favors a diathesis-stress theory; "what endogenously is latent, what exogenously stresses, and what particular resonance the one has with respect to the other" (1963, p. 577). Since this work is so often quoted as the major research favoring this thesis, let me note his comment on the four children:

> The girls seem to have had characteristics from a very early age that may best be described as constrictive. They had low energy levels (*sic*), were rather placid, 'sweet', introversive, not very talkative, communicative or outgoing, and they took little initiative either with respect to general activities or interpersonal relationships (p. 578).

This kind of mindless writing, totally insipid and thoughtless, has become the norm in American psychiatry. Rosenthal is writing about four children who were sexually mutilated surgically at age twelve, beaten daily and probably raped by their father. The work (including the psychological texts, e.g., handwriting analysis!) is, in my opinion, as 'insane' as the family, in a more subtle and pernicious way.

[28] Intimately related to the theme of screen-memories is the question of early memories, and of the reconstruction of early memories in psychoanalysis. Freud, in his paper "On Screen Memories", mentions the surprise it occasions to realize that we all possess so few memories of our own childhood. Moreover, Freud, later in his life, seems to have wondered whether there is any such thing as normal forgetting, that is, whether all holes in our memory are not occasioned by repression. From a seminal article by Schur, the theoretical importance of which has not been acknowledged, we can infer that Freud *forgot* the most highly-charged events which form the famous Irma dream of *The Interpretation of Dreams* must have been an outcome. The reasons for this forgetting are not hard to find; the 'lost' memories involve disturbing elements of sadism toward a violently-mishandled female patient (Schur, 1966b). On early memories and constructions, I have found most valuable Kris (1952, 1956), Loewald (1955), Niederland (1965a), the latter especially for the extraordinary case history it contains; Schachtel (1947) and Weiss (1942b). One can also consult Bernstein and Blacher (1967), Fine (1971), Fraiberg et al. (1975), Guillaumin (1968) Hadfield (1927), Kennedy (1972), E. Plank (1953), Rubinfine (1967), Sachs (1967), Saul et al. (1956), Schmideberg (1950), Vandendriessche (1972) and Smirnoff (1967). Munch said, "I don't paint what I see but what I saw." Cf. the moving memories of an eighteen-year-old schizophrenic artist reported in Naumberg (1950).

[29] Freud (1899, p. 320).

[30] Strachey (1934, p. 302).

[31] Fenichel (1927, p. 114). Important articles have been written on screen-memories since then by Simmel (1925), Glover (1929), Greenacre (1949), and Reider (1953, 1960).

[32] Greenacre (1949).

[33] Greenacre, op. cit., pp. 241-242.

[34] See Greenacre's article, 'The Pre-Puberty Trauma in Girls' (1950), for more on this topic.

[35] Freud (1900, p. 338).

[36] Freud, op. cit., p. 467.

[37] Freud, op. cit., p. 589.

[38] Cf. Rangell (1967, p. 177):

> But just as Freud says about the dream, that the associations to it lead to a nexus of obscurity, so do genetic reconstructions dwindle into a more and more obscure and unarticulated area of the earliest ontogenic history.

The passage from *The Interpretation of Dreams* (Freud, 1900, S.E. V, p. 525) is worth quoting in full:

> There is often a passage in even the most thoroughly-interpreted dream which has to be left obscure; this is because we become aware during the work of interpretation that at that point there is a tangle of dream-thoughts which cannot be unraveled. . . .This is the dream's navel, the spot where it reaches down into the unknown. The dream-thoughts to which we are led by interpretation cannot, from the nature of things, have any definite endings; they are bound to branch out in every direction into the intricate network of our world of thought. It is at some point where this meshwork is particularly close [the German reads *dicht*, 'dense'] that the dream-wish grows up, like a mushroom out of its mycelium.

Cf. S.E. IV, p. 111, note, where the same analogy is used.

[39] Arlow (1961, pp. 378-379).

[40] Ostow (1962, p. 229).

[41] Odier (1956, pp. 103-104).

[42] The one exception I know is a Chinese novel, the *Hsi Yu Pu* (Hsia and Hsia, 1968). In contrast to my claim is the new book by Devereux, *Dreams in Greek Tragedy* (Devereux, 1978). Of course it is possible to claim that many dream-reports in traditional literature are attempts at describing a genuine dream-experience. The distortion is the result of secondary revision, which Freud describes as a universal urge towards coherence. It is not clear, from Freud's comments on secondary revision in Chapter VI of *The Interpretation of Dreams*, whether this takes place preconsciously, immediately upon awakening, or whether it is part of our defensive equipment, a further means of disguising the true content of the dream. Does any dream escape this reworking? Unfortunately we have no means of comparing the original dream-experience with the version later reported, and so we can never gauge the degree of distortion to which a given dream is subjected. Certainly some dreams take on, in the telling, all of the logical characteristics of day-thinking. Others, however, retain their sense of strangeness and thereby impress us as being more direct communications from the unconscious. The feelings in such dreams are obscure and often defy description; they seem in some profound sense intimately linked to our most compelling preoccupations. The dreams reported in a classical literature are those most subjected to a process of cultural secondary revision and thus most rarely reveal their true nature.

[43] The dream remained, of course, the symbol par excellence of the complex working of the unconscious and the compromises it is forced to make with other parts of the mind. As

such, Lewin was able to make important analogues with phobias, treating phobias as the manifest content of a dream (Lewin, 1952). Odier, too, in the book cited (pp. 95-97), makes some telling observations about phobias and nightmares: he points out that in the phobic patient and child, "projection leaves in its wake an intimate affective relationship of a negative sort between the subject and the phobogenic object." Also: "The malevolent object is an unreal object falsely localized in an imaginary space. The neutralizing function of real space is nonexistent. For the dreamer, projection is useless" (cf. Greenson, 1959).

This is why the dream of the black frog was a nightmare; there was no place to go, no real space into which the dreamer could escape her own knowledge of her annihilating father. She may have loved the frogs, but it was a precarious kind of love, with very little hope of the affection being returned, and we can imagine the little girl feeding the loathsome toads their worms with a quivering lower lip. Her love for frogs was no doubt counterphobic; on the other hand, it was her only chance for love from her father. The analogy of dreaming with the rest of our affective life has never been taken further than in the work of the French literary critic Jacques Rivière, the discoverer of Proust, who wrote that "All our feelings are dreams; all our opinions are the exact equivalent of neurotic symptoms... In us there is a constant obstinate, ever-inventive tendency that urges us to camouflage ourselves in our own eyes." In the words of Jules Romain, the vision which refuses to acknowledge psychological realities "even when it seeks the depths allows itself to be guided by the visible surface indications. It does not suspect a deposit of iron unless the rocks above are all rusty, or of coal unless one treads upon black dust" (Rivière, 1921, p. 181).

[44] See the important book by J. S. Lincoln, *The Dream in Primitive Culture* (Lincoln, 1935).

[44] Van Gulik (1967, p. 78). While it is true that, compared to the Chinese poems, the Indian versions are poor in observation, it is nonetheless true, I believe, that the *Rāmāyaṇa* is richer in primary process material: the fantasies seem more like unconscious fantasies than the much more secondary-process, that is, logical and self-conscious, *Monkey*.

[46] I confess here to a 'wild' but very satisfying conjecture that the idea of Hanumān traveled East to inspire *Monkey* and West to inspire the vivacious tale of 'Le Chat Botté' of Charles Perrault, which is preceded (though the great French originator of the fairy tale did not know this) by the tale in the *Pentamerone* and also Straparola's *Piacevole Notti*. I have no evidence. Dudbridge (1970), in his scholarly study, while commenting on certain similarities in *Monkey* to the behavior of Hanumān in the *Rāmāyaṇa*, is justly cautious about 'sources'.

[47] One thinks of the atmosphere of magic that ought to surround these lovely beasts:

One by one in the moonlite there
Neighing far off on the haunted air
The unicorns come down to the sea (Conrad Aiken, *Evening Song*)

[48] See, especially, Yerkes and Yerkes (1929).

[49] Jane Goodall (1971), in her otherwise sane plea for the protection of chimpanzees from the rapacious use of these lovable creatures in inhumane experiments, shows to what extent we have capitulated to a completely false model of science when she says, speaking of

schizophrenia and severe depression: "Because of the similarity of the chimpanzee brain to the human brain, experiments carried out with chimpanzees will undoubtedly be of great value to those scientists who are grappling with the problems of human mental illness. . . .Chimpanzees may serve as experimental models for some of these disorders" (op. cit., pp. 248-249). I would contend that "scientists who are grappling with the problems of human mental illness" are only acting out their ill-disguised sadism on monkeys and apes. Depression is not a biological disorder, nor is it a mystery. It is, like schizophrenia, a psychological disease, which does not arrive mysteriously at birth. (Kanner's research on autistic children is a scientific and psychological disgrace.)

[50] Köhler, *The Mentality of Apes* (1925, p. 287).

[51] Kellog (1933, p. 321-322).

[52] Köhler, op. cit., p. 304.

[53] Kellog, op. cit., p. 187.

[54] Schreber may have been psychotic, but he was no fool, and he knew that *somebody* was out to get him. He thought it was God, and he wasn't far wrong: it was his psychiatrist and his father. See Masson (1974c), Niederland (1959b, 1960).

[55] Hanumān bears certain resemblances to an imaginary companion (on this charming borderland between fantasy and reality, where the phenomenon has as much potential for health as for pathology, see the literature by Svendsen, 1934; Bender and Vogel, 1941; Burlingham, 1945, 1952 – twin fantasies obviously play a decisive tole in the origin of imaginary companions – O. E. Sperling, 1954; Nagera, 1969; Bach, 1971; Myers, 1976, 1979; and my article, in press, in the *Journal of the American Oriental Society* on Hanumān as an imaginary companion), as do the other animals in the epic, especially the vulture Jaṭāyu (see, especially, Plank, 1968). It is not uncommon for a previously-feared animal to later become an all-powerful accomplice. A phobic animal is a kind of negative companion, for in the very fear and hatred one feels, a relationship is set up (cf. Ferber, 1959; A. Benjamin, 1955). Does this help to explain the strange transformations Rāvaṇa undergoes in different versions of the *Rāmāyaṇa*? In some South Indian versions, he is the hero rather than the antihero of the epic. In dreams it is not infrequent for an animal to represent a sibling. There is a charming Korean tale of a monkey who bathes a small boy, told by Seung (1971).

[56] Sen, 1920, p. 52.

[57] Vulgate IV.53.26:

alaṃ viśādena bilaṃ praviśya vasāma sarve yadi rocate vaḥ
idaṃ hi māyāvihitaṃ sudurgamaṃ prabhūtapuṣpodakabhojyapeyam
ihāsti no naiva bhayaṃ puraṃdarān na rāghavād vānararājato' pi vā

[58] This episode reminded me of another strange story in the *Rāmāyaṇa*, this one in the *Araṇyakāṇḍa*, critical edition (Divanji, 1963), III.10. Rāma is wandering through the forest,

when at dusk he comes to a beautiful lake in which elephants are bathing and birds are resting.

> *prasannasalile ramye tasmin sarasi śuśruve gītavāditranighoṣo na tu kaścana dṛśyate*
> From out of that lovely lake of pellucid waters he heard the sound of singing and of music, but nobody was to be seen.

The sage Dharmabhṛt tells him a curious story: It is called the Lake of the Five Fairies. It was created by the ascetic power of a sage called Maṇḍākarṇin. For 10,000 years he practiced *tapes*, living on air, immersed in the waters. To thwart his efforts to become immortal, the gods sent him five leading fairies (*apsaras*) "shining like flashing lightning". The sage, although he was *dṛṣṭaparāvarah*, "one who had seen higher and lower," that is one who knows the difference between the true and the false, fell in love with all five of them, and married them all. III.10.16-18 reads:

> *tātake nirmitaṃ tāsām asminn antarhitaṃ gṛham tatraivāpsarasaḥpañca nivasantyo yathā sukhaṃ ramayanti tapoyogān muniṃ yauvanam āsthitam tāsāṃ saṃrīḍa-mānānām eṣa vāditraniḥsvanaḥ śrūyate bhūṣaṇonmiśro gītaśabdo manoharaḥ* He built for them inside this lake a hidden house. It is there that the five fairies live happily and provide delight for that sage who, by the power of his austerities, has become young again. This sound of music and the beautiful song mixed with the tinkling of ornaments that one hears comes from them as they joyfully play.

[59] A certain amount of common sense is necessary in deciding what to interpret, and where to look for the mechanisms that prevail in dreams and screen-memories. Faced with the exquisite verse that describes with such evident pleasure and gusto Hanumān when he first thinks he sees Sītā:

> *āsphoṭayāmāsa cucumba pucchaṃ nananda cikrīḍa jagau jagāma*
> *stambhān arohan nipapāta bhūmau nidarśayan svāṃ prakṛtiṃ kapīnām*
> He clapped his hands and kissed his tail
> he frolicked
> he played
> he sang
> he ran to the stone pillars
> and climbed them
> Then threw himself to the ground
> Revealing his true nature as a monkey (*Sundarakāṇḍa* 10.54),

it would be insensitive to scour the verse for hidden significance. On the other hand, when we read the great lines of Blake:

> O Rose, thou art sick!
> The invisible worm
> That flies in the night,
> In the howling storm,
>
> Has found out thy bed
> Of crimson joy,

And his dark secret love
Does thy life destroy.

we are dealing with something quite different. Bowra (1950, p. 44) says of this poem: "If we ask what the poem means, we can answer that it means what it says, and that this is perfectly clear. It illustrates in an astonishing way Blake's gift for distilling a complex imaginative idea into a few marvellously telling words." But I find it hard to believe that this poem can possibly be regarded as "perfectly clear". I am not saying that the transparent symbolism is the correct one, but only that for Blake it held some particular meaning that may be lost to us today, but does not on that account cease to exist. In an article on the symbolism of bridges, Paul Friedman (1952) has shown to what deep *personal* uses a universal symbol can be put. Symbol-interpretation is at best a hazardous undertaking, and at worst a mockery of scientific investigation.

[60] I drew attention in two previous books (Masson and Patwardhan, 1969, 1970) on Sanskrit esthetics, to Ānandavardhana's opinions on the dominant esthetic experience of the *Rāmāyaṇa*. It is not an imaginative experience of the separation of lovers that Ānanda feels the *Rāmāyaṇa* is most deeply concerned with (*vipralambhaśṛṅgāra*), but with something more obdurate: *karuṇarasa*, the feeling that overcomes us when we realize that a loss is permanent. The reconciliation suggested by the *Rāmāyana* in these early books is an internal one, not totally dissimilar from what Freud meant, I think, when he said that the goal of psychoanalysis is to turn unbearable suffering into common unhappiness.

rāmāyaṇe hi karuṇo rasaḥ svayam ādikavināsūtritaḥ 'śokaḥ ślokatvam āgataḥ' ity evaṃvādinā. nirvyūḍhas ca sa eva sītātyantaviyogaparyantam eva svaprabandham uparacayatā

(*Dhvanyāloka*, pp. 529-30).

VI: NOTES ON KUBJĀ THE HUNCHBACK AND KṚṢṆA, WITH SOME OBSERVATIONS ON PERVERSIONS

In this paper I would like to examine the psychological dimensions of a strange episode in the life of Kṛṣṇa, his meeting with the hunchback Kubjā on the road to Mathurā. The story, as recounted in the earliest text to describe the childhood of Kṛṣṇa, the *Harivaṃśa* (cf. Masson, 1974), has Akrūra, the messenger of Kaṃsa, take Kṛṣṇa and his brother Saṃkarṣaṇa to his house in Mathurā. Kṛṣṇa wants to see the house of his father, Vasudeva. Akrūra tries to dissuade him, but Kṛṣṇa insists for he wants to see the king's highway and the city of Mathurā. The two go, and on the way they meet a washer-man who is so impolite that Kṛṣṇa splits his head open. Next they meet a sweet-speaking flowerseller, Guṇaka, who offers them garlands of flowers. Kṛṣṇa blesses him, but the man thinks Kṛṣṇa to be a demon and is unable to speak. The next encounter is with Kubjā, and I now give my literal translation of this episode from the *Mathurāpraveśa*, as found in the critical edition of the *Harivaṃśa*.[1]

(22) The two sons of Vasudeva as they were going on the King's Highway saw Kubjā [or 'a hunchback'] who was carrying a tray full of unguents.

(23) Kṛṣṇa said to her: "Kubjā, to whom do these unguents that you are carrying belong, O Lotus-eyed-one? Tell me quickly."

(24) She who walked as crooked as the lightning, answered him who was as dark [?] (*gambhīra*) as a cloud and whose eyes were [also] like those of a lotus, while she stood staring at him.

(25) "I am going to the bathing house of the King. So take his unguents. I am standing. Come, welcome, you are the beloved of my heart.[2]

(26) "Where, O gentle one, could you come from, that you do not know me, the beloved (*dayitā*) of the king, whom he has appointed to do his massage."[3]

(27) As she was laughing [smiling?], Kṛṣṇa said to Kubjā who was standing there: "Give us some unguent of the colour of our limbs.

(28) "For we are guests of state, wrestlers, O lovely-faced one, come to

see the heavenly bow, and the festival, and this great and prosperous kingdom."

(29) She then answered Kṛṣṇa by saying: "You are beloved in my eyes, so take this costly unguent that is fit for a king."

(30) So the two of them, their limbs wet and smeared with the unguent, shone beautifully, like two bulls going to the bathing stations of the Yamunā, their bodies shining with mud.

(31) Then Kṛṣṇa, who knew the art of flirtation (*līlāvidhānavit*), with two of his fingers, slowly lifted Kubjā.

(32) She whose smile was so beautiful and who had been sunken-chested, now became tall. She laughed aloud, her breasts prominent, like a creeper with a straight stalk.

(33) Obviously infatuated, she spoke to Kṛṣṇa out of her love: "Where are you going? I will block your path, my love. Stay, take me."

(34) The brothers laughed, clapped their hands and looked at one another, making fun of the hunchback.[4]

(35) But Kṛṣṇa, with a smile, dismissed the impassioned hunchback. Then when they were freed from the hunchback, they entered the King's palace.[5]

This, then, is the earliest version of the story of Kubjā. Already in this version, which we can date to perhaps the second century A.D., there are puzzling aspects to the story. Two elements are stressed in it, the cure of Kubjā's deformity and the sexual attraction that both feel for each other. Both are mysterious, and one of them has led the later tradition to expand the legend in interesting ways.

The second version of the story is that of the *Viṣṇupurāṇa*, which is difficult to date, but in my opinion is later than the *Harivaṃśa*. I would guess that it belongs to around the fifth century A.D. I give here a literal translation from Book 5, Chapter 20 of that text:[6]

(1) Then on the main highway Kṛṣṇa saw a hunchback coming. She was in the full bloom of youth and carrying a jar of paste.

(2) Kṛṣṇa said to her flirtatiously (*lalitam*): "Whose paste are you carrying? Tell me the truth, O you whose eyes are like a lotus."

(3) When she had been spoken to [by Kṛṣna, who seemed] in love, as it were, the hunchback [fell] in love and replied to Kṛṣṇa, flirtatiously, revished by his sight:

(4) "My beloved, how is it that you do not know me, well-known as Naikavakrā ['much-deformed'], employed by Kaṃsa to concern myself with pastes [for his use]?

(5) "For paste that has been ground by anybody else is not to his liking, and so I am the recipient of his wealth and favor."

(6) Kṛṣṇa replied: "O beautiful-faced one, give us beautiful paste that smells nice and is fit for a king and that will be the color of our skin [i.e., yellow and blue]."

(7) When she heard this, the hunchback said politely, "Take it." And she gave paste appropriate to their limbs.

(8) Then those two bulls among men with their bodies smeared with *bhakticcheda* marks[7] shone like two black and while clouds streaked through with a rainbow.

(9) Then Kṛṣṇa, who knew about flirtatious speech (*ullāpana-vidhānavit*),[8] put two fingers under her chin and, lifting her up, he pulled her.

(10) He pulled with his two feet and straightened her. And when she was straightened, she became the most beautiful of young women.

(11) She grabbed Kṛṣṇa by his clothes, and said to him in a flirtatious, playful way, her voice heavy with the burden of the embryo of love (*premagarbhabharālasam*): "Come to my house."

(12) When she had spoken to him like this, Kṛṣṇa looked at the face of his brother, laughed and told that hunchback, the faultless Naikavakrā:

(13) "I will come to your house." This is how Kṛṣṇa made fun of her. Then he dismissed her, and looking at his brother's face, laughed aloud.

Once again, we find the same elements as in the other version, only here the curious embarrassment that Kṛṣṇa feels about her direct invitation is even more prominent. Note the ambiguities of the language here: *prahasan* means both to laugh and to make fun of, and when Kṛṣṇa "laughed aloud" (*jahāsa uccaiḥ*), we are not certain whether it is in pleasure, in anticipation, or in mockery of her. Once again, it is puzzling why he would make fun of the person he has just cured. And what exactly is implied in the verb *prahasanti*, even when it does mean 'to make fun of'?

Something of the attitude of the later tradition with regard to these issues can be gleaned from a reading of the two later texts that concern themselves with the legend, namely the *Bhāgavatapurāṇa* and the later, and strange, *Brahmavaivartapurāṇa*. The elegant exchange of the *Bhāgavata* (10.42) retains the same themes as the earlier texts. In the first verse, Kṛṣṇa, called *rasapradaḥ*, is *prahasan*, and he promises the young Kubjā that he sees something good for her shortly (*śreyas tatas te na cirād bhaviṣyati*) if she will give them some unguent. The Śairandhrī (which is what the *Bhāgavata* calls her, a 'female servant') answers that she is a slave called Trivakrā ['crooked-in-three-places']. She calls Kṛṣṇa "handsome one" (*sundara*), and hands over the unguents in a most flirtatious manner. Kṛṣṇa, pleased at this, decides to make her straight, she whose face is already beautiful (*rucirānanam*). At his touch she becomes a most beautiful woman, large of breast and hip. She falls in love with him (*jātahṛcchayā*), pulls him by his shirt, and says:

> *ehi vīra gṛhaṃ yāmo na tvāṃ tyaktum ihotsahe*
> *tvayonmathitacittāyāḥ prasīda puruṣarṣabha*
> Come, virile one, let us go to my house. I cannot leave you. O Bull among men, have pity on this woman that you have infatuated.

Kṛṣṇa looks at the face of his brother and again making fun of her, says (*prahasaṃs tām uvāca ha*):

> *eṣyāmi te gṛhaṃ subhrūḥ puṃsām adhivikarṣaṇam*
> *sādhitārtho 'gṛhāṇāṃ naḥ pānthānāṃ tvaṃ parāyaṇam*
> I will come to your house, beautiful one, when I have done what I have to do, temptress of men. You are the highest refuge for travellers like us who have no home.

The suggestion here is certainly that Kubjā is a prostitute, and this would accord well with the rather mocking tone that Kṛṣṇa takes towards her. But most remarkable about the *Bhāgavata* account are the later events. In the earlier two versions of the Kubjā story, there is no further mention of her in the text. However, in the *Bhāgavata*, she appears again. After Kaṃsa's death, Kṛṣṇa takes up her invitation and visits her at night. At 10.48.6, we read:

> *āhūya kāntāṃ navasaṃgamahriyā viśaṅkitāṃ kaṅkaṇabhūṣite kare*
> *pragṛhya śayyām adhiveśya rāmayā reme 'nulepārpaṇapuṇyaleśayā*
> Calling his beloved who was shy over a new love-making, frightened even, taking her by her hand with its bangles, he took her over to the bed, and then made love to that lovely woman who had acquired some merit through having given him the unguents.

Nothing could be more explicit. Kubjā does not want Kṛṣṇa to leave, and tells him:

> *āhoṣyatām iha preṣṭa dināni katicin mayā*
> *ramasva notsahe tyaktuṃ saṅgaṃ te 'mburuhekṣaṇa*

> She said: "Most beloved, stay here some days with me. Make love to me. I do not want to leave your presence, lotus-eyed one."

Because of this explicit lovemaking, the later Vaiṣṇava tradition has a special place for Kubjā. The most explicit passage about her love for Kṛṣṇa is found in the *Bhaktisandarbha* of Jīvagosvāmin. I give the Sanskrit passage as quoted by S. K. De in his *The Early History of the Vaiṣṇava Faith and Movement in Bengal* (p. 379):

> *sairandhryās tu bhāvo riraṃsāprāyatvena śrīgopīnām iva kevala-tatatātparyābhāvāt tadapekṣayaiva nindyate, na tu svarūpataḥ,*

which I translate as:

> The feeling of the hunchback Kubjā however for Kṛṣṇa is primarily that of wanting to make love [for herself] and, unlike that of the Gopīs, is not totally directed towards Kṛṣṇa; so in comparison to their love for Kṛṣṇa it is inferior, but not completely [devoid of value].

What is recognized in this passage, even though it is theologized, is that Kubjā was sexually attracted to Kṛṣṇa and wanted, reasonably, sexual pleasure for *herself*, something that did not appeal to the Doctors of the Vaiṣṇava church.

The final text to deal with the Kubjā episode is, in many ways, the most interesting. The *Brahmavaivartapurāṇa* is a late text, and one that is replete with oddities and unorthodox sentiments. It is to the *Purāṇas* what the *Yogavāsiṣṭhamahārāmāyaṇa* is to the Vedānta: a work that is vigorous, eccentric, personal, but which cannot, by the sheer vitality of its language and content, be ignored. The meeting with Kubjā takes place in the second volume of the Ānandāśrama edition of 1935 (Adhyāya 72, p. 722). In Verse 15, we are told that Kṛṣṇa meets Kubjā, and that she is old and utterly decrepit: *vṛddhām atijarāturām*. In this version Kṛṣṇa does not even have to touch her:

> *śrīkṛṣṇadṛṣṭimātreṇa śrīyuktā sā babhūva ha*
> She became beautiful merely by the sight of Kṛṣṇa.

She becomes, the text tells us (Verse 22), as beautiful as a twelve-year-old girl (*yathā dvādaśavarṣīyā kanyā dhanyā manoharā*). She becomes enamored of Kṛṣṇa, who provides her with a marvellous palace to live in. That night he goes to visit her, and while all her servants are sleeping, he makes a remarkable statement (Verse 56):

tyaja nidrāṃ mahābhāge śṛṅgāraṃ dehi sundari
purā śūrpaṇakhā tvaṃ ca bhaginī rāvaṇasya ca
Stop sleeping, my love, and make love to me, my beautiful woman. In days gone by you were Śūrpaṇakhā, the sister of Rāvaṇa.

(57) *rāmajanmani mad dhetos tvayā kānte tapaḥ kṛtam*
tapaḥprabhāvān māṃ kāntaṃ bhaja śrīkṛṣṇajanmani
In my birth as Rāma you performed, lovely one, great asceticism for my sake. By the power of that asceticism, enjoy me, as your beloved, in my birth as Kṛṣṇa.

(58) *adhunā sukhasaṃbhogaṃ kṛtvā gaccha mamālayam*
sudurlabhaṃ ca golokaṃ jarāmṛtyuharaṃ param
Now having enjoyed the pleasure of sexual love, go to my abode, the world of cows that is so difficult to obtain and which banishes both old age and death.

(59) *ity uktvā śrīnivāsaś ca kṛtvā tām eva vakṣasi*
nagnāṃ cakāra śṛṅgāraṃ cumbanaṃ cāpi kāmukīm
Having said this Kṛṣṇa took her to his chest, and undressed her till she was naked, and kissed her and made love to her.

At the end of a long lovemaking, Kṛṣṇa finally reaches a climax and spills his seed (*niśāvasānasamaye vīryādhānaṃ cakāra saḥ*) and she, overcome with the pleasure of her own climax, faints. He then accompanies her to his heaven (i.e., she dies) where she becomes a Gopī surrounded by other Gopīs.

The association that the author of the *Brahmavaivarta* made to Śūrpaṇakhā is a telling one, for there too (as the story is told in the *Rāmāyaṇa*), a woman offers herself to Rāma, and he, in the company of his brother, turns her down in a rather crude fashion, making fun of her. In the *Rāmāyaṇa*, III.17.18, Rāma addresses Śūrpaṇakhā as *manojñāṅgī*, 'she of the beautiful body', and it is therefore not surprising that she would take these words as a declaration of sexual interest. It is interesting that at III.17.28 the same verb *prahasya* is used to denote Rāma's making fun of the woman. When the joke goes sour, Rāma makes the following comment to Lakṣmaṇa: *krūrair anāryaiḥ saumitre parihāsaḥ kathaṃ cana na kāryaḥ*. . ."One must never joke, Lakṣmaṇa, with cruel, low-class people." As we know, it is this episode which fuels the whole of the *Rāmāyaṇa*, for Rāma does not stop at making fun of her, but has his brother deform her (again the theme of deformity). It is in this condition that she returns to her brother, who then begins his long and justified vendetta against Rāma. It is no wonder that the echoes of this bizarre and grotesque episode (in which, clearly, a man is tempted toward a sexual transgression and then retaliates with sadism as a means of denying his own desire) should resound in the mind of the author of the *Brahmavaivarta*, for we find many of the same themes in the Kubjā episode. Having given what are, to my knowledge, the major texts that deal with the Kubjā episode, we are now in a position to consider some of these themes and to examine their psychological significance.

An explanation that looks to early experience, especially early childhood experience, as the underlying motivation provides some illumination. Of course, in the case of a legend, we cannot have access to genuine information about the early life of a real patient, and so 'early' here must refer to some earlier incident in some way psychologically connected to the present event. In this case, I think the association of the *Brahmavaivartapurāṇa* to the 'earlier' legend of Śūrpaṇakhā provides us with the clue: it is possible to believe that Kṛṣṇa is attempting to undo the guilt he must have felt for the disfiguring of this sexually-aroused woman. (Of course, I am speaking here with reference to the view of the redactors of this myth, for whom Kṛṣṇa represents a later reincarnation of Rāma – so the psychological comments relate to the unconscious needs of these redactors, and to readers of the legend who may react with similar feelings.) He undoes it in two ways: first, he literally repairs the disfigurement by curing the hunchback of her deformity, and then he acts out his earlier sexual desire by acceding to the desires of Kubjā. By making love to her he both admits his earlier repressed desire and also continues his act of reparation by giving her what she most wants. In the *Brahmavaivartapurāna* version, this is followed by the death of the woman (preceded by the little death of her fainting during her orgasm) as a recognition that such reparative needs cannot bear too much reality. She is transported to a land of cows, where milk and honey flow, and she is protected from old age and death, i.e., from any further disfigurement. Such a heaven is both a denial of adult sexuality (she is transformed into a twelve-year-old virgin in the *Brahmavaivartapurāṇa* version) and an overwhelming recognition of pregenital sexual needs (here symbolized by a life of being served – Kubjā is looked after, in Goloka, by innumerable female servants).

When we turn to the possible dynamic interpretations of this story, we come to more specific and more interesting psychological hypotheses.[9] We can best approach this aspect by looking more closely at the nature of sexual perversions,[10] and asking just what it is that drives certain men to feel sexually attracted to women with physical defects, in this case a hunchback. Why would a deformity, which on the surface would seem to be the opposite of sexual attractiveness, actually impassion some men?

For the answer, we can look to an important article by Fenichel (1930), 'The Psychology of Transvestitism'. In that paper he comments about a male patient: "His transvestite behavior was designed to counter his castration anxiety. We have evidence of this in a recollection that, when on one occasion he caught sight of a crippled boy, he felt an impulse to change clothes with him. The implication was a denial that the boy really was a cripple." Later in that article, Fenichel 'translates' the content of the perversion of a male wearing female clothing, as follows: "Phallic girls do exist; I myself am one." The first part of Fenichel's formula can be applied to the Kubjā incident as follows: Kṛṣṇa wished to deny his own castration anxiety. When he caught sight of a damaged person, Kubjā, he felt an impulse to cause her hump to disappear, i.e., to erase the exposure of her castration. However, this interpretation does not take into account the obviously phallic dimensions of the hump and also the subsequent sexual attraction to the woman. To understand this, we must penetrate even further into the psychology of perversions. Bak, in his article, "The Phallic Woman: The Ubiquitous Fantasy in Perversions", writes: "The need for acting out. . .derives its strength from the orgastic affirmation of the truth of the primal fantasy, on the one hand, and by the participation of the outside world, on the other. By actually engaging dramatis personae, the fantasy becomes indisputable reality."[11] We can imagine a situation in which a man masturbates to the thought of a woman with a hunchback (a displacement from a more deeply repressed thought that the woman has a penis, i.e., that he need not fear castration). But at some point, he requires the participation of somebody real in the outside world. Consequently, the dynamics in terms of artistic creation would be this: the story or legend of Kubjā was necessary because it answered some strong fusion of libidinal and aggressive drives. Kubjā had to be created in order to discharge some of the energy, but more than that, her story had to be seen not as a fantasy, but as an actual event. Why? Here we can have recourse to an important idea first suggested by Edward Glover in his 1923 article on the relation of perversion-formation to the development of reality. Glover sees the perversion as the negative of psychoses; it helps to patch over flaws in the development of a sense of reality. One can imagine the urgent necessity for this at puberty which, according to Bak,[12] is the age of the onset of most perversions. Kṛṣṇa, at the end of his adolescence, is beset with problems of sexual identity stemming from his earlier development. The danger is that these anxieties will overwhelm him to the point where he will be unable to recognize or acknowledge a difference in the sexes. By overlibidinizing the perversions (in this case, attraction to a hump), not only is the latent aggression in the perversion denied ('I do not hate and want to destroy, I love and want to caress'), but the danger of entering a psychotic universe is contained within the perversion itself. This original position of Glover is widely accepted by analysts who treat perversions. Gillespie puts it succinctly: "Splits in the ego and in the object make possible attitudes to reality confined to the sexual area, which, if more widespread, would lead to a psychosis."[13] By a split in the object, Gillespie is referring to a need to protect one's love object from imagined sadistic harm. An example he provides is that of a perversion centering around a mackintosh, in which the fetish protects the original object, the mother, from destruction by dangerous urine. (Such pregenital destructive fantasies are the rule in perversions.) The shadow of sadism is present in our stories, as we see by the constant reference to the mocking of Kubjā. It is denied in the final outcome, at least in the two later versions of the story (which read like a psychological afterthought or reaction to the more primitive, earlier stories). We might note that, statistically, sadistic perversions have a relatively low frequency, something which points to the compromise-formation involved in the perversions and supports Glover's view that they are, by and large, defensive maneuvers. We must also take into account what Hanns Sachs showed in an influential article in 1923, namely that overt perversions, or perverse fantasies, represent only the conscious part of a much larger unconscious system. This is relevant to our understanding of the Kubjā incident, which is not a clinical, overt perversion in any direct sense, but does contain perverse elements. Perversion forms a part of everybody's sexual life, whether overtly or in fantasy, to whatever degree of attenuation. During a panel discussion on perversion at the 1954 meeting of the American Psychoanalytic Association, Georges Devereux made the observation that: ". . .A sexual relationship in which the behavior is normal but the object relationship defective is essentially perverted. If this definition is taken to encompass the vast majority of human sexual relations and to place them in the category of perverted relations, then so be it. It may be regrettable, but only an infinitesimal fraction of mankind is capable of behaving and experiencing even occasionally in a mature manner befitting genital characters."[14] Kṛṣṇa's attraction to a hunchback, then, is a defect in loving of universal application. By examining some of the possible motives for such a love, we can better understand normal sexuality. In listing possible sources for this sexual attraction, I am drawing attention to the important concept of overdetermination (Waelder, 1930), namely that many varying mechanisms and needs contribute to a symptom or a perversion. There is, first of all, the nucleus of castration anxiety, to which we have already referred. We may add here that the hump must be a source of mystery to all who perceive it. The Indians, not only then but even now, deal with the anxiety it provokes by a kind of denial: a defect in the body is merely funny. But of course for the child and the child in the adult, there is nothing funny about parts of the body that can be added or subtracted. Ernst Kris once suggested that castration anxiety may owe its prominent place in the mental life of man to the peculiar visual aspect of the genitals, which seem to hang so precariously, and to be subject to a whimsical erasure, or a sudden pulling off by the hand. Judging from the literature on masturbation in Western cultures,[15] I would not be surprised to learn that Indian mothers might warn that one consequence of masturbation is the formation of a hump. Clearly, even in our earliest versions, the hump is associated in the Kṛṣṇa legend with unbridled sexuality. Kubjā is a promiscuous, sexually inflammable woman. In the *Bhāgavata* version, as we saw, she is a prostitute. Men often imagine that certain women, not attractive in the usual sense, are a greater source of sexual wisdom: they have greater needs, hence to have intercourse with them would be to learn wonderful new pleasures denied to ordinary people. Indeed, this sexualization of abnormality is very common: the witch, the giant, the hunchback, the cripple, the demon, are all creatures of strange and unspeakable sexual habits; and they are particularly attracted to us, the fantasy goes.[16] The other aspect of this fantasy is that of piety, particularly relevant to Kṛṣṇa's later sleeping with Kubjā: the alleged kindness and nobility are evident in the sacrifice. Many men cloak their own awakened sadism upon seeing a cripple and feeling sexually attracted with a sense of their own nobility: 'How kind of me to sleep with somebody so deformed that nobody else would want her.' The revulsion and hatred just beneath the surface is quickly revealed after orgasm, when the man may feel repulsed by what has taken place. Many men feel this way after a visit to a prostitute. But it is rare that they feel revulsion for themselves: only too often they blame the 'fallen' woman for providing an outlet for their lust, and thus the sadism remains hidden. The sexual contact of the penis with the damaged body part of the woman is often a reassurance: 'Look, I am whole, I am well, nothing has happened to me. It is her, she is the one to have been mutilated.' Moreover, one is relieved that one's sexuality has not been the source of the mutilation: 'I did not mutilate her, she was already that way. She is already damaged, I have done nothing.' At a level closer to consciousness one can see the following: 'Although damaged (castrated), she is not wholly sexually impotent, but can enjoy sexual intercourse. I too could suffer such damage and yet retain my sexuality.'

These are some of the mechanisms operative in a sexual attraction to a defective body. Because the episode with Kubjā lends itself to such a variety of interpretations, she is a kind of dream-figure, a condensation of many different figures from the life of the dreamer. Kubjā is an incestuous mother-figure (she belongs to Kaṃsa and is his beloved) and a sister-figure (Śūrpaṇakhā), onto whom have been projected imagined deformities. This is sexual license tempered with spiritual devotion (a major theme in the Kṛṣṇa legend). But Sachs has warned us that the perversions may serve to hide material related to the oedipal conflict. We have yet to deal with what is, after all, the most startling feature of Kṛṣṇa's encounter with Kubjā, namely the cure of her deformity. If we omit from consideration the obvious narcissistic elements in this miracle ('I am omnipotent and can undo my greatest fears, death, disease and castration'), or even the phalliclibidinal ('My penis is a healing instrument; contact with it can cure the sick'), we can see a larger design within the whole legend. Kṛṣṇa comes to Mathurā just out of boyhood; he is an adolescent, on the threshold of becoming a man. His task, his main life-goal, lies just ahead of him: to destroy Kaṃsa (clearly a thinly-disguised father-figure, the maternal uncle) and leave the life of pretense he has been leading behind him. Before the actual encounter with Kaṃsa, as a kind of practice if you like, Kṛṣṇa meets with an oddly-beloved object of Kaṃsa, Kubjā. He removes from her the special defect that must have given her some value in Kaṃsa's eyes (we can ask why it is that kings have always surrounded themselves with damaged people of one kind or another), that is, he loosens her ties to the father and then takes possession himself. Clearly this is not a myth of consummated incest; on the contrary, I am suggesting it is a legend of oedipal resolution. Kṛṣṇa disencumbers himself of his childish (and pregenital) longings and has his first genital encounter with a woman that he has won by himself. The life of the forest is left behind; Kṛṣṇa emerges from these encounters a young man, independent and ready to assume a married life, free from the trappings of deceit and magic and regression that marked his life as a cowherder. Exit the child god, enter the free man, or so at least might the legend have been read in the unconscious of those ready for such *rites de passage* themselves.

This book began with an attempt to explain the origins of mystical feelings. It went on to consider derivatives of such an experience in the creation of certain mythological figures and situations. It seems appropriate to end the book with a chapter that returns to mysticism via its concrete expression in everyday beliefs about the power of mystical attainments. The psychology of the belief in miracles has rarely been attempted without resorting to ridicule or collapsing argument into invective (needless to say that apologies for miracles display an even greater retreat from reasoned argument, as the Castañeda cult demonstrates). In looking more closely at particular miracles or claims to miracles, I hope to illuminate some features of the miraculous in general. The thesis I propound is a novel one for which I make the sanguine claim of general and universal validity.

NOTES

[1] (22) *vasudevasutau tau tu rājamārgagatāv ubhau*
kubjāṃ dadṛśatur bhūyaḥ sānulepanabhājanām
(23) *tām āha kṛṣṇah kubjeti kasyedam anulepanam*
nayasy ambujapatrākṣi kṣipram ākhyātum arhasi
(24) *sā sthitāvekṣiṇī bhūtvā pratyuvācāmbujekṣaṇam*
kṛṣṇaṃ jaladagambhīraṃ vidyutkuṭilagāminī
(25) *rājñah snānagṛhaṃ yāmi tadgṛhānānulepanam*
sthitāsmy āgaccha bhadraṃ te hṛdayasyāsi me priyaḥ
(26) *kutaś cāgamyate saumya yan māṃ tvaṃ nāvabudhyase*
mahārājasya dayitāṃ niyuktām anulepane
(27) *tām uvāca hasantīṃ tu kṛṣṇaḥ kubjām avasthitām*
āvayor gātrasadṛśaṃ dīyatām anulepanam
(28) *vayaṃ hi deśātithayo mallāḥ prāptā varānane*
draṣṭuṃ dhanur mahaṃ divyaṃ rāṣṭraṃ caiva maharddhimat
(29) *pratyuvācātha sā kṛṣṇaṃ priyo 'si mama darśane*
rājārham idam agryaṃ ca tad gṛhāṇulepanam
(30) *tāv ubhāv anuliptāṅgāv ārdragātrau virejatuḥ*
tīrthagau paṅkadigdhāṅgau yamunāyāṃ yathā vṛṣau
(31) *tāṃ tu kubjāṃ tataḥ kṛṣṇo dvyaṅgulenāgrapāṇinā*
śanaiḥ saṃtolayāmāsa kṛṣṇo līlāvidhānavit
(32) *sā tu magnastanayugā svayatāṅgi śucismitā*
jahāsoccaiḥ stanataṭā ṛjuyaṣṭir latā yathā
(33) *praṇayāc cāpi kṛṣṇam sā babhāṣe mattakāśini*
kva yāsyasi mayā ruddhaḥ kānta tiṣṭha gṛhāṇa mām
(34) *tau jātahāsāv anyonyaṃ satalākṣepam avyayau*
vīkṣamāṇau prahasitau kubjāyāḥ śrutavistarau
(35) *kṛṣṇas tu kubjāṃ kāmārtīṃ sasmitaṃ visasarja ha*
tatas tau kubjayā muktau praviṣṭau rājasaṃsadam

(From the critical edition of the *Harivaṃśa*, P.L. Vaidya (ed.), Vol. I, Chap. 71, p. 461; in the vulgate (Citraśālā) edition, *Viṣṇuparvan*, Chap. 27, p. 217).

[2] For *sthitā*, 9 mss. read *sasmitā*, 'she, smiling'. Note that the position of this verse is curious, and that Nl, the oldest manuscript Vaidya used, omits it.

[3] *Dayitā* is curious. Does Kubjā simply mean that the king is kind enough to employ her? What it seems to mean is that she is one of the king's lovers, and well-known in this capacity to the citizens of Mathurā.

[4] The verse is strange; since Kṛṣṇa has just cured the woman, one would not expect him to make fun of her. But I don't know how else to interpret *jātahāsau* and *prahasitau kubjāyāḥ*. Note that 13 mss. read *jātaharsāv*, i.e., 'delighted', which makes better sense. One Telegu ms. reads *jātarāgāv*, i.e., they fell in love with her. I cannot make sense of *śrutavistarau*, and hence have left it out of the translation. Does it mean something like: 'wide in their knowledge'? Or does it mean that they had heard the details (i.e., they had heard enough, as it were)? Tl reads *śrutịvistarau*: 'broad in their knowledge of the *Śruti*'.

[5] *Visasarja* means 'dismissed', even though this seems somewhat abrupt. Several mss. add the following half-verse at this point:

> *yatheṣṭaṃ gamyatāṃ bhadre nāhaṃ tadvidho naraḥ*
> Go as you like my dear, I am not that kind of man.

[6] (1) *rājamārge tataḥ kṛṣṇas sānulepanabhājanām*
dadarśa kubjām āyāntīṃ navayauvanagocarām
(2) *tām āha lalitaṃ kṛṣṇaḥ kasyedam anulepanam*
bhavatyā nīyate satyaṃ vadendīvaralocane
(3) *sakāmeneva sā proktā sānurāgā hariṃ prati*
prāha sā lalitaṃ kubjā taddarśanabalātkṛtā
(4) *kānta kasmān na jānāsi kaṃsena viniyojitām*
naikavakreti vikhyātām anulepanakarmaṇi
(5) *nānyapiṣṭaṃ hi kaṃsasya prītaye hy anulepanam*
bhavāmy aham atīvāsya prasādhanabhājanam
(6) *sugandham etad rājārhaṃ ruciraṃ rucirānane*
āvayor gātrasadṛśaṃ dīyatām anulepanam
(7) *śrutvaitad āha sā kubjā gṛhyatām iti sādaram*
anulepanaṃ ca pradadau gātrayogyam athobhayoḥ
(8) *bhakticchedānuliptāṅgau tatas tau puruṣarṣabhau*
sendracāpau vyarājetāṃ sītākṛṣṇāv ivāmbudau
(9) *tatas tāṃ cibuke śaurir ullāpanavidhānavit*
utpāṭya tolayāmāsa dvyaṅgulenāgrapāṇinā
(10) *cakarṣa padbhyāṃ ca tadā ṛjutvaṃ keśavo 'nayat*
tatas sā ṛjutām prāptā yoṣitām abhavad varā
(11) *vilāsalalitaṃ prāha premagarbhabharālasam*
vastre pragṛhya govindaṃ mama gehaṃ vrajeti vai
(12) *evam uktas tayā śaurī rāmasyālokya cānanam*
prahasya kubjāṃ tām āha naikavakrām aninditām
(13) *āyāsye bhavatīgeham iti tāṃ prahasan hariḥ*
visasarja jahāsoccai rāmasyālokya cānanam

(from the *Viṣṇupurāṇa*, Volume 20 [Gita Press edition, p. 432]).

[7] See H. H. Wilson's translation (1840, Vol. 5, p. 22) for an explanation of this term.

[8] Wilson translates this as "skilled in the curative art". He may be interpreting accord-ding to a commentator, but I have not been able to obtain the commentary that he used for his translation.

[9] The role of parental pathology in the etiology of perversions seems, to me, decisive. The major work is a brilliant and curious book by Robert Fliess (1973). I have touched on this issue in my paper on perversions in the *Israel Annals of Psychiatry* (Masson, 1976b) and in an unpublished article, 'The Navel of Neurosis: Trauma, Memory and Denial', as well as in an article, with T. C. Masson, 'Buried Memories on the Acropolis – Freud's Relation to Mysticism and Antisemitism', in the Jerusalem Congress issue of the *International Journal of Psycho-Analysis*. For a slightly different view, see the works of R. J. Stoller (1966, 1968, 1970, 1975) and R. R. Greenson (1966, 1968). Besides the works mentioned in this article, the following could be consulted on themes closely related to perversions: Fliess (1953a, 1956, 1961), Gillespie (1956, 1964, 1952a and 1952b), Moore (1964) and Socarides (1974).

The dynamics of sexual perversions are seen especially clearly in fetishism. I recommend the work of Greenacre (1955a, 1960, 1969) and McDougall (1972); see also Buxbaum (1960), Gillespie (1964), Bak (1953), Dickes (1963, 1965) and Chasseguet-Smirgel (1978). The 'primal scene', that is, direct observation of parental coitus, is generally blamed for the origin of most neuroses. This is, in my opinion, an antipsychological point of view. See Esman, 1973, for a good review and reconsideration.

Still the most important source of our knowledge of the seduction hypothesis is the letters to Fliess (Freud, 1954), *The Origins of Psychoanalysis*. Cf. Schur's important book (1972); also Chertok and de Saussure (1973) and McGuire (1974). Until a complete edition of these letters is published, however, the full story of Freud's withdrawal of this hypothesis will not be known. I am happy to be able to report that in cooperation with several scholars, I am now editing the unexpurgated edition of the Freud/Fliess letters. The position taken by Greenacre in her paper on a reevaluation of the process of working-through (1956) comes closest to my own. See also Devereux (1953c) on why Oedipus killed Laius; the fine case history reported in Emch (1944); and Laplanche and Pontalis (1968) on 'Fantasy and the Origins of Sexuality'. 'Real', as opposed to 'fantasied', seduction eventually leads to questions of what is constitutional and what is derived from experience. My own belief is that the evidence of "innate predispositions", as Freud called them, is not strong. However, for a good critique of this position, see Benjamin (1961), and cf. Gifford (1966). A related question involves the issue of traumatic dreams. See in particular A. Garma (1946), M. Stein (1965) and Eissler (1966).

[10] Cf. Masson (1976b), Ostow (1974), Arlow (1971), Stoller (1975), Gillespie (1956) and Greenacre (1968).

[11] Bak (1968, p. 35). Cf. the interesting article of McDougall (1972).

[12] Bak, op. cit., p. 28.

[13] Gillespie (1956, p. 144). Cf. S. M. Payne (1939).

[14] Arlow (1954, p. 337).

[15] Spitz (1952). Cf. Wermer and Leving (1967) and the important article by Huschka (1938).

[16] Witness the common Chinese story of the snake woman. See André Lévy (1971).

VII: YOGIC POWERS AND SYMPTOM FORMATION

Nun ist die Luft von
Solchem Spuk so voll
Dass niemand weiss
Wie er ihn meiden soll

When Freud first came across the mystic writing pad, which is also called a magic slate, he found it a good example of the mental apparatus: it illustrates the fact that impressions made on us do not disappear but are indelibly inscribed into the wax, though they have disappeared from the surface. The process of psychoanalysis as a clinical discipline is the recovery of these seemingly-lost messages. It follows from this that something as seemingly irrational as a symptom is only apparently so, and in fact owes its origin to an often exceedingly complex series of unconscious memories which are active far below awareness. Such memories are usually quite old. It is an interesting endeavor to apply this thesis to other apparently meaningless facts, in order to see if by means of such analysis anything of their former life can be recovered. For example, Yogic powers may be regarded as a palimpsest, or a set of symptomatic actions, concealing in their structure a hidden origin in early life. A symptom contains evidence of two opposing forces: there is the pressure from the past in the form of the repressed content of the id which demands satisfaction, and there is what is called a 'counter-cathexis' from the ego (or from the real world) opposing the satisfaction of the unconscious wish. The interaction of these two forces results in the compromise formation, the symptom, which then serves two masters. When the symptom is debilitating, as most symptoms are (consider, for a moment, the disadvantages of believing you can fly when you cannot), a third agency is automatically satisfied, namely the superego, which is appeased by the suffering the subject has to bear as a consequence of his symptom, suffering of which he may not be at all aware.[2]

The powers that a Siddha acquires are enumerated in the third chapter of the *Yogasūtras*, in the chapter called 'Vibhūtipāda'.[3] The first of these, and in many ways the most important and the most interesting, is that concerning memory, or the knowledge of earlier lives.[4] Bhoja says: *sarvam atītaṃ smarati*, "He remembers everything that is past", and finally: *krameṇa. . .pūrvajanmāntarānubhūtān api jātyādīn pratyakṣeṇa paśyati*, "Eventually he sees, directly before his eyes, his own birth and everything else that he experienced in his earlier lives." Immediately after this power comes the power to know another person's mind: *paracittajñānam*.[5] There are two interesting comments on this, one by Bhoja who says: *sarāgam asya cittaṃ vītarāgaṃ veti*, "He knows whether the mind of another person is lustful or freed from lust." The other is by Vyāsa, who writes: *raktaṃ pratyayaṃ jānāty amuṣmin ālambane raktam iti na jānāti*, which is obscure, but which I take to mean that the Yogin knows, in general, that the man whose mind he is able to read is aroused, but does not know the actual content of the sexual desire, i.e., he does not know the object toward which this lust is directed. We will see that this qualification is important. The next power to be presented is that of invisibility, *antardhānam*. As Bhoja succinctly puts it: *na kenacid asau dṛśyate*, "Nobody sees him." Concerning the next power, which has to do with knowing about the approach of death, Vyāsa writes: *viparītaṃ vā sarvam*, "Everything appears upside down", and Vācaspati specifies this to mean: "Even when there is no magic involved (*māhendrajāla*), villages and cities he takes to be heaven, and the real world of human beings to be a world of divine beings." At III.26 we are told that the Yogin knows all about that which is hidden and obscure, and Bhoja specifies that this refers to a knowledge of *rasātala*, the underworld, and the people who live on the other side of the mountain: *mervaparapārśvavarttino rasātalāder jñānam*. Similarly, *bhuvanajñānam* is the knowledge of outer space and the worlds concealed therein. Vyāsa is particularly eloquent and detailed in his description of these worlds and their inhabitants. In the world of Mahendra, for example, people have magic powers, live for a long period, are very good-looking and are especially concerned with sexual love (*kāmabhoginaḥ*). Most important, their bodies are not produced by parents![6] The men walk around surrounded by Apsarases, who are very beautiful and are not prudish.[7] At III.30 we are told of *kṣutpipāsānivṛttiḥ*, the cessation of hunger and thirst, and at III.36, of supernal organs, a *divyaṃ śrotram*, heavenly hearing, sight and smell.[8] The famous *parakāyapraveśa*, the ability to enter another person's body, is given at III.38. At III.43 we are told of *ākāśagamana*, the ability to fly through the air. And finally, at III.45 are enumerated the famous *aṇimādi*, the eight special powers. These are: the ability to become as small as an atom; to rise in the air like a piece of cotton wool; to become as large as a mountain; to be able to touch the moon with one's fingertips; to dive into the earth and swim to the surface as if in water; to make the elements appear and disappear upon command, and finally, in an epiphany of megalomania, the capacity to make all things follow one's will (*yatra kāmāvasayitvaṃ satyasaṅkalpatā yathā saṅkalpas tathā bhūtaprakṛtīnām avasthānam*). It is here that Vyāsa says: *na ca śakto 'pi padārthaviparyāsaṃ karoti. kasmāt? anyasya yatra kāmāvasayinaḥ pūr-*

vasiddhasya tathā bhūteṣu saṅkalpād iti. This sentence is somewhat obscure. According to the *Vivaraṇa* of Śaṅkara, *pūrvasiddha* refers to Īśvara. So this phrase would mean that, "Although he is quite capable of it, he does not turn things upside down. Why? Because an earlier great being has already imposed his will on the elements and he does not differ from him in his desire", i.e., he just happens to like things exactly the way God made them. One is reminded of Hotspur's reply when Owen Glendower (in *King Henry the Fourth, Part One*) tells him that he can "call spirits from the vasty deep." He answers, "Why, so can I, or so can any man; but will they come when you do call for them?" A modern commentary (Sastrin, 1931) adds to this: *pūrvayogivyavahārānusareṇaiva yogī vyavaharati anyathā tūlyabalavirodhena vyavahāralopasambhavād iti bhāvaḥ*: "A Yogin behaves like other earlier Yogins because otherwise *saṃsāra* would be in an impossible state, for his powers might conflict with those of another Yogin and both would be equal (i.e., neither could create the world)."

There has been no lack of modern authors to explain to us that these powers were not held in very high esteem in the classical texts. Eliade, in his book *Yoga: Immortality and Freedom*, says: "The uninitiated have long confused these 'powers' with the vocation of yoga."[9] He goes on to say that, "For Indian thought, all possession implies bondage to the thing possessed."[10] Similarly, in his introduction to the *Pāṭika Suttanta* of the *Dīghanikāya*, Rhys Davids writes: "In India. . .the prevailing belief was that such wonders (whether worked by humans, gods, or animals) were in accordance with laws. In a word, they were not miracles. . . . This distinction is of vital importance."[11] We have already seen that Vyāsa is careful to tell us that a man cannot know the actual content of a person's mind but only his emotional state.

The most clearly-worded statement against the *siddhis* occurs in the *Vinayapiṭaka*, in the *Cullavagga* V.8. The story reads, in Horner's translation:

> Now at that time a block of costly choice sandalwood had accrued to a [great] merchant of Rājagaha. . . .Then that [great] merchant of Rājagaha having had a bowl carved out of that block of sandalwood, having put a string round it, having hung it up on the top of a bamboo [pole], having tied it to a series of bamboo [poles], spoke thus: "Let whatever recluse or brahmin who is a perfected one as well as of psychic power get down this bowl and [to him] it is given". . . .Then the venerable Piṇḍola the Bhāradvāja, having risen above the ground, having taken hold of that bowl, circled three times round Rājagaha . . .

> Then the Lord heard the loud noise, the great noise, and having heard it, he addressed the venerable Ānanda, saying: "What on earth, Ānanda, is this loud noise, this great noise?" "Lord, the bowl of the great Rājagaha has been fetched down by the venerable Piṇḍola the Bhāradvāja".... Then the Lord on this occasion, in this connection, having had the Order of monks convened questioned the venerable Piṇḍola the Bhāradvāja, saying: "Is it true, as is said, Bhāradvāja, that the bowl of the great merchant of Rājagaha was fetched down by you?" "It is true, Lord." The Awakened One, the Lord rebuked him, saying: "It is not suiting, Bhāradvāja, it is not becoming, it is not fitting, it is not worthy of a recluse, it is not allowable, it is not to be done. How can you, Bhāradvāja, on account of a wretched wooden bowl exhibit a condition of further-men, a wonder of psychic power to householders? As, Bhāradvāja, a woman exhibits her loin-cloth, on account of a wretched stamped *māsaka*, even so by you, Bhāradvāja, was a condition of further-men, a wonder of psychic power exhibited to householders on account of a wretched wooden bowl."[12]

Note that the Buddha never denies that such powers exist, but only enjoins the monks not to display them. Similarly, the often-quoted passage from the *Yogasūtras* (whose exact meaning, like much of the *Yogasūtras*, is obscure): *te samādhāv upasargā vyutthāne siddhayaḥ*, which seems to imply that these powers are a hindrance in ecstatic states, but are useful in normal states (a strange reversal), is not the least equivocal about the *existence* of such powers. Indeed, one cannot help noticing that if Yoga, as Eliade claims, is so indifferent to these magic powers, how is it that a full third of the *Yogasūtras* is devoted to their detailed exposition? Moreover, many of these powers have played an influential role in Sanskrit literature, especially in the story literature of the Hindus, Jains and Buddhists. I have only to remind the reader of the famous commentary on the *Amaruśataka*, where the authorship of this poem is ascribed to Śaṅkara, who learned about sexual love through his ability to practice *parakāyapraveśa* when he entered the body of the dying king Amaru.

As far as I know, no Indian text has ever denied the existence of these powers, and in my personal experience in India working with traditional Pandits, I met many who were sceptical, but never one who flatly denied their existence.

Unlike Eliade then, let us not immediately close our eyes to the historical evidence and opt instead for some diffuse notion of moral values; nor let us, when forced to acknowledge historical reality, immediately spiritualize these powers and so deprive them of the influence they actually enjoyed in ancient India. This does not mean that we have to remain innocent chroniclers of historical fact, for I see no reason why we should not wish to understand such a pervasive, interesting and curious phenomenon as the belief in magic powers. The approach taken here will be a psychological one, and will try to answer the question of what needs these illusory beliefs satisfy.

There is a curious passage in the *Vyāsabhāṣya* on III.18, where Vyāsa says that Jaigiṣavya once told Āvaṭyas: *daśasu mahāsargeṣu bhavyatvād anabhibhūtabuddhisattvena mayā narakatiryagbhāvaṃ duḥkhaṃ saṃpaśyatā devamanuṣyeṣu punaḥ punar utpadyamānena yat kiñcid anubhūtaṃ tat sarvaṃ duḥkham eva pratyavaimi.* The sense of this passage is: "I have never in all my experiences, in all the many births I have taken, in all the universes I have visited, in all the times through which I have lived, experienced anything but sorrow." Since this, too, is the basic postulate of Buddhism, one is led to wonder to what genuine experience such a deep and eloquent pessimism could correspond.

Robert Fliess, in his article 'Knocking on Wood: A Note on the Preoedipal Nature of the "Magic Effect"' (1944), writes with great perception about the efficacy of magic arising from various early fears which are abrogated by a reassurance in the form of an illusion; for example, the illusory belief that one has access to a drug that gives one power over aging and dying.

> Among the many 'effects' of magic, one only is subject to clinical observation: an alteration in the performer's (or the participant's) state of mind. In defensive magic this alteration can be described as the exchange of reassurance for fear, and in all magic as, subjectively, the acquisition of a conviction or, objectively, the formation of an illusion. Since this change in the affective situation of the individual practicing magic always presents itself as the affective constant underlying the many ideational variables in the various magic procedures, it deserves to be singled out as *the* magic effect.[13]

In clinical practice, the psychoanalyst learns to recognize the manifold disguises that such an impulse will undergo. The rationalizations to which it will be subject must be undone, and this uncovering process is not one that is pleasant to the person concerned, imposing, as it does, further narcissistic injuries on a personality that resorted to magic devices in the first place because of just such injuries to his self-esteem. Such original injuries must be present, I would conjecture, before either the resort to magic or the impulse to the resort to magic would result.

At the beginning of the fourth chapter of the *Yogasūtras*, the chapter on *kaivalya,* Patañjali begins, for some unapparent reason, with a summary of the preceding chapter on magic powers. He says: *janmauṣadhimantratapaḥ samādhijāḥ siddhayaḥ*, "The magic powers come from trance states, ascetic practices, spells, drugs and finally, are constitutional." I am particularly interested in Vyāsa's gloss of *oṣadhi* as: *oṣadhibhir asurabhavaneṣu*, "by drugs in the palaces of demons." Vācaspati comments on this: "A human being, when for some cause or other, reaches the mansions of the demons, and when he makes use of elixirs-of-life brought to him by the lovely damsels of the demons, attains to agelessness and to deathlessness and to other perfections."[14] (Śaṅkara, in the *Vivaraṇa*, passes over this in silence.) Now one cannot help but be amazed at reading this. *Patañjali's sūtra*, in contrast to this fancy, has at least a resemblance to truth: undoubtedly the belief in magic powers can be occasioned by altered states of awareness (*samādhi*); the febrile states that inevitably accompany long abstinence (*tapas*); the peculiar loss of rational faculties that attends the use of *mantras*; and certain objective physical deficiencies that, in compensation, are felt as magic (they are certainly not usual – note the universal tendency to ascribe magical powers to hunchbacks, dwarves, etc.). Finally, there can be no question that the ingestion of potent psychotomimetic drugs, a practice common in India, would encourage a belief in the possession of magic powers. I do not mean that Patañjali had such psychological explanations in mind (most certainly he did not), but at least the possibility is present, given the form of the *sūtra*. But Vyāsa carries us to another realm, for he speaks of magic voyages, demons, palaces, magic potions, triumph, all in a simple *tatpuruṣa* compound of only two members!

Let us examine a further fantasy that Vyāsa, an excellent writer, offers us in his comment on III.51. We are near the end of this curious chapter about magic powers and are being prepared for a higher goal, that of *kaivalya*. Patañjali is worried about what will happen to the narcissism of the great Siddha who is invited by those in high places (*sthānyupanimantrane*) and he is not thinking, so Vyāsa allows us to infer, of the mere invitations by Mahārājas; no, these are high gods, in far-off heavens, and he is being invited in to no less a region than the mysterious Madhumatī, for he is a special kind of Yogin, who dwells in a land of sweet honey. The gods tell him:

> *bho ihāsyatām iha ramyatāṃ kamanīyo 'yaṃ bhogaḥ kamanīyeyaṃ kanyā, rasāyanam idaṃ jarāmṛtyuṃ bādhate, vaihāyasam idaṃ yānam, amī kalpadrumāḥ, punyā mandākinī, siddhā maharṣaya, uttamā*

anukūlā apsaraso, divye śrotracakṣuṣī vajropamaḥ kāyaḥ, svaguṇais sarvam idam upārjitam ayuṣmatā pratipadyatām idam akṣayam ajaram amarasthānaṃ devānāṃ priyam ity evam abhidhīyamānāḥ saṅgadoṣān bhāvayed ghoreṣu saṃsārāṅgāreṣu pacymānena mayā jananamaraṇāndhakāre viparivarttamānena kathañcid āsāditaḥ kleśatimiravināśī yogapradīpas tasya caite tṣṛṇāyonayo viṣayāvayavaḥ pratipakṣaḥ. so khalv ahaṃ labdhālokaḥ katham anayā viṣayamṛgatṛṣṇayā vāñcitas tasyaiva punaḥ pradīptasya saṃsārāgner ātmānam indhanīkūryām iti. . .svasti vaḥ svapnopamebhyaḥ kṛpanajanaprārthanīyebhyo viṣayebhya ity evaṃ niścitamatiḥ samādhiṃ bhāvayet.

I translate as follows:

"Hello! Come sit down here. Come and enjoy yourself sexually here. This is a lovely place. And this young woman is beautiful. Here is a magic potion that will counteract the effects of old age and death. And here is a carriage that flies through the air. Here are trees that fulfill all your wishes. Here is the holy Mandākinī River. Here are great sages who have all attained magic powers. And here are unrivalled Apsarases willing [to make love]. Your hearing and your vision will become supernatural. Your body will become like a diamond. All of this you have earned by your very own merits. Stay in this place, for it is deathless, it is indestructible, there is no old age here and the gods themselves love it." Thus addressed, he should reflect upon the defects to be found in attachment. He should say to himself: "I have been cooked in the terrible coals of *saṃsāra* – I have been willynilly whirled about in the darkness of [the cycle of] birth and death. Somehow I have managed to acquire the lamp of Yoga which destroys the darkness of suffering. And now these dangerous enemy winds of sensual enjoyment coming from the skies of desire have arisen to threaten it. How can I, who have found illumination, allow myself to be deluded by this mirage of sensual enjoyment and even to further offer myself as fuel to the fire of *saṃsāra* which will once again flare up? I wish you good fortune, O sensual objects – I bid you farewell. You are to be sought by pathetic people, for you are no better than dreams." This is how he should become convinced in his heart, and [finally] he should realize *samādhi*.

The desire to dissemble the underlying fantasy is overwhelming, and although I recognize that any attempt to rely on one's own empathy and imagination in searching back into one's own childhood for clues to the significance of such unrecognized metaphors is bound to be hazardous, I take heart from the fact that Fliess was able to do it with such success with regard to as innocuous a habit as touching wood. In any case, the failure can hardly do any harm. What I see underlying Vyāsa's comment and Vācaspati's gloss thereon is the feeling that any child has felt, at various times in his early life, that he is in the house of demons (see Hermann, 1949). The mother is, in Melanie Klein's terms, the "giantess of the nursery", and one's house is a magic place owned by powerful, mysterious, often evil geniuses who have absolute power over one's body and soul. But of course no growing Jack ever kills his giant without the help of that lovely woman who is herself compelled to serve the ogre, and so the magic potions that she, the mother, brings one are the very liquids the father most prizes, and which then give the small child power over age (he becomes old) and death (nobody disappears any longer). The secondary elaborations of this fantasy include, I believe, the addition of death as a specifically adult fear. 'How nice it would be', thinks the child, 'to come out of this place alive.' I have been skewing my interpretation towards more than what Freud thought of as primal and universal fantasies of early childhood, for I am indeed thinking of something much more specific, and I find that the use of an ogre's palace suits the theory very well. Put simply, the theory is this: nobody has resort to magic, especially in the totally undisguised form that it appears to us in the *Yogasūtras* and allied literature, unless he has experienced in early childhood narcissistic mortification of a particularly virulent kind. Just as, I believe, no child becomes a fetishist (see Sperling, 1963) without the collusion of his parents, and no perversion results from a home where healthy parents loved their child (it would follow that every homosexual was misused by one or both parents), so also, I believe, no ascetic, and no magician, lived a normal life in his earliest years. The hatred directed towards the child-magician was so overwhelming that it could only be controlled, in later life, by a reversion to the same protective devices the person had recourse to in childhood: a belief that revenge would eventually supervene, one would fly out of the house, over the heads of one's tormentors, raining down curses of immense potency, on one's way to adventure and love with no risks. (I am thinking, of course, of mystic love, which is the safest love because it never involves another person – only an idea, an illusion – but a much superior illusion to the illusion one had of love in that house, because at least it is under one's control and cannot be contradicted by anybody.)[15]

And this is, I believe, the attitude one must take towards magic powers.

They are the defenses of beleaguered children, taking refuge wherever they can. What gives rise to a children's song in normal development: 'I'm not small, I'm so tall I can carry the world on my back', becomes in these Yoga texts an illusion: "I'm not small, I'm as large as an elephant" (Vācaspati). How to disappear from the wrath of a psychotic parent? Become as small as an atom, fly off into the air like a piece of cotton wool – your fingers are not going to escape, unless of course they can touch the moon – and if necessary, hide yourself by diving into the floor. Better yet, Vyāsa tells us at the end of his gloss that nothing can touch this poor child: *nāpaḥ snigdhaḥ kledayanti nāgnir uṣṇo dahati, na vāyuḥ praṇami vahati. . .siddhānām apy adṛśyo bhavati*, "Water does not wet him, fire does not burn him, the wind cannot move him – [and, finally, the perfect defense:] Even the Siddhas [those great parents] cannot see him."

Since these powers are totally irrational in essence, that is, since they correspond to nothing real in the real world, it occurred to me that they may owe their origin to something that has disappeared from the real world, that is, to buried memories. A magic power, then, would replace something lost by something unreal.

What better reason could there be for the development of magic powers than the need to combat a powerful evil force, for example, a witch?[16] I am quite certain that children develop feelings of omnipotence early on, not as a natural stage in their development, as Ferenczi (1913) claimed in his well-known article, 'Stages in the Development of the Sense of Reality' (and which has been followed by analysts since), but as a means of protection against just such fears as the one of witches. And such fears are not entirely the projection of their own aggression. This is, I think, a crucial point: who develops a fear of ghosts (often disguised as a fear of nameless anxiety, of madness, of homicidal impulses, etc.)? According to Melanie Klein, everybody does, because everybody projects his own badness onto the outside world. To a certain extent this is true, but the persistence of such fears, whether in childhood, undisguised, or in later life, disguised, is not an uncaused developmental failure. It is a response to a real terror that exists in the child's life but remains disguised by his parents. Nobody who has led a happy childhood will believe in ghosts, which is to say that everybody who believes in ghosts, of whatever form, has been mistreated in a hostile, sadistic and disguised fashion. If some cultures, such as the Tibetan, seem to give greater importance to ghosts and malevolent spirits, it is not, as Tucci once explained it to be, because of the cloud formations in the Himalayas; it is because children there must be the object of greater aggression than elsewhere (though I suspect that child abuse of one kind or another has remained steady throughout history and throughout the world). The disguises may be more or less sophisticated and impenetrable, but the reality has always been the same.[17]

If one accepts my hypothesis, then many of these fantasies of magic powers yield to decoding. For example, the emphasis on the power of memory represents the feeling: 'I have repressed nothing' (in order to cover up the deep repression) – 'I remember all'. Of course, this is never accompanied by any actual remembering of early childhood. As I observed, there are no childhood memories in Sanskrit literature, and this fact continues to fascinate me. What does a leper child dream of? According to Elwin (1941), of being held by queens. What lies behind the feeling that one can fly? A child feels crippled and compensates with a dream of flying. There is an urgent necessity to escape, to be somewhere else, to get to another country, as in *The Wizard of Oz*. To be unique compensates for: 'I am nobody, I am ignored and despised.' There is no greater narcissistic blow, writes Calef (1968, 1969), than to feel unloved by one's mother, and this leads, I am sure, to another symptom, that of compassion for all people. 'My mother didn't love me', is transformed into: 'I will love everybody'. But I suspect that underlying this is: 'I will kill everybody'.[18] In perversions we often discover a kind of belated obedience: 'I will only invade anally, mother, I promise I will never love, since you didn't love me, and I must protect my memory of you. *You* are not bad, it is that nobody loves.' Since psychoanalysis is not an exercise in debate, or in philosophical speculation, but a search for the truth, it is not surprising to find these apparent contradictions. One patient responds to his mother's hatred in one way, another in a different way. The point is that both respond: the response is unconscious, and the response points to the original deed. The basic postulate is that a mother's lack of love will have profound, lasting and disguised consequences.[19]

In the *Indrajālavidyāsaṃgraha*, originally edited by Jīvānandavidyāsāgara Bhaṭṭācārya, then re-edited by his two sons, Āśubodhavidyābhūṣana and Nityabodhavidyāratna, in Calcutta in 1915, there is a text called the *Siddhanāgārjunakakṣapaṭam,* which ends with this fascinating verse (p. 360):

ravipatreṇa lepena netrayor añjanena ca
puruṣo jāyate rāmā yathā rambhā guṇānvitā,

which is a magic rite for turning oneself into a woman!

> By the application of paste from the leaf of the Ravi tree, and by the use of collyrium in the eyes, a man can become a woman, as beautiful and well-endowed as Rambhā herself.

To the psychoanalyst, there is nothing very surprising in this fantasy (cf. Kubie, 1974), for it seems very likely that the belief in omnipotence is paralleled by a degradation, or a fear of normal potency understood in its most literal sense as the renunciation of the penis. Emilio Servadio, in his article 'Magic and the Castration-Complex' (1958), gives a case history of a patient who told him,

> When I was a little boy – of 5 or 6 – I had this fantasy: I used to imagine that I might glide magically on the surface of the earth. In order to do so, however, I thought that I would have to give up my genitals, which I felt as a hindrance. I went so far as to ask our family surgeon, Professor B., if he would be willing to remove my genitals, which in my mind were only an obstacle to the possible fulfillment of my wish.

Servadio reminds us that it

> is well known that the 'magician' of the Middle Ages is a lonely figure who lives in far-away abodes, with no family and no sex-life whatsoever (often he is represented as ageless, or as an extremely old man, of whose 'maleness' in the sexual sense one could not even think!). In legends, we quite often find that the man who has gained magical powers had to pay heavily for his conquest; and this 'payment' is in several cases the mutilation of an organ – or actual castration: Wotan sacrificed an eye to partake of the wisdom of the Great Mother; in the Parsifal legend, the magician Klingsor has paid for his power with castration. . . .It may also be remembered that the priests of Cybele, again 'a great mother', paid for her protection, and for the power they got through it, by submitting to castration. There is not a single text, among those [old or recent] pretending to show the ways to the conquest of 'supernormal' [magical] powers, in which it is not stated that a condition *sine qua non* for such a supreme attainment is a complete and irreversible sexual abstinence (i.e., an equivalent of self-castration).[20]

In the Indian myths this is equally true, and we find many examples of magicians or great sages who lose their powers because of a return of the repressed. Magicians watch their semen with extraordinary diligence: not a drop must be spilled. The familiar theme of draining is evident here. It is interesting that the *Indrajālavidyāsaṃgraha* contains a whole chapter on various means of achieving arrested ejaculation.

A related hypothesis concerns the power of the *guru*. This stems, I believe, from early and malignant threats concerning masturbation. The most significant article here is that by Mabel Huschka entitled 'The Incidence and Character of Masturbation Threats in a Group of Problem Children',[21] but let me quote from a case history by Helene Deutsch in her article on female homosexuality. The mother bound Deutsch's patient's hands and feet, strapped them to crib and said, as she stood looking on:

> "Now play if you can!" This aroused. . .ungovernable rage against her mother. . .and intense sexual excitement, which she tried to satisfy by rubbing her buttocks against the bedding, regardless of her mother's presence, or perhaps to vent her spite on her mother. The most dreadful thing in this scene, for her, was the fact that her father, summoned by the mother, was a passive witness and did not offer to help his little girl despite his tender affection for her.[22]

We know very little of what went on in the day-to-day life of an Indian monastery, but I can imagine a situation in which a young adolescent monk, experiencing a natural sexual desire, would masturbate. The guru would, of course, know this. He would know that it was true of all his students, because, undoubtedly, it had been true of him and probably still was. Moreover, he had a certain psychological sense or he would not have succeeded as a guru. How does he use his knowledge? Certainly not to reassure the alarmed boy that his urges are normal and that masturbation is neither harmful nor wrong, but inevitable and universal. No, on the contrary, he calls the boy in, stares at him, hints at his enormous powers, reminds him of just one, *paracittajñāna*, and then announces, solemnly and threateningly, that he knows that the boy is masturbating. The boy, thunderstruck, guilty and anxious, confesses and is now convinced that not only does this guru possess magic powers, but he also recognizes that he is at the mercy of a merciless man. His attachment to him, perversely, mysteriously, increases, for bondage is cemented by sadism; and the guru is a sadist, a man hungry for power and control over others. But his power is dissembled by a surface humility. It is an illusion; it depends upon his knowledge of just such secrets as those of masturbation. A superficially similar, but profoundly different, situation exists between an analyst and his patient. The fact that one has told a series of painful memories to somebody increases one's fear that that person is now in a position to destroy one. Analysis is, without question, a powerful tool. Freud, early on, warned people that analysis was no joking matter, that when faced with the unconscious, curious, deep and powerful forces were let loose. It was Freud's great achievement that he subjected this force to a rigorous, uncompromising analysis. He discovered where it came from and thereby learned something, too, of its curative value. For in the end, nobody is helped in an analysis unless he develops emotional ties to the analyst; but these same ties must also be dissolved. It is the moment of disillusionment that is the central core of psychoanalysis.

Conclusion

Like the phobic, the magician has created his own dangerous universe to the avoidance of the dangers of which only he holds the key. Phobias always tend towards isolation and autism and eventually the silent solipsism of a psychosis.[23] A child, as he grows, expands his cast of play characters; personal names increase, whereas in hard magic there is a decrease of personal names, and a contraction of personal ties and intercourse with the real world.

A magician is a man who has suffered. His magic is a pathetic appeal for company and for protection, and should inspire us with genuine compassion. To believe in his magic is to do him no service; it is a perpetuation of the original forms of aggression which he had to undergo as a child. Our credulity is a disservice and an insult to the truth. Freud was correct: the object of therapy, the only kindness, is disillusion. Everything else is emotional assault.

I am reminded of the explanation that Willa Cather gave for inserting a novel within a novel. She explained that in writing this part of a novel she had in mind those Dutch paintings in which interiors are scrupulously rendered. In many of these there was a square window, open, through which one saw the masts of ships, or a stretch of gray sea, and the effect is that of an inset, a picture within a picture. Now if we imagine that this window represents the pathogenic memory, and that in fact, it is only by looking through this that far off in the distance one can perceive, faintly illuminated, the interior of another house, the one in which it all took place, the original home, and if one then realizes that the first window is closed and curtained, one begins to appreciate the difficulty, but also the beauty and challenge, of psychoanalytic work.

Notes

[1] The old Indian doctrines of *vāsanās* and of *karma* have been compared to this. It is true that the idea of responsibility for actions does bear a resemblance to Freud's notion – but the comparison cannot be carried very far, as many have tried to do (e.g., Behanan, 1937; Coster, 1934), without losing the essence of both theories. Nor must we forget that one is speculation, the other science.

[2] On symptom-formation, see Dunbar (1939), Gero (1953), Nierenberg (1963) and, for the role of aggression and sadism, Lipton (1961) and Gero (1962).

[3] On 'powers', from the Indian side I would recommend an excellent and comprehensive monograph by Lindquist (1935), Schmidt (1908), Bloomfield (1917), Hopkins (1901, 1905, 1915), Filliozat (1946, 1952, 1974), Filliozat and Renou (1953), Brown (1928), Poussin (1931, 1937), Senart (1900), Deussen (1906) and Dubois (1936). From the psychoanalytic point of view, I would recommend in particular a scathing review of the literature on parapsychology by a Swedish analyst, Börje Löfgren (1968a); see too Holzman and Ekstein (1959), Rosenman (1956), Caruth (1968), Saul (1938), Feigenbaum (1963), Horton (1918-1919), Frumkes (1953) and, from a literary point of view, Kurtz (1910). From an anthropological point of view, see Wax and Wax (1963), Whitehead (1974) Truzzo (1972). On supernormal phenomena in classical antiquity, see Dobbs (1971). Of significance is what has become known as the Urbantschitsch phenomenon, where a visual stimulus is rendered invisible by covering it with sheets of paper. The fact, discovered by Urbantschitsch, is that the stimulus still registers through the paper upon the perceptual apparatus. Friedman and Fisher, in a valuable article (1960), point out that "The Urbantschitsch phenomenon is based upon a physical premise; namely, that light passes through the screening material – that there is a very faint retinal stimulation." This is a valuable means of refuting much parapsychological 'research' based on the mistaken belief that the eye only perceives what is conveyed to consciousness.

On Yoga generally, the most comprehensive work is by Eliade (1954, 1962), but it is marred by a naive point of view. More objective is the work by Barber (1970). See too Edgerton (1924), Dasgupta (1941), Filliozat and Renou (1953), Oltramare (1906) and Deussen (1906). Psychological studies of Yoga have not been as valuable as was once expected. The most elaborate is by Brosse (1963). See, for criticism, Wenger and Bagchi (1961), Barber (1970), Mahotra (1963), and especially Heonig (1968).

Of great interest to this topic is the belief in fairies. The startling case of the Cottingly fairy photographs, which Sir Arthur Conan Doyle did so much to popularize, is one of the most fascinating cases of credulity on record. I have said something about it in an earlier note (p. 102) above. I know of no literature (except Bose, 1948, which contains some interesting data) on this or allied subjects (the belief in supernatural beings) in Indian studies, though there is valuable material in the translation of the *Ocean of Story*. A careful search of the primary literature in this area would doubtless lead to fruitful and unsuspected insights. I should think that there would be some literature on the belief in supernatural beings in the anthropological literature on India, but I have not seen anything. As for the predisposition to believe in magic, one is likely to learn most from a study of children. I recommend in particular Greenacre's (1957a) article on experiences of awe in childhood and her earlier work (1947) on vision, headache and the halo. See, too, Mahler (1942) on pseudoimbecility as a magic cap of invisibility.

For the text and commentaries of the *Yogasūtras*, I have used Jhā (1907), Prasāda (1924), Sastri (1952), Śāstrin (1931) and Bodas (1917). I have also used the translation by Woods (1927).

[4] On these memories, the best bibliography is by Lamotte, in *Le Traité de la Grande Vertu de Sagesse*, Vol. I, p. 329. Also, Demiéville (1927). See also E. Senart (1900). The worst article is by M. Eliade (1974).

[5] Saul, 1938, writes of one of his 'clairvoyant' patients:

> From being sensitive to the emotional states of others, she became hypersensitive. . .she could sense situations and psychological states of others so unerringly that she began to believe she possessed telepathic powers. She was not over-critical of this conclusion since it afforded her a great narcissistic satisfaction.

In the same essay (p. 332), he writes:

> The well-known observation that most clairvoyant predictions of the future are of wars, floods, earthquakes, and other dire and destructive events. . .and certainly, as Freud has pointed out, such predictions tell a lot about the unconscious wishes of the predictor.

It seems to me that, underlying the belief in extrasensory perception, is an inverted sexual fantasy: if only we had remained pure (i.e., asexual) we would not have lost some mysterious and magical supersense. Saul (1938) says that in a personal communication to him, the analyst Franz Alexander said that one extra sense had become overlaid and underdeveloped, like our sense of smell!

[6] *Aupapādikadehāḥ*, on which Nāgojibhaṭṭa specifies: *pitroḥ saṃyogam antareṇa akasmād eva divyaṃ śarīram.*

[7] Woods (1927, p. 256).

[8] I believe that one can explain the preponderance of the physical senses by observing the concern that children exhibit over their own senses, and in particular in their limitations with respect to the parents. The emphasis on the superacuity of hearing is certainly to be traced back to fears of being overheard. (See the fine article by Knapp, 1953.) Spoken words in dreams almost always refer to prohibitory speech uttered in real life by the parents. (Cf. Isakower, 1945, 1954.) A compensation for the fear of being overheard would naturally entail the ability to hear everything. It denies the fear that one hears nothing. The inevitable overdetermination would involve also auditory impressions from primal-scene material, both the longing for its repetition, and the need to seek protection against it. (The Yogin can hear everything, but he can also make himself immune to external noises). Similar considerations apply to seeing. (See the article by Hart, 1949.) With specific reference to the terrifying eyes of the parents in anger, I recommend the article by Peto (1969). Valuable, too, are the penetrating studies on blindness by Blank (1957). On smell, see Bose (1921).

[9] Eliade (1954, p. 88).

[10] Ibid., p. 90.

[11] Rhys Davids, *Dialogues of the Buddha*, Vol. 3, London: OUP, 1921, rpt. PTS 1965, p. 2.

[12] *The Book of the Discipline* (*Vinayapiṭaka*), Vol. V (Collavagga), translated by I. B. Horner. London: Luzac and Co., 1963 (1st edition, 1952). For the text, see Hermann Oldenberg (1880). *The Vinaya Pitakam: One of the Principal Buddhist Holy Scriptures in the Pali Language*. Vol. II (Cullavagga). London: PTS: Luzac and Co., 1964. The crucial passage reads (p. 112):

> *ananucchaviyaṃ bhāradvāja ananulomikam. . .akaraṇīyam. kathaṃ hi nāma tvaṃ bhāradvāja chavassa dārupattassa kāraṇā gihīnaṃ uttarimanussadhammaṃ iddhipāṭihāriyaṃ dassessasi. seyyathāpi bhāradvāja mātugāmo chavassa māsakarūpassa kāraṇā kopīnaṃ dasseti.*

[13] Fliess (1944, p. 327).

[14] Woods, translation, p. 300.

[15] In a panel on childhood omnipotence (*Journal of the American Psychoanalytical Association*, Vol. 22 [1974], p. 588), James Anthony described the remarkable case of "Jim, whose father, Mr. R., 47, had been manic-depressive for many years before the birth of Jim, now 15. All decisions in the family are based upon the anticipation of Mr. R.'s mania or depression. He has dominated his entire family by his strength when megalomanic or his weakness when depressed. Mrs. R., a petite, seductive woman, lives under her husband's intellectual shadow, hates him for keeping her in hell most of the time, yet admits that he is the most charming and brilliant person she has ever known and the greatest figure in his professional area. Mrs. R. feels that she has a ringside seat to a struggle between her husband and son. . . The mother said: 'He always has to show that he is the greatest; now I do think he is great, but not all that great, and certainly not as great as his father.' Jim wore numerous strange medallions and was dressed very eccentrically (a persistence in magical thinking). He openly wanted Dr. Anthony's admiration and was pleased to share in Anthony's omnipotence. He alluded to the magical powers of a medallion he wore: 'as long as I have this I can't be hurt.' He referred to his tremendous luck, and then to his tremendous brains which enabled him to know things other people cannot know because they are so stupid."

Thus omniscience, omnipotence, and at the same time, magical thinking, a belief in luck, and a continued optimism, all serve to screen the one real fact of his life, a deep depression. The denial is continual and frantic: 'I am not weak, I am not impotent', and behind that, deeper still: 'I am not the object of my father's hatred, nor of my mother's depreciation.'

There seems to me little doubt that had Jim lived in ancient India, he would have fallen prey to the belief in the possession of *siddhis*. See, too, the panel report on the vicissitudes of infantile omnipotence in Kramer (1974), and Tarachow's influential article on ambiguity and human imperfection (1965).

[16] The fear of witches is a common device for forcing a child to be obedient: "In Austria this spirit is an old witch who sits in the corn; she is naked and black and has glowing red iron-fingers, by which she stings out the children's eyes; she pecks at them till they are roasted. This spirit is close akin to the deadly 'old one' in the corn, a being who eats children, sucks blood out of them, forces them to drink deadly black milk, blood, or tar out of her long

black iron breasts. In Silesia, people thus say, to keep their children from the field: 'The old one sits there; she will take you.' Here the rustle of the trees is spoken of as the whispering of the witches" (A. Runeberg, *Witches, Demons and Fertility Magic*, Helsinki, 1947, pp. 135-136; I have quoted it from Widdowson, 1973.) Connected is the opposing fantasy of the good, all-providing mother (see Patch's 1927 work on the goddess Fortuna).

[17] Most ghosts are pictorial representations of the unconscious – something hidden, mysterious, and probably dangerous. Freud, in speaking of making the unconscious conscious, notes that ghosts disappear in the light of day. What is hidden is more frightening than what is exposed. See the interesting comments by Loewald (1960).

[18] Cf. Spring (1939) on world-destruction fantasies.

[19] Following the lead of Fenichel, who has coined the term 'counterphobic' for somebody who seeks out the very situations of which he is afraid, one could posit a counterparanoia, the persistent belief, in the face of evidence to the contrary, that nobody is after one, that conflict with the external world is unreal, and that all events of any importance are endopsychic. Witness the defensive incredulity with which child-abuse is generally met.

[20] I think of a patient of Nunberg's reported in his classic paper, 'Homosexuality, Magic and Aggression' (1935), where the patient had succeeded in making a woman out of the man with whom he was sleeping. This led to a particular form of a belief in magic, his magic powers. Nunberg writes (p. 163): "The fulfillment of his homosexual desires resulted indeed in an increase in his self-esteem, in the confirmation of his infantile feelings of omnipotence, and gave him an exalted feeling that a certain magic power emanated from his personality. Magic was the main means by which he tried to outbalance the disturbance of his narcissistic equilibrium." Note Löfgren (1968c): "It may even be that an ordinary narcissistic investment is difficult: most men harbor a vague feeling that there is something wrong with their penis. . . it almost certainly *changes* appearance at puberty and starts a new autonomous activity – nocturnal emissions – and one can indeed say that the relation of the penis to the body ego is quite indistinct, vague and precarious."

[21] Huschka (1938, pp. 338-356). Cf. Spitz (1952), Reich (1951), the article by Hare (1962) on masturbatory insanity, and Marcus and Francis (1975).

[22] Deutsch (1932).

[23] Cf. Ferber (1959), Greenson (1959), Odier (1956).

A PERSONAL EPILOGUE

Dark waters in far-off oceans: I can remember sensations from a dream I had as a child which seemed inexpressible. Walking down a deserted street on the outskirts of Bombay at dusk, or during a long windy rain-storm in the hills of Mahabaleshwar, I often experienced, for a brief moment, feelings which seemed to lead me back to that dream, or to others like it. Moments neither of happiness nor unhappiness, but closer to the latter, tinged with a certain sadness or regret, nostalgia or loneliness – perhaps a longing for some life as yet only glimpsed in strange tides of emotion, analogous to those in dreams. And the personal relations that I formed in those dreams, with dream figures unrecognizable in my waking life, were intense, passionate, and mysteriously significant.

At one period in my life I thought I had found an expression and an explanation of these feelings in Indian mystical texts. I thought the *Upaniṣads* put into words what I felt, or that the atmosphere conjured up by reading early Pali texts was what I knew. I was wrong. These feelings were not religious. Were they, then, psychologically explicable, based as they were on very early experiences and inchoate sexual sensations? My research into psychoanalytic theory and my reading of an entire clinical literature (searching, no doubt, for personal parallels) appears to have ground to a halt at the same point as my earlier research.

Yet I have been brought back again and again to that dark centre of the dream that Freud called the navel, the most obscure point, where the dream appears to drop away into complete blackness. Somehow it seems that the key for which I am searching is contained in the transformation of a deeply-felt experience into the strange but engrossing language of a dream. The house on a hill that I inhabit in a dream bears a resemblance to houses I lived in as a child, but it is different. That likeness and that difference obsess me.

I began with the ocean, and I return to it at the end. I know a little bit more about the real ocean, and a great deal more about the oceans that ancient writers talked about in Sanskrit texts. But the ocean I create at night is still a dark place, in which sunlight never filters down to the depths, and where even the best diver, after all, can only swim so deep.

BIBLIOGRAPHY*

ABBREVIATIONS

Am. Imago	American Imago
B.O.R.I.	Bhandarkar Oriental Research Institute
Br. J. Med. Psychol.	British Journal of Medical Psychology
Int. J. Psycho-Anal.	International Journal of Psycho-Analysis (London)
J. Am. Or. Soc.	Journal of the American Oriental Society
J. Am. Psychoanal. Assoc.	Journal of the American Psychoanalytic Association
J. Hillside Hosp.	Journal of the Hillside Hospital (New York)
J. Ind. Phil.	Journal of Indian Philosophy (The Netherlands)
Psychoanal. Q.	Psychoanalytical Quarterly (New York)
Psychoanal. Study Child	The Psychoanalytic Study of the Child (New Haven)
S.E.	Standard Edition, Volumes, 1-24. (London)

Abraham, Karl: (1910), 'Hysterical Dream-states' in *Selected Papers of Karl Abraham,* with an Introductory Memoir by Ernest Jones, translated by Douglas Bryan and Alix Strachey, London, The Hogarth Press, 1927, pp. 90–124.

____________: (1911), 'Notes on the Psychoanalytical Investigation and Treatment of Manic-Depressive Insanity and Allied Conditions', ibid., pp. 137–156.

____________: (1922), 'Rescue and Murder of the Father in Neurotic Phantasies', *Int. J. Psycho-Anal.* **3**, 467–474.

____________: (1924), 'A Short Study of the Development of the Libido, Viewed in the Light of Mental Disorders', ibid., 418–502.

*____________: (1925), 'The History of an Imposter in the Light of Psychoanalytical Knowledge' in *Clinical Papers and Essays on Psycho-Analysis*, with a Preface by Ernest Jones, London, The Hogarth Press, 1955, pp. 210–261.

*Starred items are of particular interest.

Agarwala, Vasudeva S.: (1963), *Matsya Purāṇa: A Study* (An exposition of the ancient Purāṇa Vidyā), Banaras, All India Kashiraj Trust.

Akhtar, Jamna Das: (1972), *The Matsya Purāṇam*, Notes by B. C. Majumdar, S. C. Vasu, H. H. Wilson, etc., *The Sacred Books of the Aryans*, Vol. I, Delhi, Oriental Publishers.

Alexander, Franz: (1929), 'The Need for Punishment and the Death-instinct', *Int. J. Psycho-Anal.* **10**, 256–269.

Alsdorf, Ludwig: (1961), *Beiträge zur Geschichte von Vegetarismus und Rinderverehrung in Indien,* Wiesbaden, F. Steiner Verlag. (Akademie der Wissenschaften und der Literatur in Mainz – Abhandlungen der Geistes – und Sozialwissenschaftlichen Klasse, Jahrgang 1961, No. 6, pp. 559–625).

Altschul, Sol: (1968), 'Denial and Ego Arrest', *J. Am. Psychoanal. Assoc.* **16**, 301–318.

Anthony E. James and Koupernik, Cyrille (eds.): (1973), *The Child in his Family: The Impact of Disease and Death,* Vol. 2 of Yearbook of the Int. Assoc. for Child Psychiat., New York, John Wiley and Sons.

__________ and Chiland, Colette (eds.): (1978), *The Child in his Family* (The Ahmedabad Conference on the Effects of Change in a slowly Developing Country), Vol. 5, New York, John Wiley and Sons.

Archer, W. G.: (1957), *The Loves of Krishna in Indian Painting and Poetry,* London, George Allen and Unwin.

__________: (1973), *Indian Paintings from the Punjab Hills: A Survey and History of Pahari Miniature Painting,* Foreward by Sherman E. Lee, 2 Vols., London, Sotheby Parke Bernet.

Arlow, Jacob A.: (1954), reporter on 'Perversions: Theoretical and Therapeutic Aspects', *J. Am. Psychoanal. Assoc.* **2**, 336–345.

__________: (1957), 'On Smugness', *Int. J. Psycho-Anal.* **38**, 1–8.

__________: (1959), 'The Structure of the *Déjà Vu* Experience', *J. Am. Psychoanal. Assoc.* **7**, 611–631.

__________: (1961), 'Ego Psychology and the Study of Mythology', *J. Am. Psychoanal. Assoc.* **9**, 371–393.

__________: (1966), 'Depersonalization and Derealization' in *Psychoanalysis – A General Psychology: Essays in Honor of Heinz Hartmann*, ed. R. M. Loewenstein, New York, Int. Univ. Press, 1966, pp. 456–478.

____________: (1971), 'Character Perversions' in *Currents in Psychoanalysis*, I. M. Marcus, (ed.), New York, Int. Univ. Press, pp. 317–336.

____________: (1972), 'The Only Child', *Psychoanal. Q.* **41**, 507–536.

Aṣṭāvakra-saṃhitā: (1854), ed. with Bengali translation at the Vinduvāśini Press, Calcutta.

Auden, W. A.: (1951), *The Enchafèd Flood, or The Romantic Iconography of the Sea*, London, Faber and Faber.

Avery, Gillian: (1975), *Childhood's Pattern: A Study of the Heroes and Heroines of Children's Fiction, 1770-1950*, London, Hodder and Stoughton.

*Axelrad, Sidney: (1960), 'On some uses of psychoanalysis', *J. Am. Psychoanal. Assoc.*, **8**, 175–218.

____________: (1962), 'Infant care and personality reconsidered', *Psychoanal. Study Society* **2**, 75–132.

Bach, S.: (1971), 'Notes on some imaginary companion', *Psychoanal. Study Child* **26**, 159–171.

Bachelard, Gaston: (1942), *L'eau et les rêves: Essai sur l'imagination de la matière*, Paris, Librairie José Corti.

____________: (1948), *La terre et les rêveries du repos*, Paris, Librairie José Corti.

*Bacot, Jacques: (1925), *Milarépa – ses méfaits – ses épreuves – son illumination*, Paris, Fayard, 1971.

____________: (1937), *La vie de Marpa le 'Traducteur' suivie d'un chapitre de l'Avadāna de l'oiseau Nīlakaṇṭha*, Paris, Librairie Orientaliste Paul Geuthner.

Bagchi, Prabodh Ch.: (1939), *Studies in the Tantras*, Calcutta, University Press.

Bak, R. D.: (1953), 'Fetishism', *J. Am. Psychoanal. Assoc.* **1**, 285–298.

____________: (1968), 'The Phallic Woman: The Ubiquitous Fantasy in Perversions', *Psychoanal. Study Child* **23**, 15–36.

Balint, Enid: (1963), 'On Being Empty of Oneself', *Int, J. Psycho-Anal.* **44**, 471–480.

Bapat, P. V.: (1958), *The Majjhima Nikāya*, Pali text ed. in the Nālandā-Devanāgarī-Pāli Series, Bihar Government, Pāli Publications Board.

Barber, T. X.: (1970), *LSD, Marihuana, Yoga, and Hypnosis*, Chicago, Aldine.

Bareau, André: (1963), *Recherches sur la biographie du Buddha dans les Sūtrapiṭaka et les Vinayapiṭaka anciens: De la quête de l'éveil à la conversion de Sāriputra et de Maudgalyāyana,* Paris, École Francaise d'Extrême-Orient.

__________: (1965), 'La Légende de la jeunesse du Buddha dans les Vinayapiṭaka anciens', *Oriens Extremus* **9**, 6–33.

__________: (1971), *Recherches sur la biographie du Buddha dans les Sūtrapiṭaka et les Vinayapiṭaka anciens.* II. *Les derniers mois, Le parinirvāṇa et les funérailles,* Paris, École Française d'Extrême-Orient.

Barrère, Jean Bertrand: (1955), *Romain Rolland par Lui-Même,* Écrivains de Toujours, Paris, Edition au Seuil.

__________: (1966), *Romain Rolland: L'âme et l'art,* Paris, Albion Michel.

Bartlett, F. C.: (1920), 'Psychology in Relation to the Popular Story', *Folklore* **3**, 264–293.

Barzun, Jacques: (1972), 'History: The Muse and Her Doctors', *Am. Historical Rev.* **7**, 36–64.

Bas, Francis: (1946), *Les routes de l'autre monde: Descentes aux enfers et voyages dans l'audelà,* Paris, Presses Universitaires de France.

Bates, Stuart E.: (1936), *Inside Out: An Introduction to Autobiography,* Oxford, Basil Blackwell.

*Bauer, Wolfgang: (1971), *China and the Search for Happiness: Recurring Themes in Four Thousand Years of Chinese Cultural History,* translated from the German by M. Shaw, New York, Seabury Press, 1976.

Behanan, Kovoor T.: (1937), *Yoga: A Scientific Evaluation,* New York, Dover Publications.

Bell, (Sir) Charles: (1931), *The Religion of Tibet,* Oxford, Clarendon Press.

Bender, E.: (1962), *Indological Studies in Honor of W. Norman Brown,* New Haven, Conn., American Oriental Society.

Bender, L. and Vogel, F.: (1941), 'Imaginary Companions of Children', *Am. J. Orthopsychiat.* **11**, 56–66.

Benedek, Therese: (1934), 'Dominant Ideas and Their Relation to Morbid Cravings' in *Psychoanalytic Investigations: Selected Papers of Therese Benedek,* New York, Quadrangle, 1973, pp. 71–90.

__________: (1956), 'Toward the Biology of the Depressive Constellation', *J. Am. Psychoanal. Assoc.* **4**, 389–427.

Benedict, Ruth: (1949), 'Child Rearing in Certain European Countries', *Am. J. Orthopsychiat.* **19**, 342–350.

Benjamin, Anne: (1955), reporter on 'Childhood Phobias', *J. Am. Psychoanal. Assoc.* **3**, 309–313.

*Benjamin, J. D.: (1961), 'The Innate and the Experiential in Child Development' in *Lectures on Experimental Psychiatry,* H. W. Brosin (ed.), Pittsburgh, Univ. of Pittsburgh Press, pp. 19–42.

Bennet, Glin: (1974), 'Psychological Breakdown at Sea: Hazards of Singlehanded Ocean Sailing', *Brit. J. Med. Psychol.* **47**, 189–210.

Benton, John F.: (1970), *Self and Society in Medieval France: The Memoirs of Abbot Guibert of Nogent* (? 1064–c.1125), ed. with Introduction and notes, translated by C. C. Swinton Bland, New York, Harper and Row.

Beres, D. and Obers, S. J.: (1950), 'The Effects of Extreme Deprivation in Infancy on Psychic Structure in Adolescence, *Psychoanal. Study Child* **5**, 212–235.

Beres, David: (1959), 'The Contribution of Psychoanalysis to the Biography of the Artist', *Int. J. Psycho-Anal.* **40**, 26–36.

__________: (1966), 'Superego and Depression' in *Psychoanalysis – A General Psychology,* R. N. Loewenstein et al. (ed.), New York, Int. Univ. Press, pp. 479–498.

Berkeley-Hill, A. R. Owen: (1933), *Collected Papers,* Calcutta, The Book Co. Ltd.

Berman, Leon: (1978), 'Sibling Loss as an Organiser of Unconscious Guilt: A Case Study', *Psychoanal. Q.* **47**, 568–587.

*Bernfeld, Siegfried: (1944), 'Freud's Earliest Theories and the School of Helmholtz', *Psychoanal. Q.* **13**, 341–362.

*__________: (1949), 'Freud's Scientific Beginnings', *Am. Imago* **6**, 165–196.

*__________: (1951), 'Sigmund Freud, M.D., 1882-1885', *Int. J. Psycho-Anal.* **32**, 204–217.

*__________: (1952), 'Freud's First Year in Practice, 1886-1887', *Bull. Menninger Clinic* **16**, 37–49.

*__________: (1953), 'Freud's Studies on Cocaine, 1884-1887', *J. Am. Psychoanal. Assoc.* **1**, 581–613.

*__________ and Bernfeld, Suzanne Cassierer: (1944), 'Freud's Early Childhood', *Bull. Menninger Clinic* **8**, 107–115.

Bernstein, A. E. H. and Blacher, R. S.: (1967), 'The Recovery of a Memory from Three Months of Age', *Psychoanal. Study Child* **22**, 156–161.

Bettelheim, Bruno: (1959), 'Feral Children and Autistic Children', *Am. J. Sociology* **64**, 455–467.

———: (1975), 'The Uses of Enchantment', *New Yorker*, Dec. 8, 50–114.

———: (1976), *The Uses of Enchantment: The Meaning and Importance of Fairy Tales*, New York, Knopf.

Bhāgavatapurāṇa, Vāsudeva Lakṣmaṇa Śarman Paṇśīkar (ed.), Bombay, Nirnayasagara Press, 19 29.

Bhandari, L. C.: (1960), 'Some Aspects of Psychoanalytic Therapy in India', *Progress in Psychotherapy* **5**, 218–220.

Bharati, Agehananda: (1965), *The Tantric Tradition*, London, Rider and Co.

———: (1971), 'Anthropological Approaches to the Study of Religion, Ritual and Belief Systems', *Biennial Review of Anthropology*, B. J. Siegel (ed.), Standford, Conn:, Standford University Press, pp. 230–282.

———: (1976), *The Light at the Center: Context and Pretext of Modern Mysticism*, Santa Barbara, Ross-Erikson.

Bhatt, G. H.: (1960), *The Bālakāṇḍa: The First Book of the Vālmīki Rāmāyaṇa*, Baroda, Oriental Institute.

*Bhattacharya, Vidhushekhara: (1943), *The Āgamaśāstra of Gauḍapāda*, Calcutta, University of Calcutta.

Bibring, Edward: (1943), 'The Conception of the Repetition Compulsion', *Psychoanal. Q.* **12**, 486-519.

———: (1947), 'The so-called English school of psychoanalysis', *Psychoanal. Q.* **16**, 69–93.

———: (1953), 'The Mechanism of Depression' in *Affective Disorders*, P. Greenacre (ed.), New York, Int. Univ. Press.

Bibring. G. et al.: (1961), 'A Study of the Psychological Processes in Pregnancy and of the Earliest Mother-Child Relationship: I: Some Propositions and Comments. II: Methodological Considerations', *Psychoanal. Study Child* **16**, 9–72.

Bies, Jean: (1974), *Littérature Française et pensée Hindoue des origines à 1950*, Paris, C. Klincksieck.

Bigandet, P.: (1888), *The Life or Legend of Gaudama the Buddha of the Burmese*, 3rd ed., 2 Vols, London, Trubner.

Bird, Brian: (1957), 'Feelings of Unreality', *Int. J. Psycho-Anal.* **38**, 256–265.

———: (1958), 'Depersonalization', *Am. Med. Assoc., Arch. Neur. Psychiat.* **80**, 467–476.

Blank, H. Robert: (1954), 'Depression, Hypomania and Depersonalization', *Psychoanal. Q.* **23**, 20–37.

———: (1957), 'Psychoanalysis and Blindness', *Psychoanal. Q.* **26**, 1–24.

———: (1975), 'Reflections on the Special Senses in relation to the Development of Affect with Special Emphasis on Blindness', *J. Am. Psychoanal. Assoc.* **23**, 32–50.

Blitzsten, N. L. (1936), 'Amphithymia: Some Syndromes of Depression and Elation', *Archives of Neurology and Psychiatry* **36**, 1021–1036.

Bloomfield, Maurice: (1917), 'On the Art of Entering Another's Body: A Hindu Fiction Motif', *Proceedings of the American Philosophical Society* **56**, 1–43.

Bodas, L. R. S.: (1917), *The Yogasūtras of Patañjali, with Vyāsa and Vācaspati's Gloss*, L. Rajaram Shastri Bodas (ed.), with the commentary of Nāgojibhaṭṭa, 2nd ed. Vasudev Shastri Abhyankar, Bombay Sanskrit and Prakrit Series, No. 46, Bombay.

Bødker, Laurits: (1957), *Indian Animal Tales: A Preliminary Survey*, Folklore Fellows Communication, No. 170 (Helsinki, Academia Scientiarum Fennica, 1957).

Boisen, A. T.: (1936), *The Exploration of the Inner World: A Study of Mental Disorder and Religious Experience*, New York, Willett Clark.

Bonaparte, Marie: (1933), *Edgar Poe: Étude psychanalytique*, Paris, Trans. *The Life and Works of Edgar Allan, Poe*, London, 1949.

———: (1946), 'The Legend of the Unfathomable Waters', *Am. Imago* **4**, 20–31.

———: (1948), *Chronos, Eros, Thanatos*, Paris, Presses Universitaires de France, London, Imago, 1952.

Bonser, Anthony: (1960), *The Complete Works of François Villon*, introduction by William Carlos Williams, New York, David McKinnon.

Bose, Girindrashekhar: (1921), 'Psychology of smell' in *Concept of Repression*, Calcutta, Sri Gouranga Press, pp. 162–182.

———: (1937), 'The duration of coitus', *Int. J. Psycho-Anal.* **18**, 235–255.

———: (1943), '"All or None" Attitude in Sex', *Yearbook of Psychoanalysis* **4**, 86–98.

———: (1945), *Everyday Psychoanalysis*, Calcutta, Susil Gupta,

Bose, Nirmal Kumar: (1952), 'Some facts of psychoanalytic interest on Gandhiji's life', *Samīkṣā* **6**, 163–175.

Bose, Uma: (1948), 'A Psychological Approach to the Origin of Religion and the Development of the Concepts of God and Ghost in Children', *Samīkṣā* **2**, 25–64.

Bowlby, J.: (1951), *Maternal Care and Mental Health*, W.H.O. Monographs, No. 2, New York, Columbia Univ. Press.

———: (1960), 'Grief and Mourning in Infancy and Early Childhood', *Psychoanal. Study Child* **21**, 9–52.

———: (1963), 'Pathological mourning and childhood mourning', *J. Am. Psychoanal. Assoc.* **11**, 500–541.

———, Robertson, James and Rosenbluth, Dina: (1952), 'A Two-Year-Old Goes to Hospital', *Psychoanal. Study Child* **7**, 82–94.

Bowra, C. M.: (1950), *The Romantic Imagination*, London, Oxford Univ. Press.

Brahmapurāṇa: (1895), edited by the Pandits of the Ānandāśrama, Vol. 17 of the series, Poona, Anandāśrama Press.

Brahmavaivartapurāṇa (Kṛṣṇajanmakhāṇḍa): (1909), *Poṭhi form*, Bombay, Veṅkateśvara, Press.

Brenman, M.: (1952), 'On Teasing and Being Teased: and the Problem of "Moral Masochism"', *Psychoanal. Study Child* **7**, 264–285.

Brenner, C.: (1953), 'An Addendum to Freud's Theory of Anxiety', *Int. J. Psycho-Anal.* **34**, 18–24.

———: (1957a), 'The Nature and Development of the Concept of Repression in Freud's Writings', *Psychoanal. Study Child* **12**, 19–46.

———: (1957b), 'The Reformulation of the Theory of Anxiety', Appendix to *A General Selection from the Works of Sigmund Freud*, J. Rickman (ed.), New York, Doubleday and Co.

———: (1959), 'The Masochistic Character: Genesis and Treatment', *J. Am. Psychoanal. Assoc.* **7**, 197–226.

———: (1974), 'On the Nature and Development of Affects: A Unified Theory', *Psychoanal. Q.* **43**, 532–556.

———: (1975), 'Affects and Psychic Conflict', *Psychoanal. Q.* **44**, 5–28.

Brigg, K. M.: (1959), *The Anatomy of Puck*, London, Routledge and Kegan Paul.

———: (1967), *The Fairies in Tradition and Literature*, London, Routledge and Kegan Paul.

Brill, A. A.: (1945), 'The Universality of Symbols', *The Yearbook of Psychoanalysis* **1**, 63–78.

Brody, Sylvia: (1956), *Patterns of Mothering: Maternal Influence During Infancy*, introduction by René A. Spitz, New York, Int. Univ. Press.

Brosse, Thérèse: (1963), *Études instrumentales des techniques du yoga: expérimentation psychosomatique*. Publications de l'École Française D'Extrême-Orient, No. 52, Paris, Adrien – Maisonneuve.

Brower, R. H. and Miner, E. R.: (1966), *Japanese Court Poetry*, Stanford, Stanford Univ. Press.

Brown, W. Norman: (1928), *The Indian and Christian Miracles of Walking on the Water*, Chicago, Open Crt. Pub. Co.

———: (1933), *The Story of Kālaka*, Freer Gallery of Art, Oriental Studies. No. 1 Washington, Smithsonian Institution.

———: (1957), 'The sanctity of the cow in Hinduism', *J. Madras University* (Section A), Vol. 28, No. 2, Jan. 1957, 29–49.

Bruch, Hilde: (1973), *Eating Disorders: Obesity, Anorexia Nervosa and the Person Within*, New York, Basic Books.

Buchan, J.: (1931), *The Novel and the Fairy Tale*, The English Association, No. 49.

Burlingame, E.W.: (1921), Buddhist Legends Translated from the Original Pali Text of the Dhammapada Commentary, 3 Vols., Harvard Oriental Series, Cambridge, Harvard University Press, pp. 28–30.

Burlingham, Dorothy: (1945), 'The Fantasy of Having a Twin', *Psychoanal, Study Child* **1**, 205–210.

———: (1952), *Twins: A Study of Three Pairs of Identical Twins*, New York, Int. Univ. Press.

__________ and Freud, A.: (1944), *Infants Without Families: The Case for and Against Residential Nurseries*, London, George Allen and Unwin.

Burnett, Frances Hodgson: (1911), *The Secret Garden*, New York, Dell Pub. Co. 1975.

Burnouf, E.: (1844), *Introduction à l'histoire du Bouddhisme Indien*, Paris.

*__________: (1884), *Le Bhāgavata Purāṇa, ou histoire poétique de Krichna*, 4 Vols. Book 10, translated by Hauvette-Besnault, Paris, Imprimerie Nationale.

Bush, Susan: (1971), *The Chinese Literati on Painting: Su Shih (1037-1101) to Tung Chi'i'ch'ang (1555-1636)*, Harvard Yenching Institute Studies. No. 27, Cambridge, Harvard Univ. Press.

Buxbaum, E.: (1941), 'The role of detective stories in child analysis', *Psychoanal. Q.* **10**, 373–381.

__________: (1960), 'Hair pulling and fetishism', *Psychoanal. Study Child* **15**, 243–261.

Bychowski, Gustov: (1968), 'A Brief Visit to India: Observations and Psychoanalytic Implications', *Am. Imago* **25** 59–76.

Cahill, James: (1967), *Fantastics and Eccentrics in Chinese Painting*. N.Y., *Asia Soc.*, (Ed. by V. Field).

Calef, V.: (1954), 'Color in Dreams', *J. Am. Psychoanal. Assoc.* **2**, 453–461.

__________: (1968), 'The Unconscious Fantasy of Infanticide Manifested in Resistance', *J. Am. Psychoanal. Assoc.* **16**, 697–710.

__________: (1969), 'Lady Macbeth and Infanticide, or "How Many Children Had Lady Macbeth Murdered?"', *J. Am. Psychoanal. Assoc.* **17**, 711–739.

Cannon, Walter B.: (1942), '"Voodoo" Death', *Am. Anthropologist* **44**, 169–181.

Carey, George: (1969), 'Enchanted Island Traditions of the Sixteenth and Seventeenth Centuries', *Am. Neptune* **29**, 275–281.

Carstairs, G. Morris: (1957), *The Twice-Born: A Study of a Community of High-Caste Hindus*, London, The Hogarth Press.

Carstairs, G. and Kapur, R. L.: (1976), *The Great Universe of Kota: Stress, Change and Mental Disorder in an Indian Village*, Berkeley, Univ. of Calif. Press.

Caruth, Elain: (1968), 'Hercules and Superman: The Modern-day Mythology of the Comic Book: Some Clinical Applications', *Am. Acad. Child Psychiat.* **7**, 1–12.

Castelnuovo-Tedesco, P.: (1974), reporter on 'Toward a Theory of Affects', *J. Am. Psychoanal. Assoc.* **22**, 612–626.

Chakravarti, Chintaharan: (1963), *The Tantras: Studies on their Religion and Literature,* Calcutta, Punthi Pustak.

Chang, Garma C. C.: (1962), *The Hundred Thousand Songs of Milarepa: The Life-story and Teaching of the Greatest Poet-Saint Ever to Appear in the History of Buddhism,* 2 Vols., New York, University Books.

Chasseguet-Smirgel, J.: (1978), 'Reflection on the Connexions between Perversion and Sadism'. *Int. J. Psycho-Anal.* **59**, 27–36.

Chertok, L. and de Saussure, R.: (1973), *Naissance du psychanalyste: de Mesmer à Freud,* Paris, Payot (Collection Science de l'Homme).

Choissy, Maryse: (1947), *La métaphysique des yogas: Essai sur les techniques indiennes de la sublimation,* Foreward by Paul Masson-Oursel, Genève, Mont Blanc.

Chombart de Lauwe, Marie-José: (1971), *Un monde autre: l'enfance: de ses représentations à son mythe,* Paris, Payot.

Claparède, E.: (1911), 'Recognition and "Me-ness" ' in David Rapaport, *Organization and Pathology of Thought: Selected Sources,* New York, Columbia Univ. Press, 1951, pp. 58–75.

Clark, (Sir) Kenneth: (1954), *Moments of Vision,* Oxford, Clarendon.

*Clark, W. E.: (1930), 'Some Problems in the Criticism of the Sources for Early Buddhist History', *Harvard Theological Review* **23**, 121–147.

Cohn, Franz S.: (1957), 'Time and the ego', *Psychoanal. Q.* **26**, 168–189.

Cohn, Norman: (1957), *The Pursuit of the Millenium: Revolutionary Millenarians and Mystical Anarchists of the Middle Ages* rev. and expanded ed., New York, Oxford Univ. Press, 1970.

Compton, A.: (1972), 'A Study of the Psychoanalytic Theory of Anxiety. I: The Development of Freud's Theory of Anxiety', *J. Am. Psychoanal. Assoc.* **20**, 3–44.

Conrad, Joseph: (1906), *The Mirror of the Sea: Memories and Impressions,* London, Methuen.

Cornubert, Colette: (1966), *Freud et Romain Rolland: Essai sur la Découverte de la Pensée Psychanalytique par Quelques Écrivains Français,* Thèse No. 453 pour Le Doctorat en Médecine. Paris, Faculté de Médecine de Paris, Thèse présentée et soutenue le 9 Juin, 1966, Président: M. Jean Delay, Professeur agrégé.

Coster, Geraldine: (1934), *Yoga and Western Psychotherapy: A Comparison,* London, Oxford Univ. Press.

Cowell, E. B.: (1897), *The Jātaka, or Stories of the Buddha's Former Births,* translated by H. T. Francis, 5 Vols., London, Luzac and Company, Ltd. for the Pali Text Society, 1957.

Cox, George W.: (1883), *An Introduction to the Science of Comparative Mythology and Folklore,* 2nd ed., London, Kegan Paul, Trench.

Cross, Wilbur L.: (1924), *An Outline of Biography from Plutarch to Strachey,* New York, Henry Holt and Co.

Cumont, Franz: (1922), *After Life in Roman Paganism,* New Haven, Yale Univ. Press.

Daly, Claude D.: (1927), 'Hindu-Mythologie und Kastrationskomplex', *Imago* **13**, 145–198.

Dandekar, R. N.: (1966a), The *Anuśāsanparvan:* Being the Thirteenth Book of the *Mahābhārata,* the Great Epic of India, Vol. 17, Part I, critical edition, Poona, Bhandarkar Oriental Research Institute.

———: (1966b), The *Anuśāsanaparvan:* Being the Thirteenth Book of the *Mahābhārata,* the Great Epic of India, Vol. 17, Part II, Appendices, critical notes and concordance, Poona, Bhandarkar Oriental Research Institute.

Daniels, Cora Linn and Stevans, C. M.: (1903), *Encyclopaedia of Supersitions, Folklore and the Occult Sciences of the World,* 3 Vols, Chicago, J.W. Yewdale.

Danto, Arthur C.: (1972), *Mysticism and Morality: Oriental Thought and Moral Philosophy,* New York, Basic Books.

*Dasgupta, Shashibusan: (1946), *Obscure Religious Cults as a Background to Bengali Literature,* Calcutta, Univ. of Calcutta.

Dasgupta, Surendranath: (1941), 'Yoga Psychology' in *Philosophical Essays,* Calcutta, Univ. of Calcutta Press, pp. 179–197.

David, Christian: (1971), 'Quelqu'un manque' in *L'État amoureux: Essais psychanalytiques,* Paris, Payot, 247–266.

David-Neel, Alexandra: (1929), *Mystiques et magiciens du Tibet,* Paris.

De, S. K.: (1919), *Bengali Literature in the Nineteenth Century (1757-1857),* 2nd ed. Calcutta, Firma K. L. Mukhopadhyay, 1962.

———: (1942), *The Early History of the Vaishnava Faith and Movement in Bengal,* Calcutta, 2nd ed., Calcutta, K. L. Mukhopadhyay, 1961.

De La Mare, Walter: (1930), *Desert Islands and Robinson Crusoe,* with decorations by Rex Whisterl, London, Faber and Faber.

Deikman, A.: (1966), 'De-automatization and the Mystic Experience', *Psychiatry* **22**, 329–343.

Delatte, A.: (1934), 'Les conceptions de l'enthousiasme chez les philosophes présocratiques', *L'Antiquité Classique* **III**, 5–79.

Delehaye, H.: (1907), *The Legends of the Saints: An Introduction to Hagiography*, translated by V. M. Crawford, London, Longmans, Green and Co.

Demiéville, Paul: (1927), 'Sur la memoire des existences antérieures', *Bulletin de l'École Française d'Extrême-Orient* **27**, 283–298.

*____________: (1952), *Le Concile de Lhasa: Une controverse sur le quiétisme entre Bouddhistes de l'Inde et de la Chine au VIIIe siècle de l'ère Chrétienne*, Paris, Imprimerie Nationale de France, P. U. F.

____________: (1972), *Entretiens de Lin-tsi*, Paris, Fayard.

____________: (1973), *Choix d'études sinologiques: 1921-1970*, A. Bareau et al. (ed.), Leiden, E. J. Brill.

Desmonde, W.: (1951), 'Jack and the Beanstalk', *Am. Imago* **8**, 287–288.

Deussen, Paul: (1906), *The Philosophy of the Upaniṣads*, translated by A. S. Geden, Edinburgh, T. and T. Clark.

Deutsch, Helene: (1930), 'Hysterical fate neurosis' in *Neuroses and Character Types: Clinical Psychoanalytic Studies*, New York, Int. Univ. Press, 1965, pp. 14–28.

____________: (1932), 'On Female Homosexuality', *Psychoanal. Q.* **1**, 484–510.

*____________: (1937), 'Absence of Grief', *Psychoanal. Q.* **6**, 12–22.

____________: (1938), 'Folie à deux', *Psychoanal. Q.* **7**, 307–318.

____________: (1942), 'Some Forms of Emotional Disturbance and Their Relationship to Schizophrenia', *Psychoanal. Q.* **11**, 301–321.

____________: (1955), 'The Impostor: Contribution to Ego Psychology of a Type of Psychopath' in *Neuroses and Character Types: Clinical Psychoanalytic Studies*, New York, Int. Univ. Press, 1965, pp. 319–338.

Devereux, G.: (1947), 'Mohave Orality: An analysis of Nursing and Weaning Customs', *Psychoanal. Q.* **16**, 519–546.

____________: (1951a), *Reality and Dream: The Psychotherapy of a Plains Indian*, New York, Int. Univ. Press; rev. ed., 1969.

———: (1951b), 'Logical Status and Methodological Problems of Research in Clinical Psychiatry', *Psychiatry* **14**, 327–330.

———: (1951c), 'Cultural and Characterological Traits of the Mohave Related to the Anal Stage of Psychosexual Development', *Psychoanal. Q.* **20**, 394–422.

———: (1951d), 'The Oedipal Situation and Its Consequences in the Epics of Ancient India', *Samīkṣā* **5**, 5–13.

———: (1953a), ed. *Psychoanalysis and the Occult*, New York, Int. Univ. Press.

*———: (1953b), 'Cultural Factors in Psychoanalytic Therapy', *J. Am. Psychoanal. Assoc.* **1**, 629–655.

*———: (1953c), 'Why Oedipus Killed Laius: A Note on the Complementary Oedipus Complex', *Int. J. Psycho-Anal.* **34**, 132–141.

———: (1954a), 'The Denial of the Anus in Neurosis and Culture', *Bull. Philadelphia Assoc. Psychoanal.* **4**, 24–47.

———: (1954b), 'Belief, Supersition, and Symptom', *Samīkṣā* **8**, 210–215.

———: (1955a), *A Study of Abortion in Primitive Societies*, New York, Int. Univ. Press.

———: (1955b), 'Anthropological Data Suggesting Unexplored Unconscious Attitudes toward and in Unwed Mothers', *Archives of Criminal Psychodynamics* **1**, 564–576.

———: (1956), 'Normal and abnormal' in *Some Uses of Anthropology: Theoretical and Applied*, Washington, D. C., The Anthropological Society of Washington, pp. 23–48.

———: (1957), 'The Awarding of a Penis as Compensation for Rape: A Demonstration of the Clinical Relevance of the Psycho-analytic Study of Cultural Data', *Int. J. Psycho-Anal.* **38**, 398-401

———: (1958), 'The Significance of the External Female Genitalia and of Female Orgasm for the Male', *J. Am. Psychoanal. Assoc.* **6**, 278–286.

———: (1959), 'The Nature of the Bizarre', *J. Hillside Hosp.* **8**, 266–278.

*———: (1961), *Mohave Ethnopsychiatry and Suicide*, Bureau of American Ethnology, Washington, D. C., 2nd ed., rev., **175**, 1969.

———: (1965), 'Weeping, Urination and Grand Mal', *J. Hillside Hosp.* **14**, 97–107.

*___________: (1967), 'Observation and belief in Aischylos' accounts of dreams', *Pschother. Psychosom.* **15**, 114–134.

___________: (1968?), 'La naissance d'Aphrodite' in *Échange et communications: Mélanges offerts á Claude Levi-Strauss,* J. Pouillon and P. Maranda (eds.), Mouton. The Hauge.

___________: (1970), *Essais d'ethnopsychiatrie générale,* Bibliothèque des sciences humaines, Paris, Gallimard.

___________: (1972), *Ethnopsychanalyse complémentariste,* Nouvelle bibliothèque scientifique, Paris, Flammarion.

___________: (1973), 'The Self-blinding of Oidipous in Sophokles: Oidipous Tyrannos', *J. of Hellenic St.* **93**, 36–49.

___________: (1976), *Dreams in Greek Tragedy: An Ethno-Psycho-Analytical Study,* Berkeley, Univ. of Calif. Press.

Dhvanyāloka of Ānandavardhana, edited with Abhinavaguptą's *Locana* by Paṭṭābhirāma Śāstrī, Haridas Skt. Series, No. 135, Banaras, Chowkhambha Skt. Series Office, 1940.

Dickes, Robert: (1963), 'Fetishistic Behaviour: A Contribution to Its Complex Development and Significance', *J. Am. Psychoanal. Assoc.* **11**, 303–330.

*___________: (1965), 'The Defensive Function of an Altered State of Consciousness. A Hypnoid State', *J. Am. Psychoanal. Assoc.* **13**, 365–403.

Dikshitar, V. R. Ramachandra: (1951), *The Purana Index,* 3 Vols., Madras Univ. Historical Series, No. 19, Madras, Univ. of Madras.

Dimock, Edward C.: (1966), *The Place of the Hidden Moon: Erotic Mysticism in the Vaiṣṇava-Sahajīya Cult of Bengal,* Chicago, Univ. of Chicago Press.

Divanji, P. C.: (1963), *The Araṇyakāṇḍa: The Third Book of the Vālmīki Rāmāyaṇa, the National Epic of India,* Baroda, The Oriental Institute.

Dodds, E. R.: (1951), *The Greeks and the Irrational,* Berkeley, Univ. of Calif. Press.

___________: (1973), 'Supernormal Phenomena in Classical Antiquity' in *The Ancient Concept of Progress and Other Essays on Greek Literature and Belief,* Oxford, Clarendon Press, pp. 156–210.

Doi, Takeo: (1971), *The Anatomy of Dependence,* Translated John Bester, Tōkyō, Kōdansha Int., 1973.

Dorson, Richard: (1972), *Folklore: Selected Essays,* Indiana, Indiana Univ. Press.

*Dubois, J. N.: (1936), *Hindu Manners, Customs and Ceremonies,* Translated from the French by H. K. Beauchamp, 3rd ed., Oxford. Clarendon Press.

Dudridge, Glen: (1970), *The Hsi-yu Chi: A Study of Antecedents to the Sixteenth-Century Chinese Novel,* Cambridge, Cambridge Univ. Press.

Dunbar, Flanders: (1939), 'Character and Symptom Formation', *Psychoanal. Q.* **8**, 18–47.

Dundes, Alan (ed.),: (1965), *The Study of Folklore,* Englewood Cliffs, Prentice-Hall.

__________: (1975), *Analytic Essays in Folklore,* The Hague, Mouton.

Edel, Leon: (1957), *Literary Biography,* Toronto, Univ. of Toronto Press, rev. 1959; rpt. Bloomington, Indiana Univ. Press, 1973.

__________: (1961), 'The Biographer and Psycho-analysis', *Int. J. Psycho-Anal.* **42**, 458–466.

Edgerton, Franklin: (1924), 'The Meaning of Sāṃkhya and Yoga', *Am. J. Philology* **45**, 1–46.

__________: (1926), *Vikrama's Adventures, or The Thirty-two Tales of the Throne,* Cambridge, Harvard Univ. Press.

__________: (1929), 'The Upaniṣads: What Do They Seek and Why?', *J. Am. Or. Soc.* **49**, 97–121.

Edwards, Richard: (1962), *The Field of Stones: A Study of the Art of Shen Chou (1427-1509),* Smithsonian Institute, Oriental Studies, No. 5, Washington, Freer Gallery of Art.

__________: (1967), *The Painting of Tao 'chi,* Ann Arbor.

*Eissler, K. R.: (1955), *The Psychiatrist and the Dying Patient,* New York, Int. Univ. Press.

__________: (1961), *Leonardo da Vinci: Psychoanalytic Notes on the Enigma,* New York, Int. Univ. Press.

__________: (1963), *Goethe: A Psychoanalytic Study, 1775-1786,* 2 Vols., Detroit, Wayne State Univ. Press.

__________: (1965), *Medical Orthodoxy and the Future of Psychoanalysis,* New York, Int. Univ. Press.

__________: (1966), 'A Note on Trauma, Dream, Anxiety and Schizophrenia', *Psychoanal. Study Child* **21**, 17–50.

Ekvall, Robert B.: (1964), *Religious Observances in Tibet: Patterns and Functions,* Chicago, Univ. of Chicago Press.

Eliade, Mircea: (1954), *Yoga: Immortality and Freedom,* translated from the French by Willard R. Trask, Bollingen Series. No. 56, New York, Pantheon Books, 1958.

___________: (1959), 'The Yearning for Paradise in Primitive Tradition', *Daedalus* **88**, 255–267.

___________: (1962), *Patañjali et le Yoga,* Paris, Éditions du Seuil.

___________: (1974), 'The Occult and the Modern World', *J. Philadelphia Assoc. Psychoanal.* **1**, 195-213.

Eliot, (Sir) Charles; (1921), *Hinduism and Buddhism: An Historical Sketch,* 3 Vols., London, Edward Arnold.

Elliott, Robert C.: (1970), *The Shape of Utopia: Studies in a Literary Genre,* Chicago, Univ. of Chicago Press.

Ellwood, Gracia Fay: (1970), *Good News from Tolkien's Middle Earth,* Michigan, William B. Eerdmans Pub. Co.

Elwin, V.: (1941), 'Dreams of Indian Aboriginal Lepers', *Man* **41**, 55–60.

___________: (1943), 'The Vagina Dentata Legend', *Br. J. Med. Psychol.* **19**, 439–453.

___________: (1947), *The Muria and their Ghotul,* Bombay, Oxford Univ. Press.

Emch, Minna: (1944), 'On "the need to know" as related to identification and acting out', *Int. J. Psycho-Anal.* **25**, 13–18.

Erikson, Erik H.: (1969), *Gandhi's Truth: On the Origins of Militant Nonviolence,* New York, W. W. Norton and Company.

*Esman, Aaron H.: (1973), 'The Primal Scene: A Review and a Reconsideration', *Psychoanal. Study Child* **28**, 49–81.

Fairweather, J. A.: (1974), 'Fiction in the Biographies of Ancient Writers', *Ancient Society* **5**, 231–275.

Farber, Maurice L.: (1950), 'The Problem of National Character: A Methodological Analysis' in *Personality and Social Systems,* N. J. Smelser (ed.), New York, J. Wiley and Sons, 1963.

*Farinelli, Arturo: (1916), *La Vita e un Sogno,* 2 Vols., Vol. 1: *Preludi al dramma di Calderón,* Torino, Fratelli Bocca.

*Farquhar, J. N.: (1920), *An Outline of the Religious Literature of India,* Oxford, Oxford Univ. Press.

Fausbøll, V.: (1903), *Indian Mythology According to the Mahābhārata in Outline*, Luzac's Oriental Religious Series, No. 1, London, Luzac and Co.

Feigenbaum, Dorian: (1926), 'A Case of Hysterical Depression', *Psychoanal. Rev.* **13**, 404–423.

———: (1937), 'Depersonalization as a Defense Mechanism', *Psychoanal. Q.* **6**, 4–11.

*Fenichel, O.: (1927), 'The Economic Function of Screen Memories' in *The Collected Papers of Otto Fenichel*, Vol. 1, New York, W. W. Norton, 1953, pp. 113–116.

———: (1930), 'The Psychology of Transvestitism', *Int. J. Psycho-Anal.* **11**, 211–227.

———: (1934), 'On the Psychology of Boredom' in *Collected Papers*, 1st Series, New York, Norton, 1953, pp. 292–302.

———: (1935), 'A Contribution to the Psychology of Jealously' in *Collected Papers*, 1st Series, New York, Norton, 1953, pp. 349–362.

*———: (1939a), 'The Counter-phobic Attitude', *Int. J. Psycho-Anal.* **20**, 263–274.

*———: (1939b), 'The Economics of Pseudologia Phantastica', *The Collected Papers of Otto Fenichel*, 2nd Series, New York, Int. Univ. Press, pp. 129–140.

*———: (1942), 'Symposium on Neurotic Disturbances of Sleep', *Int. J. Psycho-Anal.* **23**, 49–68.

———: (1944), 'Remarks on the Common Phobias', *Psychoanal. Q.* **13**, 313–326.

*———: (1945), *The Psychoanalytic Theory of Neurosis*, New York, W. W. Norton and Co.

Ferber, Leon: (1959), reporter on 'Phobias and their Vicissitudes', *J. Am. Psychoanal. Assoc.* **7**, 182–192.

Ferenczi, S.: (1913), 'Stages in the Development of the Sense of Reality', *Contributions to Psychoanalysis* (later retitled *Sex in Psychoanalysis*), translated by Ernest Jones. New York, Basic Books, 1950, pp. 213–239.

———: (1914), 'The Ontogenesis of the Interest in Money' in ibid, pp. 319–331.

———: (1929), 'The Unwelcome Child and His Death Instinct', *Int. J. Psycho-Anal.* **10**, 124–129.

*———: (1933), 'Confusion of Tongues between Adults and the Child' in *Final Contributions to the Problems and Methods of Psychoanalysis*, London, The Hogarth Press, 1955, pp. 156–167.

Festugière, André-Jean: (1954), *Personal Religion Among the Greeks,* Berkeley, Univ. of Calif. Press.

____________: (1961), *Les Moines d'Orient.* Vol. 1, *Culture ou sainteté, introduction au monachisme oriental,* Paris, Les Editions du Cerf.

*Feuerbach, A. von: (1832), *Caspar Hauser,* translated by H. Linberg. London, Simpkin and Marshall, 1834.

Fiedler, Leslie: (1974), Introduction, *Beyond the Looking Glass: Extraordinary Works of Fantasy and Fairy Tale,* Jonathan Cott (ed.), London, Hart-Davis, McGibbon Ltd.

____________: (1978), *Freaks: Myths and Images of the Secret Self,* New York, Simon and Schuster.

Filliozat, Jean: (1946), 'Les origines d'une technique mystique indienne', *Revue Philosophique,* pp. 208–220.

____________: (1947), 'Le sommeil et les rêves selon les médecins indiens et les physiologues grecs' in *Laghuprabandhāḥ:* Choix d'Articles d'Indologie, C. Caillat et al. (ed.), Leiden, E. J. Brill, 1974, pp. 212–232.

____________: (1952), 'Continence et sexualité dans le bouddhisme et les disciplines de yoga' in *Mystique et continence. Études Carmélitaines,* **41**, Paris, pp. 70–81.

____________: (1953), 'Les limits des pouvoirs humains dans l'Inde' in *Limites de l'humain. Études Carmélitaines,* **43**, Paris, pp. 23–38.

____________: (1972), 'Les théories psychologiques de l'Inde', *Bull. de la Société française de Philosophie* (juil-sept), pp. 73–96.

____________: (1974), *Laghu-Prabandhāḥ:* Choix d'Articles d'Indologie, C. Caillat et al. (ed.), Leiden, E.J. Brill.

____________ and Renou, Louis: (1953), 'Le Yoga' in *L'Inde classique: Manuel des études indiennes,* Vol. 2, Paris, Imprimerie Nationale.

Fine, Bernard D. (ed.): (1969), *The Mechanism of Denial,* Monograph Series of the Kris Study Group of the N. Y. P. I., New York, Int. Univ. Press, No. 3.

____________: (1971), *Recollection and Reconstruction,* Monograph 4 of the Kris Study Group, New York, Int. Univ. Press.

Fischer, J. L.: (1963), 'The Sociopsychological Analysis of Folktales', *Current Anthropology* **4**, 235–295.

Fisher, Charles: (1945), 'Amnesic States in War Neurosis: The Psychogenesis of Fuges', *Psychoanal. Q.* **14**, 437–468.

__________: (1947), 'The Psychogenesis of Fugue States', *Am. J. Psychotherapy* **1**, 211–220.

__________: (1949), 'Fugue with Awareness of Loss of Personal Identity', *Psychoanal. Q.* **18**, 480–493.

*__________: (1954), 'Dreams and Perception: The Role of Preconscious and Primary Modes of Perception in Dream Formation', *J. Am. Psychoanal. Assoc.* **2**, 389–445.

Fischer, D. J.: (1976), 'Sigmund Freud and Romain Rolland: The Terrestrial Animal and His Great Oceanic Friend', *Am. Imago* **33**, 1–59.

Fleming, Jean and Altschul, Sol: (1963), 'Activation of Mourning and Growth by Psychoanalysis', *Int. J. Psycho-Anal.* **44**, 419–431.

Fliess, Robert: (1942), 'The Metapsychology of the Analyst', *Psychoanal. Q.* **11**, 211–227.

__________: (1944), 'Knocking on Wood: A Note on the Preodipal Nature of the "Magic Effect" ', *Psychoanal. Q.* **13**, 327–340.

__________: (1953a), 'The Hypnotic Evasion: A Clinical Observation', *Psychoanal. Q.* **22**, 497–511.

*__________: (1953b), *The Revival of Interest in the Dream: A Critical Study of Post-Freudian Psychoanalytic Contributions*, New York, Int. Univ. Press.

__________: (1956), *Erogeneity and Libido. Addenda to the Theory of the Psychosexual Development of the Human*, New York, Int. Univ. Press.

__________: (1961), *Ego and Body Ego: Contributions to their Psychoanalytic Psychology*, New York, Int. Univ. Press.

*__________: (1973), *Symbol, Dream and Psychosis*, Psychoanalytic Series, Vol. 3, New York, Int. Univ. Press.

Flournoy, Th.: (1900), *From India to the Planet Mars: A Study of a Case of Somnambulism with Glossolalia*, translated by D. B. Vermile, New York, Harper.

__________: (1915), *Une mystique moderne: Documents pour la psychologie religieuse*, rpt. from *Archives de Psychologie*, Vol. 15, Geneva, Kundig, 1928.

Fodor, Nander: (1949), *The Search for the Beloved: A Clinical Investigation of the Trauma of Birth and Pre-Natal Conditioning*, New York, Hermitage Press.

__________: (1950), 'Varieties of Nostalgia', *Psychoanal. Rev.* **37**, 25–38.

Fontein, Jan and Hickman, Mary L.: (1970), *Zen Painting and Calligraphy*, Boston, Museum of Fine Arts, Dist. by New York Graphic Society.

Formichi, Carlo: (1912), *Açvaghosa poeta del Buddhismo,* Biblioteca di Cultura Moderna, Vol. 54, Bari, Laterza.

Foster, Grace: (1945), 'The psychotherapy of William James', *Psychoanal. Rev.* **32**, 300–318.

*Foucher, A: (1949), *La vie du Bouddha d'après les textes et les monuments de l'Inde,* Bibliothèque Historique, Paris, Payot.

*————: (1955), *Les vies antérieures du Bouddha d'après les textes et les monuments de l'Inde,* Publications du Musée Guimet, 6, Paris, Presses Univ. de France.

Fraiberg, Selma: (1954), 'Tales of the Discovery of the Secret Treasure', *Psychoanal. Study Child* **9**, 218–241.

————, Adelson, Edna and Shapiro, Vivian: (1975), 'Ghosts in the Nursery: A Psychoanalytic Approach to the Problems of Impaired Infant-Mother Relationships', *J. Am. Acad, Child Psychiat.* **14**, 387-421.

Frankfort, Henri: (1948), *Ancient Egyptian Religion: An Interpretation,* New York, Columbia Univ. Press.

Freedman, A.: (1956), 'The Feeling of Nostalgia and Its Relationship to Phobia', *Bull. Philadelphia Assoc. Psychoanal.* **6**, 84–92.

*Freedman, D.: (1975), 'Congenital and Perinatal Sensory Deprivations: Their Effect on the Capacity to Experience Affect', *Psychoanal. Q.* **44**, 62–80.

*Freedman, D. and Browns, S. L.: (1968), 'On the Role of Coenesthetic Stimulation in the Development of Psychic Structure', *Psychoanal. Q.* **37**, 418-438.

*Frere, Mary: (1867), *Old Deccan Days, or Hindoo Fairy Legends Current in Southern India (Collected from Oral Tradition),* 3rd ed., London, John Murray, 1881; rpt. New York, Dover, 1966, introduction and notes by Sir Bartle Frere.

Freud, Anna: (1936), *The Ego and the Mechanisms of Defense,* translated by C. Baines, New York, Int. Univ. Press, rev. ed., 1966.

————: (1953), 'Some remarks on infant observation', *Psychoanal. Study Child* **8**, 9–19.

————: (1958), 'Child observation and prediction of development: A memorial lecture in honor of Ernst Kris', *Psychoanal. Study Child* **13**, 92–124.

*————: (1965), *Normality and Pathology in Childhood,* New York, Int. Univ. Press.

Freud, Ernest L. (ed.): (1961), *Letters of Sigmund Freud: 1873-1939,* translated by Tania and James Stern, London, The Hogarth Press.

Freud, Sigmund: (1895), 'Studies on Hysteria', *S.E.* 2.

*__________: (1896), 'The Aetiology of Hysteria', *S. E.* 3, 189–221.

*__________: (1899), 'Screen memories', *S. E.* 3, London, The Hogarth Press, 1962, pp. 301–322.

*__________: (1900), *The Interpretation of Dreams, S.E.* 4–5, London, The Hogarth Press, 1953.

__________: (1901), *The Psychopathology of Everyday Life, S. E.* 6.

__________: (1907), 'Delusions and Dreams in Jensen's "Gradiva" ', *S. E.* 9, London, The Hogarth Press, 1959, pp. 3–95.

__________: (1910), 'Leonardo da Vinci and a Memory of His Childhood', *S. E.* 11, 63–138.

*__________: (1911), 'Psychoanalytic Notes on an Autobiographical Account of a Case of Paranoia (Dementia Paranoides)', *S. E.* 12, 3–84.

__________: (1913a), 'The Occurrence in Dreams of Material from Fairy Tales', *S. E.* 12, London, The Hogarth Press, 1958, pp. 279–287.

__________: (1913b), 'The Theme of the Three Caskets', *S. E.* 12, London, The Hogarth Press, 1958, pp. 289–302.

__________: (1914a), 'Remembering, Repeating and Working-through (Further Recommendations on the Technique of Psycho-analysis, II)', *S. E.* 12, 145–156.

__________: (1914b), 'Observations on Transference-Love', *S.E.* 12, 157–171.

__________: (1914c), 'On Narcissism: An Introduction', *S.E.* 14, 73–104.

*__________: (1915a), 'Instincts and Their Vicissitudes', *S.E.* 14, 117–140.

*__________: (1915b), 'Repression', *S.E.* 14, 146–158.

*__________: (1915c), 'The Unconscious', *S. E.* 14, 166–216.

__________: (1916), 'On Transience', *S.E.* 14, London, The Hogarth Press, 1957, pp. 304–307.

*__________: (1917a), 'Mourning and Melancholia', *S. E.* 14, 243–258.

__________: (1917b), 'A Metapsychological Supplement to the Theory of Dreams', *S. E.* 14, 222–236.

____________: (1918), 'From the History of an Infantile Neurosis', *S. E.* 17, London, The Hogarth Press, 1955, pp. 3–122.

____________: (1920), *Beyond the Pleasure Principle, S. E.* 8, 7–64.

*____________: (1926), *Inhibitions, Symptoms, and Anxiety, S. E.* 20, 75–176.

____________: (1927), 'Humour', *S. E.* 21, London, The Hogarth Press, 1961, pp. 159–166.

____________: (1930), *Civilization and its Discontents, S. E.* 21, London, The Hogarth Press, 1961, pp. 59–145.

*____________: (1936), 'A Disturbance of Memory on the Acropolis', *S. E.* 22, 239–248.

*____________: (1937a), 'Analysis Terminable and Interminable', *S.E.* 23, 211–253.

*____________: (1937b), 'Constructions in analysis', *S. E.* 23, 256–267.

*____________: (1938), *An Outline of Psycho-Analysis, S. E.* 23, 141–207.

*____________: (1954), *The Origins of Psychoanalysis: Letters to Wilhelm Fliess, Drafts and Notes: 1887-1902.* Marie Bonaparte, Anna Freud, Ernst Kris (eds.), translated by Eric Mosbacher and James Strachey, London, Imago Publishing Co.

Friedlander, Kate: (1940), 'On the longing to Die', *Int. J. Psycho-Anal.* **21**, 416–426.

____________: (1942), 'Children's Books and Their Function in Latency and Prepuberty', *Am. Imago* **3**, 129–150.

Friedman, Paul: (1952), 'The Bridge: A Study in Symbolism', *Psychoanal. Q.* **21**, 49–80.

Friedman, S. M. and Fisher, Charles: (1960), 'Further Observations on Primary Modes of Perception: The Use of a Masking Technique for Subliminal Visual Stimulation', *J. Am. Psychoanal. Assoc.* **8**, 100–129.

Frodsham, J.D.: (1970), *The Poems of Li Ho (791-817),* Oxford, Clarendon Press.

Frumkes, G.: (1953), 'Impairment of the sense of reality as manifested in psychoneuroses and everyday life', *Int. Int. J. Psycho-Anal.* **34**, 123–131.

Furman, E.: (1974), *A Child's Parent Dies,* New Haven, Yale Univ. Press.

Furman, R. A.: (1964), 'Death of a Six-Year-Old's Mother during His Analysis', *Psychoanal. Study Child* **19**, 377–397.

Furst, S. S. (ed.): (1967), *Psychic Trauma,* New York, Basic Books.

Garma, Angel: (1946), 'The Traumatic Situation in the Gensis of Dreams', *Int. J. Psycho-Anal.* **27**, 134–139.

———: (1968), 'The Deceiving Superego and the Masochistic Ego in Mania', *Psychoanal. Q.* **37**, 63–79.

Garma, C. C. Chang: (1962), *The Hundred Thousand Songs of Milarepa,* 2 Vols., New York, University Books.

Gedo, John F.: (1972), 'The Methodology of Psychoanalytic Biography, *J. Am. Psychoanal Assoc.* **20**, 638–649.

Geleerd, E.: (1956), 'Clinical Contribution to the Problem of the Early Mother-Child Relationship: Some Discussion of Its Influence on Self-destructive Tendencies and Fugue States', *Psychoanal. Study Child* **11**, 336–351.

———: (1965), 'Two Kinds of Denial: Neurotic Denial and Denial in the Serivce of the Need to Surivive' in *Drives, Affects, Behaviour: Essays in Memory of Marie Bonaparte,* Vol. 2., Max Schur (ed.), New York, Int. Univ. Press.

Geleerd, E. et al.: (1945), 'Contribution to the Study of Amnesia and Allied Conditions', *Psychoanal. Q.* **14**, 199–220.

Gerhardt, Mia I.: (1963), *The Art of Story-telling: A Literary Study of the Thousand and One Nights,* Leiden, E.J. Brill.

———: (1967), *Old Men of the Sea: From Neptunus to Old French "luiton": Ancestry and Character of a Water-Spirit,* Amsterdam, Polak and Van Gennep.

Gero, George: (1951), 'The Concept of Defense', *Psychoanal. Q.* **20**, 565–578.

———: (1953), 'Defenses in Sympton Formation', *J. Am. Psychoanal. Assoc.* **1**, 87–103.

———: (1962), 'Sadism, Masochism, and Aggression: Their Role in Symptom Formation', *Psychoanal. Q.* **31**, 31–42.

Gesell, A.: (1941), *Wolf Child and Human Child,* New York, Harper and Brothers.

*Getty, Alice: (1914), *The Gods of Northern Buddhism: Their History, Iconography and Progressive Evolution through the Northern Buddhist Countries,* translated from the French by J. Deniher, London: O. U. P., 1914, rev. 1928; rpt., Rutland, Charles E. Tuttle, 1962.

Ghosh, P. R.: (1973), 'Sri Ramakrishna's teaching: A contribution to Bengali literature', *Bulletin of the Ramakrishna Mission Institute of Culture* **24**, 430–439.

Giamatti, A. Bartlett: (1966), *The Earthly Paradise and the Renaissance Epic,* Princeton, Princeton Univ. Press.

Gifford, Sanford: (1964), reporter on 'Repetition Compulsion', *J. Am. Psychoanal. Assoc.* **12**, 632–649.

____________: (1966), 'Differences in Individual Development within a Pair of Identical Twins', *Int. J. Psycho-Anal.* **47**, 261–268.

*Gill, Merton M. and Brenman, Margaret: (1959), *Hypnosis and Related States: Psychoanalytic Studies in Regression,* New York, Int. Univ. Press.

Gillespie, W. H.: (1952a), 'A Contribution to the Study of Fetishism', *Int. J. Psycho-Anal.* **21**, 401–415.

____________: (1952b), 'Notes on the Analysis of Sexual Perversions', *Int. J. Psycho-Anal.* **33**, 397–402.

____________: (1956), 'The General Theory of Sexual Perversions', *Int. J. Psycho-Anal.* **37**, 396-403.

____________: (1964), 'The Psychonalytic Theory of Sexual Deviation with Special Reference to Fetishism' in *The Pathology and Treatment of Sexual Deviation,* I. Rosen (ed.), New York, Oxford Univ. Press, pp. 123–145.

Giovacchini, Peter L.: (1967), 'Frustration and Externalization', *Psychoanal. Q.* **36**, 571–583.

Glauber, I. P.: (1949), 'Observations on a Primary Form of Anhedonia', *Psychoanal. Q.* **18**, 67–78.

Glover, E.: (1929), 'The Screening Function of Traumatic Memories' in *On the Early Development of Mind,* New York, Int. Univ. Press, 1956, pp. 108-111.

____________: (1933), 'The Relation of Perversion-Formation to the Development of Reality Sense', *Int. J. Psycho-Anal.* **14**, 486–504.

____________: (1938), 'A Note on Idealization', *Int. J. Psycho-Anal.* **19,** 91–96.

____________: (1939), The Psycho-analysis of Affects' in *On the Early Development of Mind,* New York, Int. Univ. Press, 1956, pp. 297–306.

____________: (1945), 'Examination of the Kleinian System of Child Psychology', *Psychoanal. Study Child* **1**, 75–118.

____________: (1964), 'Aggression and Sado-masochism' in Rosen, I., pp. 146–162 (see under Gillespie, 1964).

Goldman, R. P. (1976), *Gods, Priests and Warriors,* New York, Columbia Univ. Press.

*__________: (1978), 'Fathers, Sons and Gurus: Oedipal Conflict in the Sanskrit Epics', *J. Ind. Phil.* **6**, 325–392.

*__________: (1979 – forthcoming), 'Rāmaḥ Sahalakṣmaṇaḥ: Psychological and Literary Aspects of the Composite Hero of Vālmīki's *Rāmāyaṇa, J. Ind. Phil.*

Goldman, R. P. and Masson, J.: (1969), 'Who Knows Rāvaṇa – A Narrative Difficulty in the Vālmīki Rāmāyaṇa, *Annals of the B. O. R. I.* **50**, 95–100.

Gonda, Jan: (1950), *Notes on Brahman,* Utrecht, J. L. Beyers.

__________: (1954), *Aspects of Early Viṣṇuism,* Utrecht, N. V. A. Oosthoek's Uitgevers Mij.

Goodall, Jane Van Lawick: (1971), *In the Shadow of Man.* London, William Collins.

Gorer, G.: (1938), *Himalayan Village: An Account of the Lepchas of Sikkim,* 2nd ed., New York, Basic Books, 1967.

__________: (1948), *The American People: A Study in National Character,* New York, W. W. Norton.

__________: (1955), *Exploring English Character,* London, Cresset Press.

__________, and Rickman, J.: (1949), *People of Great Russia: A Psychological Study,* London, Cresset Press.

Grahame, Kenneth: (1887), *The Golden Age,* London, John Lane.

__________: (1892), Preface to *Lullaby-Land: Songs of Childhood* by Eugene Field. New York Charles Scribner's.

*__________: (1898), 'The Reluctant Dragon' in *Dream Days,* New York, John Lane.

Gray, Basil: (1959), *Buddhist Cave Paintings at Tun-haung,* Preface by Arthur Waley, London, Faber and Faber.

Green, Peter: (1957), *Kenneth Grahame: A Biography,* Cleveland, The World Publishing Co.

Green, Roger Lancelyn: (1965), *Teller of Tales: Children's Books and Their Authors from 1800 to 1964,* rev. ed., London, Edmund Ward.

Greenacre, Phyllis: (1941), 'The Predisposition to Anxiety' in *Trauma, Growth and Personality,* New York, Norton, 1952, pp. 27–28.

___________: (1947), 'Vision, Headache and the Halo' in *Trauma, Growth and Personality,* London, The Hogarth Press, 1953, pp. 122–137.

*___________: (1949), 'A Contribution to the Study of Screen Memories', *Psychoanal. Study Child* **3/4**, 73–84.

*___________: (1950), 'The Prepuberty Trauma in Girls', *Psychoanal. Q.* **19**, 298–317.

___________: (1953), 'Certain Relationships between Fetishism and the Faulty Development of the Body Image', *Psychoanal. Study Child* **8**, 79–98.

___________: (1955a), 'Further Considerations regarding Fetishism', *Psychoanal. Study Child* **1**, 187–194.

___________: (1955b), ' "It's My Own Invention" ', *Psychoanal. Q.* **24**, 200–244.

___________: (1955c), *Swift and Carroll: A Psychoanalytic Study of Two Lives,* New York, Int. Univ. Press.

*___________: (1956), 'Re-evaluation of the Process of Working-Through', *Int. J. Psycho-Anal.* **37**, 439–444.

___________: (1957a), 'Experiences of Awe in Childhood', *Psychoanal. Study Child* **11**, 9–30.

___________: (1957b), 'The Childhood of the Artist', *Psychoanal. Study Child* **12**, 47–72.

___________: (1958a), 'The Family Romance of the Artist', *Psychoanal. Study Child* **13**, 9–43.

___________: (1958b), 'The Relation of the Imposter to the Artist', *Psychoanal. Study Child* **13**, 521–540, rpt. in *Emotional Growth,* New York, Int. Univ. Press, 1971.

___________: (1960), 'Further Notes on Fetishism', *Psychoanal. Study Child* **15**, 191–207.

___________: (1968), 'Perversions: General Considerations regarding their Genetic and Dynamic Background', *Psychoanal. Study Child* **23**, 47–62.

___________: (1969), 'The fetish and the transitional object', *Psychoanal. Study Child* **24**, 144–164.

Greenson, Ralph R.: (1949), 'The Psychology of Apathy', *Psychoanal. Q.* **18**, 270–302.

*___________: (1959), 'Phobia, Anxiety, and Depression', *J. Am. Psychoanal. Assoc.* **7**, 663–675.

————: (1962), 'On Enthusiasm', *J. Am. Psychoanal. Assoc.* **10**, 3–21.

————: (1966), 'A Transvestite Boy and a Hypothesis', *Int. J. Psycho-Anal.* **47**, 396–403.

————: (1968), 'Dis-identifying from Mother', *Int. J. Psycho-Anal.* **49**, 370–374.

Groff, W. L.: (1956), *Rainer Maria Rilke: Creative Anguish of a Modern Poet,* Princeton, Princeton Univ. Press.

Grotjahn, Martin: (1939-40), 'Ferdinand the Bull: Psychoanalytical Remarks about a Modern Totem Animal', *Am. Imago* **1**, 33–41.

*Grouse, Frederick Salmon: (1874), *Mathurā: A District Memoir,* 1st ed., Allahabad, North-Western Provinces Govt. Press, 2nd enlarged ed., 1880; 3rd ed. rev. and abridged, 1883.

Guillaumin, Jean: (1968), *Le Genèse du souvenir: Essai sur les fondements de la psychologie de l'enfant,* Paris, Presses Universitaries de France.

Gusdorf, Georges: (1956), 'Conditions et limites de l'autobiographie' in *Formen der Selbstdarstellung,* Analekten zu einer Geschichte des literarischen Selbstportraits, Festgabe für Fritz Neubert, G. Reichenkron and E. Hasse (eds.), Berlin, Dunckher and Humblot.

Haark, Erik: (1969), *The Yar-Lun Dynasty: A Study with Particular Regard to the Contribution by Myths and Legends to the History of Ancient Tibet and the Origin and Nature of its Kings,* Copenhagen, G. C. C. Gad's Forlag.

Hadfield, J. A.: (1927), 'The Reliability of Infantile Memories', *Br. J. Med. Psychol.* **35**, 31–46, 1962.

Haim, A.: (1974), *Adolescent Suicide,* New York Int. Univ. Press.

Hall, F.: (1840), H. H. Wilson (ed.), *The Vishnu Purāṇa, A System of Hindu Mythology and Tradition,* 5 Vols., London, John Murray.

*Hanly, C. and Masson, J.: (1976), 'A Critical examination of the New Narcissism', *Int. J. Psycho-Anal.* **57**, 49–66.

Hare, E. M.: (1962), 'Masturbatory Insanity: The History of an Idea', *J. Mental Science (Br. J. Psychiat.)* **108**, 2–25.

Harivaṃśa: (1936), printed with Nīlakaṇṭha's *Bhāratabhāvadīpa,* Pandit Ramachandrashastri Kinjawadekar (ed.), Poona, Chitrashala Press.

The Hariavaṃśa. Being the Khila, or Supplement to the Mahābhārata: (1969–1971), Vol. I, critical text, Introduction and Notes, Poona, Bhandarkar Oriental Research Institute, 1969, P. L. Vaidya (ed.), Vol. II, appendices, Poona, B. O. R. I.

Harlow, Harry F.: (1958), 'The Nature of Love', *Am. Psychologist* **12**, 673–685.

____________: (1959), 'Love in Infant Monkeys', *Scientific American*, June 1959, 1–8.

____________ and Zimmermann, Robert R.: (1958), 'The Development of Affectional Responses in Infant Monkeys', *Proceedings of the American Philosophical Society* **102**, 501–509.

Harrison, Irving B.: (1966), 'A Reconsideration of Freud's "A Disturbance of Memory on the Acropolis" in Relation to Identity Disturbance', *J. Am. Psychoanal. Assoc.* **14**, 518–529.

____________: (1975), 'On the Maternal Origins of Awe', *Psychoanal. Study Child* **30**, 181–196.

____________: (1979), 'On Freud's View of the Infant-Mother Relationship and of the Oceanic Feeling – Some Subjective Influences', *J. Am. Psychoanal. Assoc.* **27**, 399–422.

*Hart, Henry Harper: (1949), 'The Eye in Symbol and Symptom', *Psychoanal. Rev.* **36**, 1–21.

Hauschild, Richard: (1967), *Die Aṣṭāvakra-Gītā*, edited and translated with notes and Introduction in *Abhandlungen der Sächsischen Akademie der Wissenschaften zu Leipzig*, Vol. 58, Berlin, Akademie-Verlag.

*Hawkes, David: (1959), *Ch'u Tz'ŭ: The Songs of the South. An Ancient Chinese Anthology*, Oxford, Clarendon Press.

Haynal, André: (1977), 'Le sens du désespoir', *Rev. Fr. de Psychoanalyse* **41**, 5–186.

Hazard, Paul: (1933), *Books, Children and Men*, translated by Mitchell. Boston, The Horn Book, Inc., 1944.

Helfer, Ray E. and Kempe, C. Henry (eds.): (1968), *The Battered Child*, Chicago, Univ. Chicago Press.

Heonig, J.: (1968), 'Medical Research on Yoga', *Confin. Psychiat.* **11**, 69–89.

Hermann, I.: (1949), 'The Giant Mother, the Phallic Mother, Obscenity', *Psychoanal. Rev.* **36**, 302–306.

Hightower, James Robert: (1970), *The Poetry of T'ao Chi'ien*, Oxford, Clarendon Press.

Holzman, Philip S. and Ekstein, Rudolf: (1959), 'Repetition-functions of Transitory Regressive Thinking', *Psychoanal. Q.* **28**, 228–235.

Hooykaas, C.: (1955), *The Old-Javanese Ramayana Kakawin*, The Hague, Martinus Nijhoff.

Hopkins, E. Washburn: (1901), 'Yoga-technique in the Great Epic', *J. Am. Or. Soc.* **22**, 333-379.

———: (1905), 'The fountain of youth', *J. Am. Or. Soc.* **26**, 1–67.

*———: (1915), *Epic Mythology* in *Grundriss der Indo-Arischen Philologie und Altertumskunde*, Strassburg, Verlag von Karl J. Trübner.

Horner, I. B.: (1954), *The Collection of Middle-Length Sayings (Majjhima-Nikāya)*, Vol. I, Pali Text Society Translation Series 29, London, Luzac.

*Horney, Karen: (1932), 'The Dread of Women: Observations on a Specific Difference in the Dread Felt by Men and by Women Respectively for the Opposite Sex', *Int. J. Psycho-Anal.* **13**, 348–360.

———: (1922-1936), *Feminine Psychology: Previously Uncollected Essays*, Harold Kelman (ed.), New York, W. W. Norton, 1967.

———: (1948), 'The value of vindictiveness', *Am. J. Psychiat.* **8**, 3–13.

Horton, Lydiard H.: (1918-1919), 'The illusion of levitation', *J. Ab. Psych.* **13**, 42–53, 119–127.

Hsia, C. T. and Hsia, T. A.: (1968), 'New Perspectives on Two Ming Novels: Hsi Yu Chi and Hsi Yu Pu: The Hsi Yu Pu as a Study of Dreams in fiction' in *Wen-Lin: Studies in the Chinese Humanities*, Chow Tse-Tsung (ed.), Madison, Univ. of Wis. Press.

Hsun, Lu: (1959), *A Brief History of Chinese Fiction*, Peking, Foreign Languages Press.

Huckel, Helen: (1957), 'One Day I'll Live in the Castle! Cinderella as a Case History', *Am. Imago* **14**, 303–314.

Hudson, W. H.: (1905), *A Little Boy Lost*, London, Duckworth and Co.

*Huschka, M.: (1938), 'Incidence and Character of Masturbation Threats in a Group of Problem Children', *Psychoanal. Q.* **7** 338–356.

Ingalls, Daniel H. H.: (1965), *An Anthology of Sanskrit Court Poetry: Vidyākara's Subhāṣitaratnakoṣa*, Harvard Oriental Series, Vol. 44, Cambridge, Harvard Univ. Press.

*———: (1968), *The Harivaṃśa as a Mahākāvya* in *Mélanges d'Indianisme à la Mémoire de L. Renou*, Paris, Editions E. de Boccard, pp. 381–394.

Isaacs, Neil D. and Zimbardo, Rose (eds.): (1968), *Tolkien and the Critics: Essays on J. R. R. Tolkien's The Lord of the Rings*, Notre Dame, Univ. of Notre Dame Press.

*Isakower, Otto: (1936), 'A Contribution to the Pathopsychology of Phenomena associated with Falling Asleep', *Int. J. Psycho-Anal.* **19**, 331–345, 1938.

*__________: (1945), 'Self-observation, Self-experimentation, and Creative Vision', *Psychoanal. Study Child* **29**, 451–472, 1974.

__________: (1954), 'Spoken words in Dreams: A Preliminary Communication', *Psychoanal. Q.* **23**, 1–6.

Isherwood, Christopher: (1959), *Ramakrishna and his Disciples,* New York, Simon and Schuster, 1964.

__________: (1964), *A Single Man,* London, Methuen.

Jackson, Stanley W.: (1968), reporter on 'Aspects of Culture in Psychoanalytic Theory and Practice', *J. Am. Psychoanal. Assoc.* **16**, 651–670.

Jacobs, Hans: (1961), *Western Psychotherapy and Hindu Sādhanā: A Contribution to Comparative Studies in Psychology and Metaphysics,* London, George Allen and Unwin.

Jacobs, Joseph: (1892), *Indian Fairy Tales,* London, David Nutt; rpt. Dover, 1969.

Jacobson, Edith: (1957a), 'On Normal and Pathological Moods', *Psychoanal. Study Child* **12**, 73–113.

*__________: (1957b), 'Denial and Repression', *J. Am. Psychoanal. Assoc.* **5**, 61–92.

__________: (1959), 'Depersonalization', *J. Am. Psychoanal. Assoc.* **7**, 581–610.

__________: (1971), *Depression,* New York, Int. Univ. Press.

James, William, (1901-02), *The Varieties of Religious Experience: A Study in Human Nature, Being the Gifford Lectures on Natural Religion Delievered at Edinburgh,* enlarged ed. with appendices and Introduction by James Ratner, New York, Univ. Books, 1963.

__________: (1901), *The Varieties of Religious Experience,* New York, Collier Books, 1972.

Jan, Isabelle: (1969), *On Children's Literature,* Catherine Storr (ed.), London, Allen Lane, 1973.

Janet, P.: (1910-1919), *De l'angoisse à l'extase: Études sur les croyances et les sentiments,* 2 Vols., Paris, Félix Alcan, 1926.

__________: (1921), 'A Case of Sleep Lasting Five Years with Loss of Sense of Reality', *Archives of Neurology and Psychiatry* **6**, 467–475.

Jhā, Gaṅgānātha: (1907), *The Yoga-Darshana Comprising the Sūtras of Patañjali with the Bhāṣya of Vyāsa,* 2nd rev. ed., Madras, Theosophical Pub. Hse., 1934.

*Johnston, E. H.: (1932), *The Saundarananda, or Nanda the Fair,* Punjab Univ. Oriental Publication No. 14, London, Oxford Univ. Press.

__________: (1936), *The Buddhacarita, or Acts of the Buddha.* Part II: Cantos I to XIV, translated from the original Sanskrit supplemented by the Tibetan version, Panjab Univ. Oriental Publication No. 32, Calcutta, Baptist Mission Press.

Jones, Ernest: (1916), 'The Theory of Symbolism' in *Papers on Psycho-Analysis,* London, Baillère, Tindall and Cox, 1912; 5th ed., 1948; rpt., 1961, pp. 87–144.

__________: (1923), 'The Nature of Auto-suggestion' in *Papers on Psychoanalysis,* 5th ed., Boston, Beacon, 1948, pp. 273–293.

*__________: (1929), 'Fear, Guilt and Hate', ibid., pp. 304–309.

__________: (1957), *Sigmund Freud: Life and Work,* Vol. III, *The Last Phase, 1919-1939,* London, The Hogarth Press.

Kane, P. V.: (1930-1962), *History of Dharmaśāstra,* 7 Vols., Poona, B. O. R. I.

Kanner, Leo: (1973), *Childhood Psychosis: Initial Studies and New Insights,* Washington, V. H. Winston and Sons.

Kanzer, Mark: (1955), 'The Communicative Function of the Dream', *Int. J. Psycho-Anal.* **36**, 260–266.

__________: (1969), 'Sigmund and Alexander Freud on the Acropolis', *Am. Imago* **26**, 324–354.

Kaufman, R. M. and Heiman, M. (eds.): (1964), *Evolution of Psychosomatic Concepts: Anorexia Nervosa: A Paradigm,* New York, Int. Univ. Press.

Keene, Donald: (1971), 'The Portrait of Ikkyū' in *Landscapes and Portraits: Appreciation of Japanese Culture,* Tōkyō, Kōdansha Int.

Keith, A. B.: (1917), 'Indian Mythology' in *The Mythology of All Races,* 13 Vols., Vol. 6, Boston, Marshall Jones Co.

*__________: (1925), *The Religion and Philosophy of the Veda and Upanishads,* Harvard Oriental Series 31–32, 2 Vols, Cambridge, Harvard Univ. Press.

Kellogg, Wintrop N. and Kellogg, L. A.: (1933), *The Ape and the Child: A Study of Environmental Influence upon Early Behaviour,* New York, Hofner Pub. Co., 1967.

Kennedy, Hanna: (1972), 'Reconstruction in Child Analysis', *Psychoanal. Study Child* **26**, 386–402.

Kepecs, J. G.: (1952), 'A Waking Screen Analogous to the Dream Screen', *Psychoanal. Q.* **21**, 167–171.

———: (1954), 'Observations on Screens and Barriers in the Mind', *Psychoanal. Q.* **22**, 62–77.

Kepecs, J. G. et al.: (1951), 'Relationship between Certain Emotional States and Exudation into the Skin', *Psychosom. Med.* **13**, 10–19.

Kern, H.: (1901), *Histoire du Bouddhisme dans l'Inde,* translated by G. Huet, Vol. 1, Paris, Ernst Leroux (orig. in Dutch; Eng. translation 1896).

Kernberg, O.: (1974), 'Contrasting Viewpoints regarding the Nature and Psychoanalytic Treatment of Narcissistic Personalities: A Preliminary Communication', *J. Am. Psychoanal. Assoc.* **22**, 255–267.

Kety, S. S.: (1960), 'A Biologist Examines the Mind and Behaviour', *Science* **172**, 1861–1870.

Khan, Masud, R. M.: (1964), 'Ego Distortion, Cumulative Trauma, and the Role of Reconstruction in the Analytic Situation', *Int. J. Psycho-Anal.* **45**, 272–279.

Kirkland, Edwin Capers: (1966), *A Bibliography of South Asian Folklore,* Indiana Univ. Folklore Series, No. 21, Bloomington, Indiana Research Center in Anthropology, Folklore, Linguistics.

Kiṣkhindhākāṇḍa Vol. 4 of the Rāmāyaṇa of Vālmīki: n. d., edited with three commentaries *(Tilaka Śiromaṇi* and *Bhūṣana)* by S. K. Mudhokar, Bombay, Gujarati Printing Press.

Kiṣkhindhākāṇḍa. The Fourth Book of the Vālmīki Rāmāyaṇa, the National Epic of India: 1965, critically edited by D. R. Mankad, Baroda, Oriental Institute.

Klein, Melanie: (1932), *The Psycho-Analysis of Children,* translated by Alix Strachey, London, The Hogarth Press, 1948.

———: (1934): 'A Contribution to the Psychogenesis of Manic-Depressive States' in *Contribution to Psycho-Analysis, 1921-1945,* London, The Hogarth Press, 1948.

Kleiner, J.: (1970), 'On Nostalgia', *Bull. Philadelphia Assoc. Psychoanal.* **20**, 11–30.

Klineberg, O.: (1944), 'A Science of National Character', *J. Soc. Psychol.* **19**, 141–162.

*Knapp, Peter H.: (1953), 'The Ear, listening and hearing', *J. Am. Psychoanal. Assoc.* **1**, 672–689.

———: (1957), 'Conscious and Unconscious Affects: A Preliminary Approach to Concepts and Methods of Study', *Psychiatric Research Reports* **8**, 55–74.

——— et al.: (1966), 'Asthma, Melancholia, and Death. 1. Psychoanalytic considerations', *Psychosom. Med.* **28**, 114–133.

Köhler, Wolfgang: (1925), *The Mentality of Apes*, trans. by Ella Winter, New York.

Kohut, Heinz: (1957a), '*Death in Venice* by Thomas Mann: A Story about the Disintegration of Artistic Sublimation', *Psychoanal. Q.* **26**, 206–228.

———: (1957b), 'Observations on the Psychological Functions of Music', *J. Am. Psychonal. Assoc.* **5**, 389–407.

———: (1960), 'Beyond the Bounds of the Basic Rule: Some Recent Contributions to Applied Psychoanalysis', *J. Am. Psychoanal. Assoc.* **8**, 567ff.

———: (1966), 'Forms and Transformations of Narcissism', *J. Am. Pscyhoanal. Assoc.* **14**, 243–272.

———: (1971), *The Analysis of the Self*, New York, Int. Univ. Press.

———: (1972), 'Thoughts on Narcissism and Narcissistic Rage', *Psychoanal. Study Child* **27**, 36–400.

Korczak, Janusz: (1925), *Mathew the Young King*, adapted by Edith and Sidney Sulkin, New York, Roy Publisher, 1948.

Kramer, Selma: (1974), reporter on 'Viscissitudes of Infantile Omnipotence', *J. Am. Psychoanal. Assoc.* **22**, 588–602.

Krappe, Alexander Haggerty: (1929), *The Science of Folklore*, New York, Barnes and Noble.

Kris, Ernst: (1952), 'The Image of the Artist: A Psychological Study of the Role of Tradition in Ancient Biographies' in *Psychoanalytic Explorations in Art*, New York, Int. Univ. Press, pp. 64–84.

———: (1952), 'On Preconscious Mental Processes' in *Psychoantlytic Explorations in Art*, New York, Int. Univ. Press.

———: (1956a), 'The Recovery of Childhood Memories in Psychoanalysis', *Psychoanal. Study Child* **11**, 54–88.

———: (1956b), 'The Personal Myth: A Problem in Psychoanalytic Technique', *J. Am. Psychoanal. Assoc.* **4**, 653–681.

____________: (1956c), 'On Some Vicissitudes of Insight in Psychoanalysis', *Int. J. Psycho-Anal.* **37**, 445–455.

____________: (1956d), 'Decline and Recovery in the Life of a Three-Year-Old', *Psychoanal. Study Child* **17**, 175–215, 1962.

____________ and Kurz, Otto: (1934), *Legend, Myth and Magic in the Image of the Artist: A Historical Experiment,* Preface by E. H. Gombrich, translated by Alastair Laing and revised by Lotti M. Newman, New Haven, Yale Univ. Press, 1979.

Kubie, Lawrence S.: (1937), 'The Fantasy of Dirt', *Psychoanal. Q.* **6**, 388–425.

____________: (1939), 'A Critical Analysis of the Concept of a Repetition Compulsion', *Int. J. Psycho-Anal.* **20**, 390–402.

*____________: (1941), 'The Repetitive Core of the Neurosis', *Psychoanal. Q.* **10**, 23–43.

____________: (1953), 'The Distortion of the Symbolic Process in Neurosis and Psychosis', *J. Am. Psychoanal. Assoc.* **1**, 59–85.

____________: (1956), 'Some Unsolved Problems of the Scientific Career', rpt. in *Identity and Anxiety: Survival of the Person in Mass Society,* M. R. Stein et al. (eds.), Illinois, The Free Press, 1960.

*____________: (1958), *Neurotic Distortion of the Creative Process,* New York, Noonday Press, 1975.

____________: (1964), 'Multiple Determinants of Suicide' in *Essays in Self-Destruction,* ed. by E. S. Shneidman, New York, Science House, 1967, pp. 455–462.

*____________: (1974), 'The Drive to Become Both Sexes', *Psychoanal. Q.* **43**, 349–426.

Kurtz, Benjamin P.: (1910), *Studies in the Marvellous,* Berkeley, Univ. of Calif. Press.

*Lacôte, Félix: (1908), *Bṛhatkathāślokasaṅgraha de Budhasvāmin, I-IX. Texte sanskrit. . .accompagné d'une traduction française,* Paris, Imprimerie Nationale.

Laforgue, René: (1932), *The Defeat of Baudelaire: A Psycho-Analytical Study of the Neurosis of Charles Baudelaire,* translated by Herbert Agar, London, The Hogarth Press.

Lagache, Daniel: (1947), 'Fugue et fuite de soi-même', *Evolution Psychiatrique* **4**, 1–15.

*Lamotte, E.: (1944), *Le traité de la grande vertu de sagesse de Nāgārjuna (Mahāprajñāpāramitāśāstra),* Vol. 1, Bibliotheque du Muséon, Vol. 18, Louvain, Bureaux du Muséon.

__________: (1947-1948), 'La légende du Buddha', *Revue de l'histoire des religions* **134**, 37–71.

__________: (1955), 'La personalité et l'esprit de Śākyamuni', *Bulletin de la classe des lettres et des sciences morales et politiques,* 5e Série – Tome XLI, Bruxelles, Palais des Academies, pp. 199–218.

*__________: (1958), *Histoire du Bouddhisme Indien des origines à l'ère Śaka,* Bibliothèque du Muséon, Vol. 43, Louvain, Institut Orientaliste.

*__________: (1962), *L'enseignement de Vimalakīrti,* Bibliothèque du Muséon, Vol. 51, Louvain, Publications Universitaires.

*Landauer, K.: (1938), 'Affects, Passions and Temperament', *Int. J. Psycho-Anal.* **19**, 388–415.

Laplanche, Jean and Pontalis, J. B.: (1968), 'Fantasy and the Origins of Sexuality', *Int. J. Psycho-Anal.* **49**, 1–18.

Latham, Minor White: (1930), *The Elizabethan Fairies: The Fairies of Folklore and the Fairies of Shakespeare,* New York, Columbia Univ. Press.

Lee, Sherman E.: (1954), *Chinese Landscape Painting,* 2nd rev. ed. The Cleveland Museum of Art, New York, Harry N. Abrams.

Lefmann, S.: (1902), *Lalita Vistara. Leben und Lehre des Cākya-Buddha,* Vol. I, *Text,* Halle, Buchhandlung des Waisenhauses.

Lehman, E.: (1949), 'Feeding Problems of Psychogenic Origins: A Survey of the Literature', *Psychoanal. Study Child* **3/4**, 461–488.

Lehman, Herbert: (1966), 'A Conversation between Freud and Rilke', *Psychoanal. Q.* **35**, 423–427.

Lessa, William A.: (1961), *Tales from Ulithi Atoll: A Comparative Study in Oceanic Folklore,* Univ. of Calif. Publications Folklore Studies, 13, Berkeley, Univ. of Calif. Press.

Leuba, J.: (1925), *The Psychology of Religious Mysticism,* London, K. Paul Trench and Trubner.

Lévi, Sylvain: (1885-1886), 'La *Bṛihatkathāmañjarī* de Kshemendra', *Journal Asiatique, 8e* Serie, **6** (1885), 397–479, 8e Serie, **7**(1886), 178–222.

Levin, H.: (1969), *Myth of the Golden Age in the Renaissance,* Bloomington, Indiana Univ. Press.

Levitan, Harold L.: (1968), 'The Turn to Mania', *Psychoanal. Q.* **37**, 56–62.

__________: (1969), 'The Depersonalizing Process', *Psychoanal. Q.* **38** 97–109.

__________: (1970), 'The Depersonalization Process: The Sense of Reality and of Unreality', *Psychoanal. Q.* **39**, 449–470.

*Lévy André: (1971), 'Études sur le conte et le roman chinois', Paris, *Bulletin de l'École Francaise d'Extrême-Orient,* Vol. 83, 'Le serpent blanc en Chine et au Japon: Excursions à travers les variations d'une thème', pp. 97–113.

Lewin, B.D.: (1932), 'Analysis and Structure of a Transient Hypomania', *Psychoanal. Q.* **1**, 43–58.

__________: (1937), 'A Type of Neurotic Hypomania Reaction', *Arch. Neurol. Psychiatry* **37**, 868–873.

__________: (1941), 'Comments on Hypomania and Related States', *Psychoanal. Rev.* **28**, 86–91.

*__________: (1949), 'Mania and Sleep', *Psychoanal. Q.* **18**, 419–433.

*__________: (1950), *The Psychoanalaysis of Elation,* New York, The Psychoanalysis Quarterly, 1961.

*__________: (1952), 'Phobic Symptoms and Dream Interpretation' in *Selected Writings of Bertram D. Lewin,* Jacob A. Arlow (ed.), New York, The Psychoanalytic Quarterly, Inc., 1973.

__________: (1959), 'Some Psychoanalytic Ideas Applied to Elation and Depression', *Am. J. Psychiatry* **116**, 38–43.

Lewinsky, H.: (1951), 'Pathological generosity', *Int. J. Psycho-Anal.* **32**, 185–189.

Lewis, C. S.: (1941), 'Psychoanalysis and Literary Criticism' in *They Asked for a Paper: Papers and Addresses,* London, G. Bles, 1962, pp. 120–138.

Lewy, Ernst: (1954), 'On Micropsia', *Int. J. Psycho-Anal.* **35**, 13–19.

Lidz, Theodore: (1964), 'August Strindberg: A Study of the Relationship between his Creativity and Schizophrenia', *Int. J. Psycho-Anal.* **45**, 399–410.

Lienhard, Siegfried: (1975), 'Sur la structure poétique des *Theratherīgāthā, Journal Asiatique* **263**, 375–396.

*Lincoln, J. S.: (1935), *The Dream in Primitive Culture,* Introduction by C. G. Seligman, Preface by G. Devereux, New York, Cresett Press; rpt. New York, Johnson rpt. Co., 1970: Landmarks in Anthropology.

*Lindquist, Sigurd: (1935), *Siddhi und Abhiññā: Eine Studie über die klassischen Wunder des Yoga,* Uppsala, A. B. Lundequistska Bokhandeln.

Lipton, Samuel D.: (1961), 'Aggression and Symptom Formation', *J. Am. Psychoanal. Assoc.* **9**, 585–592.

*Loewald, Hans W.: (1955), 'Hypnoid State, Repression, Abreaction and Recollection', *J. Am. Psychoanal. Assoc.* **3**, 201–210.

———: (1960), 'On the Therapeutic Action of Psychoanalysis', *Int. J. Psycho-Anal.* **41**, 16–33.

———: (1962), 'Internalization, Separation, Mourning and the Superego', *Psychoanal. Q.* **31**, 483–504.

———: (1971), 'Some Considerations on Repetition and Repetition Compulsion', *Int. J. Psycho-Anal.* **52**, 59–66.

Loewenstein, R. M.: (1957), 'A Contribution to the Psychoanalytic Theory of Masochism', *J. Am. Psychoanal. Assoc.* **5**, 197–234.

*Löfgren, L. Börge: (1968a), 'Recent Publications on Parapsychology', *J. Am. Psychoanal. Assoc.* **16**, 146–178.

———: (1968b), reporter on 'Psychoanalytic Theory of Affects', *J. Am. Psychoanal. Assoc.* **16**, 638–650.

———: (1968c), 'Castration Anxiety and the Body Ego', *Int. J. Psycho-Anal.* **49**, 408–410.

Lorand, Sandor: (1935), 'Fairy Tales and Neurosis', *Psychoanal. Q.* **4**, 234–243.

Lovejoy, Arthur A. and Boas, George: (1935), 'The noble savage in antiquity' in *Primitivism and Related Ideas in Antiquity,* Baltimore, Johns Hopkins Press.

Lubin, A. J.: (1958), 'A Feminie Moses: A Bridge between Childhood Identification and Adult Identity', *Int. J. Psycho-Anal.* **39**, 1–12.

———: (1959), 'A Boy's View of Jesus', *Psychoanal. Study Child* **14**, 155–168.

———: (1969), 'A psychoanalytic view of religion', *International Psychiatry Clinics* **5**, 49–60.

——— et al.: (1968), *The Psychic Function of Religion in Mental Illness and Health,* formulated by the Committee on Psychiatry and Religion, Group for the Advancement of Psychiatry, Vol. 6, 67, New York, The Mental Health Materials Center.

__________ et al.: (1976), *Mysticism: Spiritual Quest or Psychic Disorder?*, formulated by the Committee on Psychiatry and Religion, Group for the Advancement of Psychiatry, Vol. 9, 97, New York, The Mental Health Materials Center.

Lüthi, Max: (1962), *Once Upon a Time: On the Nature of Fairy Tales.* translated by L. Chadeayre and P. Gottwald, New York, Frederick Ungar Pub. Co., 1970.

*Macalpine, I. and Hunter, R. A.: (1955), *Memoirs of My Nervous Illness* (A translation of D. P. Schreber's 1903 *Denkwürdigkeiten eines Nervenkranken*), London, Dawson and Sons.

MacDonald, George: (1870), *At the Back of the North Wind,* New York, Airment Pub. Co., 1966.

__________: (1872), *The Princess and the Goblin,* London, Puffin Books, 1974.

Macdonnell, Alexander: (1899), *A selection of Games at Chess,* London, T. Hurst.

Mack, John: (1971), 'Psychoanalysis and Historical Biography', *J. Am. Psychoanal. Assoc.* **19**, 143–179.

Mahābhārata with the *Bhāratabhāvadīpa* of Nīlakaṇṭha: (1933), Vol. 6, by Pandit Ramachandrashastri Kinjawadekar (ed.), Poona, Chitrashala Press.

The *Mahābhārata* of Krishna-Dwaipayana Vyasa: c. 1890, translated into English prose from the original Sanskrit text by Pratap Chandra Roy, Vol. 10, Calcutta, Oriental Publishing Co., N. D.

Mahler, Margaret G.: (1942), 'Pseudo-imbecility: A Magic Cap of Invisibility', *Psychoanal. Q.* **11**, 149–164.

__________: (1961), 'Sadness and Grief in Childhood', *Psychoanal. Study Child* **16**, 332–351.

__________: (1966), 'Notes on the Development of Basic Moods: The Depressive Affect in Psychoanalysis' in *Psychoanalysis – A General Psychology,* R. W. Loewenstein et al. (eds.), New York, Int. Univ. Press, pp. 152–168.

Mahotra, J. C.: (1963), 'Yoga and Psychiatry: A Review', *J. Neuropsychiatry* **4**, 375–385.

Malamud, Bernard: (1979), *Dubin's Life,* New York, Farrar, Straus, Giroux.

Malson, Lucien: (1964), *Wolf-Children and the Problem of Human Nature,* New York, Monthly Review Press, 1972.

Mandelbaum, D. G.: (1943), 'Wolf-child Histories from India', *J. Soc. Psychol.* **17**, 25–44.

Manuel, Frank E.: (1965), 'Toward a Psychological History of Utopias and the Golden Age: A Mythic Prehistory for Western Utopia' in *Freedom from History and Other Untimely Essays*, New York, N. Y. Univ. Press, 1971.

——— and Manuel, Fritzie P.: (1971), 'Sketch for a Natural History of Paradise' in *Myth, Symbol and Culture*, Clifford Geertz (ed.), New York: W. W. Norton and Co., 1972.

Marasse, Henry F.: (1959), reporter on 'Isolation', *J. Am. Psychoanal. Assoc.* **7**, 163–172.

Marcovitz, Eli: (1952), 'The Meaning of *Déjà Vu*', *Psychoanal. Q.* **21**, 481–489.

Marcus, Irwin M. and Francis, John J. (eds.): (1975), *Masturbation from Infancy to Senescence*, New York, Int. Univ. Press.

Marechel, Joseph: (1927), *Studies in the Psychology of the Mystics*, translated by Algar Thorold, London, Burns Oates and Washburn.

Masson, J.: (1968), 'Yeats' *The Ten Principal Upaniṣads'*, Jadavpur *Journal of Comp. Lit.* **9**, 24–31.

———: (1969a), 'Who killed Cock Krauñca? Abhinavagaputa's Reflections on the Origins of Aesthetic Experience', *Journal of the Oriental Institute* **18**, 207–224.

———: (1969b), 'A Note on the Sources of Bhāsa's *Avimāraka'*, *Journal of the Oriental Institue* **17**, 60–74.

———: (1969c), 'Spoken Sanskrit', *Proceedings of the Forty-third International Congress of Orientalists, Munich, 1969.*

———: (1970), 'Abhinavagupta as a poet', *Journal of the Oriental Institute* **19**, 247–251.

———: (1971a), 'Philosophy and Literary Criticism in Ancient India', *Journal of Indian Philosophy* **1**, 167–180.

———: (1971b), 'Effort vs. Imagination in Indian Poetics', *Journal of Indian Philosophy* **1**, 296–299.

———: (1971c), 'Obscenity in Sanskrit Literature', *MAHFIL: A Quarterly of South Asian Literature* **3**, 197–207.

———: (1972a), 'A Note on the Authenticity of the *Bhamāhavivaraṇa attributed to Udbhaṭa'*, *Indo-Iranian Journal* **13**, 250–254.

———: (1972b), 'Did Dharmakīrti Write the Kārikās of the *Alaṅkāraśekhara*?', *Indo-Iranian Journal* **14**, 32–39.

___________: (1973), 'Telling, Not Conveying – *Svaśabdavācya*', *Journal of Indian Philosophy* **2**, 145–155.

___________: (1974a), 'The Childhood of Kṛṣṇa: Some Psychoanalytic Observations', *J. Am. Or. Soc.* **94**, 454–459.

___________: (1974b), 'India and the Unconscious: Erik Erikson on Gandhi', *Int. J. Psycho-Anal.* **55**, 519–526.

___________: (1974c), 'Schreber and Freud', paper presented at the Annual Meeting of the American Psychoanalytic Association, Denver.

___________: (1974d), 'Sex and Yoga: Psychoanalysis and the Indian Religious Experience', *Journal of Indian Philosophy* **2**, 307–320.

___________: (1975a), 'When is a Poem Artificial? – A Note on the *Ghaṭakarparvivṛti*', *Journal of the American Oriental Society* **95** (April-June 1975), 264–266.

___________: (1975b), 'Fratricide and the Monkeys: Psychoanalytic Observations on an Episode in the *Vālmīkirāmāyaṇam*', *J. Am. Or. Soc.* **95**, 672-678.

*___________: (1976a), 'The Psychology of the Ascetic', *Journal of Asian Studies* **35**, 611–625.

___________: (1976b), 'Perversions: Some Observations', *The Israel Annals of Psychiatry and Related Disciplines* **14**, 354–361.

___________: (1977a), 'The *Dhvanyāloka* and the *Dhvanyālokalocana:* A Translation of the Fourth Uddyota, Part 1', *J. Am. Or. Soc.* **97**, 285–304.

___________: (1977b), 'The *Dhvanyāloka* and the *Dhvanyālokalocana:* A translation of the fourth Uddyota, Part 2', *J. Am. Or. Soc.* **97**, 423–440.

___________: (1977c), 'Two Views on the Value of Human Love', *Journal Ind. Phil.* **5**, 85–89.

___________: (in press), 'Hanumān as an Imaginary Companion', *J. Am. Or. Soc.*

___________: (1979), 'Indian Psychotherapy?', *J. Ind. Phil.* **7**, 327-332.

___________: (1979), 'Philology *vs* Theology', *J. Ind. Phil.* **7**, 223–228.

___________: (in press), 'Melancholia and the Buddha: Unconscious Love in the Lives of the Indian Mystics', *Dialogue* (Bulletin of the Friends of the San Francisco Psychoanalytic Society).

___________ and R.P. Goldman: (1969), 'Who Knows Rāvaṇa? A Narrative difficulty in the *Vālmīkirāmāyaṇa*', *Annals of the Bhandarkar Oriental Research Institute* **50**, 95–100.

*___________ and C. Hanly: (1976), 'A Critical Examination of the New Narcissism', *Int. J. Psycho-Anal.* **57**, 49–66.

——— and D. D. Kosambi: (1970), *Avimāraka – Love's Enchanted World*, UNESCO Series of Representative Works, Motilal Banarsidas, New Delhi.

——— and T. C. Masson: (1976), 'The Study of Mysticism: A Criticism of W. T. Stace', *Journal of Indian Philosophy* **4**, 109–125.

*——— and T. C. Masson: (1978a), 'Buried Memories on the Acropolis: Freud's Relation to Mysticism and Anti-semitism', *Int. J. Psycho-Anal.* **59**, 199–208

——— and T. C. Masson: (1978b), 'The Navel of Neurosis: Trauma, Memory and Denial', paper presented to the *San Francisco Psychoanalytic Society*, May 1978.

——— and T. C. Masson: (1979), 'Affects', *Bulletin of the Southern California Psychoanalytic Institute and Society*, 56: 4–8.

——— and Matilal, B. K.: (1966), 'A Love Story from Eighth-Century India', *Jadavpur Journal of Comp. Lit.* (Calcutta) **4**, 56–67.

——— and W. S. Merwin: (1977), *Sanskrit Love Poetry*, Introduction, notes and annotated Bibliography by J. Masson, translation by W. S. Merwin, *UNESCO Series of Representative Works*, New York, Columbia Univ. Press.

——— and Patwardhan, M. V.: (1969), *Śāntarasa and Abhinavagupta's Philosophy of Aesthetics*, Poona, Bhandarkar Oriental Research Institute.

——— and Patwardhan, M. V.: (1970a), 'The *Rasagaṅgādhara* on the definition and source of poetry', *Journal of the Oriental Institute* **19**, 416–427.

*——— and Patwardhan, M. V.: (1970b), *Aesthetic Rapture: The Rasādhayāya of the Nāṭyasāstra*, 2 vols. Poona, Deccan College.

——— and Patwardhan, M. V.: (1974a), 'The *Dhvanyāloka* and the *Gaüḍavaho*' in *Science and Human Progress*, Prof. D. D. Kosambi Commemoration Volume, Bombay, Popular Prakashan, pp. 176–183.

——— and Patwardhan, M. V.: (1974b), *Dhvanigāthāpañjikā*', *Annals of the Bhandarkar Oriental Research Institute* **55**, 219–225.

*Matilal, B.K.: (1972), *Epistemology, Logic and Grammar in Indian Philosophical Analysis*, The Hague, Mouton.

———: (1977), *The Logical Illumination of Indian Mysticism: An Inaugural Lecture Delivered Before the University of Oxford on 5 May 1977*, Oxford, Clarendon Press.

*McDougall, J.: (1972), 'Primal Scene and Sexual Perversions', *Int. J. Psycho-Anal.* **53**, 371–384.

McGregor, R. S.: (1973), *Nanddar: The Round Dance of Krishna and Uddhav's Message*, London, Luzac and Co.

*McGuire, William (ed.), (1974), *The Freud/Jung Letters,* translated by Ralph Manheim and R. F. C. Hull, Bollingen Series 94, Princeton, Princeton Univ. Press.

Mead, Margaret: (1953), 'National character' in *Anthropology Today: An Encyclopedic Inventory,* A. L. Kroeber (ed.), Chicago, Univ. of Chicago Press, pp. 642–667.

__________ and Metraux, Rhoda (eds.): (1949), *The Study of Culture at a Distance,* Chicago, Univ. of Chicago Press.

__________ and Wolfenstein, Martha W.: (1955), *Childhood in Contemporary Cultures,* Chicago, Univ. of Chicago Press.

Mendelson, Myer: (1974), *Psychoanalytic Concepts of Depression,* 2nd ed., New York, Spectrum Publications.

Menking, Manfred et al.: (1969), 'Rumination – A Nearly Fatal Psychiatric Disease of Infancy', *New England J. Med.* **280**, April 10.

*Meyer, John Jacob: (1909), *Hindu Tales,* an English translation of Jacobi's *Ausgewählte Erzählungen in Māhārāshṭrī,* London, Luzac and Co.

Miller, J. and Menes, B.: (1961), 'Children's Reactions to the Death of a Parent: A Review of the Psychoanalytic Literature', *J. Am. Psychoanal. Assoc.* **19**, 697-719.

*Miller, Stuart C.: (1962), 'Ego-autonomy in Sensory Deprivation, Isolation and Stress', *Int. J. Psycho-Anal.* **43**, 1–20.

Misch, Georg: (1907), *A History of Authobiography in Antiquity,* 2 Vols., translated by E. W. Dickes, in collaboration with the author, London, Routledge and Kegan Paul.

*Mitra, Vihārīlāla: (1899), *The Yoga-vāsiṣṭha-Mahārāmāyaṇa of Vālmīki,* translated from the original Sanskrit by Vihārīlāla, Mitra, Calcutta, Metropolitan Printing Works.

Moloney, James Clark: (1954), 'Mother, God and Superego', *J. Am. Psychoanal. Assoc.* **2**, 120–151.

Mookerjee, Satkari: (1940), Introduction to *Aṣṭāvakra Saṁhitā* translated by Swami Nityaswarupanand, 3rd ed., Calcutta, Advaita Āshrama, 1969.

Moore, B.: (1964), 'Frigidity: A Review of the Psychoanalytic Literature', *Psychoanal. Q.* **33**, 323–349.

*Morel, Ferdinand: (1918), *Essai sur l'introversion mystique: Étude psychologique de Pseudo-Denys l'Aréopagite et de quelques autres cas de mysticisme,* Geneva, Librarie Kundig.

Muckle, J. T.: (1964), *The Story of Abelard's Adversities: A Translation with Notes of the Historia Calamitatum*, Preface by Etienne Gilson, Toronto, Pontifical Institute of Medieval Studies.

Mukhopadhyaya, Sujitkumar: (1963), *The Aśokāvadāna: Sanskrit Text Compared with Chinese Versions,* New Delhi, Sahitya Akademi.

Mullane, Harvey: (1965), 'Unconscious Emotion', *Theoria* **21**, 181–190.

Müller, F. Max: (1898), *Rāmakrishna, His Life and Sayings* in *Collected Works of the Right Honorable F. Max Müller,* London, Longmans Green and Co. 1923.

Murray, Gilbert: (1922), *Essays and Addresses,* London, G. Allen and Unwin.

Murray, Henry A.: (1967), 'Dead to the World: The Passions of Herman Melville' in *Essays in Self-Destruction,* Edwin S. Shneidman (ed.), New York, Science House, 1967, pp. 7–29.

Myers, W. A.: (1976), 'Imaginary Companions, Fantasy Twins, Mirror Dreams and Depersonalization', *Psychoanal. Q.* **45**, 503–524.

__________: (1979), 'Imaginary Companions in Childhood and Adult Creativity', *Psychoanal. Q.* **48**, 292–307.

Nagera, Humberto: (1969), 'The Imaginary Companion: Its Significance for Ego Development and Conflict Solution', *Psychoanal. Study Child* **24**, 165–196.

Nair, Balakrishna N.: (1959), *The Dynamic Brahmin: A Study of the Brahmin Peasants in Indian Culture with Special Reference to South India,* Bombay, Popular Book Depot.

Narain, Dhirendra: (1957), *Hindu Character (A Few Glimpses),* Univ. of Bombay Pub. Sociology Series, No. 8, Bombay, Univ. of Bombay.

Naranjo, C. and Ornstein, R. E.: (1971), *On the Psychology of Meditation,* New York, Viking.

Naumberg, Margaret: (1950), *Schizophrenic Art: Its Meaning in Psychotherapy,* New York, Greene and Stratten.

Nedeljkovic, Dragan: (1970), *Romain Rolland et Stefan Zweig,* Paris, C. Klincksieck.

Neruda, Pablo: (1930), *Residencia en la Tierra,* Buenos Aires, Losada.

*Nicolson, Harold: (1928), *The Development of English Biography,* New York, Harcourt Brace and Co.

Niederland, W. G.: (1951), 'Three Notes on the Schreber Case', *Psychoanal. Q.* **20**, 579–591.

*__________: (1956), 'River Symbolism Part I', *Psychoanal. Q.* **25**, 469–504.

__________: (1957), 'River Symbolism Part II', *Psychoanal. Q.* **26**, 50–75.

———: (1959a), 'The "Miracled-up" World of Schreber's Childhood', *Psychoanal. Study Child* **14**, 383–413.

*———: (1959b), 'Schreber: Father and Son', *Psychoanal. Q.* **28**, 151-169.

———: (1960), 'Schreber's Father', *J. Am. Psychoanal. Assoc.* **8**, 492-499.

———: (1963), 'Further Data and Memorabilia pertaining to the Schreber case', *Int. J. Psycho-Anal.* **44**, 201-207.

*———: (1965a), 'The Role of the Ego in the Recovery of Early Memories', *Psychoanal. Q.* **34**, 564–571.

———: (1965b), reporter on 'Memory and Repression', *J. Am. Psychoanal. Assoc.* **13**, 619–633.

*———: (1968), 'Schreber and Flechsig: A Further Contribution to the "Kernel of Truth" in Schreber's Delusional System', *J. Am. Psychoanal. Assoc.* **16**, 740–748.

Nierenberg, Harry H.: (1963), 'Symptom Formation', *J. Am. Psychoanal. Assoc.* **11**, 161–172.

*Nikhilananda, Swami: (1952), *The Gospel of Sri Ramakrishna: Originally Recorded in Bengali by M., a Disciple of the Master,* translated into English with an Introduction, New York, Ramakrishna-Vivekananda Center.

Nityaswarupananda, Swami: (1929), *Ashtavakra Samhita: Text with word-for-word translation, English rendering,* 2nd ed., Almora, Advaita Ashrama, 1953.

Nityatmananda, Swami: (1967), *"M" – the Apostle and the Evangelist: A Continuation of M's Gospel of Sri Ramakrishna,* Vol. I, Rohtak, Sri Ramakrishna-Sri Ma Prakashan.

Norman, R. K.: (1969), *The Elder's Verses I. Theragāthā,* Pali Text Society Translation Series, No. 38, London, Luzac.

*———: (1971), *The Elder's Verses II. Therīgāthā.* Pali Text Society Translation Series, No. 40, London, Luzac.

Novey, Samuel: (1959), 'A Clinical View of Affect Theory in Psychoanalysis', *Int. J. Psycho-Anal.* **40**, 94–104.

———: (1961), 'Further Considerations of Affect Theory in Psychoanalysis', *Int. J. Psycho-Anal.* **42**, 21–31.

———: (1968), *The Second Look: The Reconstruction of Personal History in Psychiatry and Psychoanalysis,* Baltimore, Johns Hopkins Press.

Nunberg, H.: (1922), 'States of Depersonalization in the Light of Libido Theory' in *Practice and Theory of Psychoanalysis,* New York, Int. Univ. Press, 1956.

————: (1935), 'Homosexuality, Magic and Aggression' in *Practice and Theory of Psychoanalysis,* Vol. 1, New York, Int. Univ. Press, pp. 150–164.

Oberndorf, C.: (1951), 'Transference and Reality', *Int J. Psycho-Anal.* **32**, 1–9.

————: (1935), 'The Genesis of the Feeling of Unreality', *Int. J. Psycho-Anal.* **16**, 296–306.

————: (1936), 'Feelings of Unreality', *Archives of Neurology and Psychiatry* **36**, 322–330.

————: (1939), 'On Retaining the Sense of Reality in States of Depersonalization', *Int. J. Psycho-Anal.* **20**, 137–147.

————: (1941a), 'Co-conscious Mentation', *Psychoanal. Q.* **10**, 44–65.

————: (1941b), Erroneous Recognition (fausse reconnaissance)', *Psychiatric Q.* **15**, 316–326.

————: (1950), 'The Role of Anxiety in Depersonalization', *Int. J. Psycho-Anal.* **31**, 1–5.

*Odier, Charles: (1956), *Anxiety and Magic Thinking,* translated by Marie-Louise Schoelly and Mary Jane Sherfey, New York, Int. Univ. Press.

*Oldenberg, Hermann: (1882), *Buddha: His Life, His Doctrine, His Order*, translated from the German by W. Hoey, London, Williams and Norgate.

———— and Pischel, R.: (1883), *Thera- and Therī-Gāthā*, 2nd ed. by K.R. Norman and L. Alsdorf, London, Pali Text Society, Luzac and Co., 1966.

Oltramare, Paul: (1906), *L'histoire des idées théosophiques dans l'Inde,* Vol. 1. *La théosophie Brahmanique,* Paris, Ernest Leroux.

*Oman, John Campbell: (1903), *The Mystics, Ascetics and Saints of India. A Study of Sadhuism, With an Account of the Yogis, Sanyasis, Bairagis and Other Strange Hindu Sectarians,* London, T. Fisher Unwin.

Opie, Iona and Opie, Peter: (1974), *The Classic Fairy Tales*. London, Oxford Univ. Press.

Opler, Morris E.: (1959), review of *The Twice Born, Am. Anthropoligist* **61**, 140–142.

Orgel, Shelley: (1965), 'On Time and Timelessness', *J. Am. Psychoanal. Assoc.* **13**, 102–121.

————: (1974), 'Sylvia Plath: Fusion with the Victim and Suicide', *Psychoanal. Q.* **43**, 262–287.

Orlans, Harold: (1949), 'Infant Care and Personality' (orig. pub. in *Psychol. Bull.* **46**) rpt. in

Critical Essays on Psychoanalysis, S. Rachman (ed.), New York, Macmillan Co., 1963, pp. 141-197.

Orr, W.G.: (1947), *A Sixteenth-Century Indian Mystic: Dadu and his Followers*, London, Lutterworth Press.

Ostow, Mortimer: (1962), *Drugs in Psychoanalysis and Psychotherapy*, New York, Basic Books.

____________: (1970), *The Psychology of Melancholy*, New York, Harper and Row.

____________ (ed.): (1974), *Sexual Perversions*, New York, Quadrangle/New York Times.

____________ and Scharfstein, Ben-Ami: (1954), *The Need to Believe: The Psychology of Religion*, New York, Int. Univ. Press.

Otto, Rudolf: (1924), *Mysticism East and West: A Comparative Analysis of the Nature of Mysticism*, New York, Macmillan, 1932.

____________: (1931), *The Idea of the Holy: An Inquiry into the Nonrational Factor in the Idea of the Divine and its Relation to the Rational*, London, Oxford Univ. Press.

Padmapurāṇa: (1894), R. Maṇḍalīha Viśvanātha Nārāyaṇa (ed.), Ānandāśrama Sanskrit Series, No. 131, Poona, Ānandāśrama Press.

Panofsky, Erwin: (1936), 'Et in Arcadia Ego', rpt. in *Pastoral and Romance: Modern Essays in Criticism*, E. T. Lincoln (ed.), Englewood Cliffs, Prentice-Hall, 1969.

*Pascal, Roy V.: (1960), *Design and Truth in Autobiography*, Cambridge, Harvard Univ. Press.

Patai, Raphael: (1973), *The Arab Mind*, New York, Charles Scribner's Sons.

Patch, Howard Rollin: (1927), *The Goddess Fortuna in Mediaeval Literature*, Cambridge, Harvard Univ. Press.

*____________: (1950), *The Other World According to Descriptions in Mediaeval Literature*, Cambridge, Harvard Univ. Press.

Paṭṭābhirāmaśāstrī: (1940), *Dhvanyāloka*, edited with Abhinavagupta's *Locana*, Banaras, Chowkhamba Sanskrit Series.

*Payne, Robert: (1949), *The White Pony: An Anthology of Chinese Poetry from the Earliest Times to the Present Day*, London, Allen and Unwin.

Payne, S. M.: (1939), 'Some Observations on the Ego Development of the Fetishist', *Int. J. Psycho-Anal.* **20**, 161–170.

Peller, Lili: (1958), 'Reading and Daydreams in Latency, Boy-Girl Differences', *J. Am. Psychoanal. Assoc.* **6**, 57–70.

____________: (1959), 'Daydreams and Children's Favourite books', *Psychoanal. Study Child* **14**, 414–436.

*Penzer, N. M.: (1924-1928), *The Ocean of Story* (orig. translation by C. H. Tawney), 10 Vols., London, Charles J. Sawyer.

Peto, Andrew: (1949), 'Infant and Mothers: Observations on Object Relations in Early Infancy', *Int. J. Psycho-Anal.* **30**, 260–264.

____________: (1960), 'On the Transient Disintegrative Effect of Interpretation', *Int. J. Psycho-Anal.* **41**, 413–417.

____________: (1969), 'Terrifying Eyes: A Visual Superego Fore-runner', *Psychoanal. Study Child* **24**, 197–212.

Petty, T. A.: (1953), 'The Tragedy of Humpty-Dumpty', *Psychoanal. Study Child* **8**, 404–412.

Plank, Emma N.: (1953), 'Memories of Early Childhood in Autobiographies', *Psychoanal. Study Child* **8**, 381–393.

Plank, Robert: (1957), 'On "Seeing the Salamander"', *Psychoanal. Study Child* **12**, 379–398.

*____________: (1968), *The Emotional Significance of Imaginary Beings: A Study of the Interaction between Psychopathology, Literature and Reality in the Modern World*, Springfield, Ill., Charles C. Thomas.

Poggioli, Renato: (1959), 'The Pastoral of the Self', *Daedalus* **88**, 686–699.

Pollock, George: (1961), 'Mourning and Adaptation', *Int. J. Psycho-Anal.* **42**, 341–361.

____________: (1970), 'Anniversary Reactions, Trauma and Mourning', *Psychoanal. Q.* **39**, 347–371.

____________: (1975), 'On Mourning, Immortality and Utopia', *J. Am. Psychoanal. Assoc.* **23**, 354–362.

Poussin, Louis de la Vallée: (1931), 'Le Bouddha et les Abhijñās', *Le Muséon* **44**, 1–8.

____________: (1937), 'Le Bouddhisme et le Yoga de Patañjali', *Mélanges Chinois et Bouddhiques* **5**, 223–242.

Powys, John Cowper: (1934), *Autobiography*, Introduction by J. B. Priestley, London, Macdonald, 1967.

Prasāda, Rāma: (1924), *Patañjali's Yoga Sūtras with the Commentary of Vyāsa and the Gloss of Vāchaspati Miśra,* translated by Rāma Prasāda, Introd. by Rai Bahadur Śrīsā Chandra Vasu, 3rd ed. Sacred Books of the Hindus, Vol. 4, Allahabad, Panini Office, 1924.

Pratt, James B.: (1920), *The Religious Consciousness: A Psychological Study,* New York, Macmillan.

Przyluski, Jean: (1920), 'Le parinirvāṇa et les funérailles du Buddha', Extrait du *Journal Asiatique* (1918-1920), Paris, Imprimerie Nationale.

Pulver, S. E.: (1971), 'Can Affects be Unconscious?', *Int. J. Psycho-Anal.* **52**, 347–354.

———: (1974), 'Unconscious versus Potential Affects', *Psychoanal. Q.* **43**, 77–84.

Rabindranatha Tagore et Romain Rolland: Lettres et autres écrits: 1961, in *Cahiers Romain Rolland,* No. 2., Paris, Albin Michel.

Rado, Sandor: (1928), 'The Problem of Melancholia', *Int. J. Psycho-Anal.* **9**, 420–438.

Raffel, Burton: (1968), '*The Lord of the Rings* as Literature' in Isaacs and Zimbardo, pp. 218–246.

Ramadas, G.: (1925), 'The Aboriginal Tribes in the *Rāmāyaṇa*', *Man in India* **5**, 22–45.

Ramana, C. V.: (1952), 'Observations of the Analysis of a Musician', *Samīkṣā* **6**, 229-242.

———: (1964), 'On the Early History and Development of Psychoanalysis in India', *J. Am. Psychoanal. Assoc.* **12**, 110–134.

*Ramanujan, A. K.: (1967), *The Interior Landscape: Love Poems from a Classical Tamil Anthology,* London, Peter Owen, 1970.

Rāmāyaṇa, [Sundarakāṇḍa]: (1966), critical ed., G. C. Jhala (ed.), Baroda, Oriental Institute.

Rangell, Leon: (1967), 'Psychoanalysis, Affects and the "human core": On the Relationship of Psychoanalysis to the Behavioral Sciences', *Psychoanal. Q.* **37**, 172–202.

Rao, S. K. Ramachandra: (1963), *Development of Psychological Thought in India,* Mysore, Kavyalaya.

Rapaport, David: (1951), *Organization and Pathology of Thought. Selected Sources. Translations and Commentaries,* New York, Columbia Univ. Press.

———: (1953), 'On the Psychoanalytic Theory of Affects' in *Collected Papers,* New York, Basic Books, 1967, pp. 313–328.

Rathborne, Isabel E.: (1937), *The Meaning of Spenser's Fairyland,* New York, Columbia Univ. Press.

Regamey, K: (1938), *Three Chapters from the Samādhirājasūtra*. Publications of the Oriental Commission, No. 1, Warsaw, The Warsaw Society of Sciences and Letters.

Regnard, P. (1887), *Sorcellerie, magnetisme, morphinisme, délire de grandeurs*, Paris, Lib. Plon.

Reich, A.: (1951), 'The Discussion of 1912 on Masturbation and Our Present-day View', *Psychoanal. Study Child* **6**, 80–94.

*Reider, N.: (1953), 'Reconstruction and Screen Function', *J. Am. Psychoanal. Assoc.* **1**, 389–405.

__________: (1959), 'Chess, Oedipus and the Mater Dolorosa', *Int. J. Psycho-Anal.* **40**, 320–333.

__________: (1960), 'Percept as a Screen: Economic and Structural Aspects', *J. Am. Psychoanal. Assoc.* **8**, 82–99.

Reilly, R. J.: (1968), 'Tolkien and the Fairy Story' in Isaacs and Zimbardo, pp. 128–150.

*Renou, Louis and Filliozat, Jean: (1947), *L'Inde classique: Manuel des études indiennes*, 2 Vols., Paris, Payot.

Rhys Davids, T.W.: (1880), *Buddhist Birth-Stories (Jātaka Tales). The Commentarial Introduction Entitled Nidāna-Kathā, the Story of the Lineage*, rev. ed. by Mrs. Rhys Davids, London, George Routledge, n.d.

Ribble, Margaret. A.: (1943), *The Rights of Infants: Early Psychological Needs and their Satisfaction*, New York, Columbia Univ. Press, 1965.

Rie, Herbert E.: (1966), 'Depression in Childhood: A Survey of Some Pertinent Contributions', *J. Am. Acad. Child Psychiat.* **5**, 653–685.

Ries, Hannah: (1945), 'An "Unwelcome Child" and Her Death Instinct', *Int. J. Psycho-Anal.* **26**, 153–161.

Rivière, Jacques: (1921), *The Ideal Reader: Selected Essays by Jacques Rivière*, translated by Blance A. Price (ed.), New York, Meridian Books, 1960.

Robichez, Jacques: (1961), *Romain Rolland*. Connaissance des Lettres, Vol. 57, Paris, Hatier.

Rockhill, W. W. (1884), *The Life of the Buddha Derived from Tibetan Works*, London.

Rohde, Erwin: (1894), *Seelencult und Unsterblichkeitsglaube der Griechen*, Leipzig, J. C. B. Mohr; English translation: *Psyche*, London, Routledge and Kegan Paul, 1925.

Roheim, G.: (1923), 'Psychoanalysis and the Folktale: A Rejoinder to a Recent Article', *Int. J. Psycho-Anal.* **3**, 180–186.

Rolland, Romain: (1929), *Essai sur la mystique et l'action de l'Inde vivante*. Vol. I *La vie de Ramakrishna*. Vols. II and III. *La vie de Vivekananda et l'évangile universel*, Paris, Librairie Stock, Delemain et Boutelleau.

____________: (1930), *Prophets of the New India*, translated by E. F. Malcolm-Smith, London, Casell and Co., 1930.

____________: (1960), *Inde: Journal (1915-1943)*, 2nd ed., enlarged, Paris, Éditions Albin Michel; 1st ed., Lausanne, 1951.

*Rosen, Victor H.: (1953), 'The Reconstruction of a Traumatic Childhood Event in a Case of Derealization', *J. Am. Psychoanal. Assoc.* **3**, 211–221.

Rosenberg (Zetzel), Elizabeth: (1949), 'Anxiety and the Capacity to Bear It', *Int. J. Psycho-Anal.* **30**, 1–12.

Rosenman, S.: (1956), 'Black Magic and Superego Formation', *Psychoanal. Rev.* **43**, 272–319.

*Rosenthal, David (ed.): (1963), *The Genain Quintuplets: A Case Study and Theoretical Analysis of Heredity and Environment in Schizophrenia*, New York, Basic Books.

Roshco, M.: (1967), 'Perception, Denial and Depersonalization', *J. Am. Psychoanal. Assoc.* **15**, 243–260.

Ross, Harry: (1938), *Utopias Old and New*, London, Nicolsen and Watson.

Ross, Nathaniel: (1958), 'Psychoanalysis and religion', *J. Am. Psychoanal. Assoc.* **6**, 519–529.

____________: (1968a), 'The "As If" Concept', *J. Am. Psychoanal. Assoc.* **16**, 59–82.

____________: (1968b), 'Beyond "The Future of an Illusion" ', *J. Hillside Hosp.* **17**, 259–276.

____________: (1975), 'Affect as Cognition: With Observations on the Meanings of Mystical States', *Int. Rev. Psycho-Anal.* **2**, 79–93.

Rowley, J. L.: (1951), 'Rumpelstilzkin in the Analytical Situation', *Int. J. Psycho-Anal.* **32**, 190–195.

Ruben, Walter: (1941), 'The Kṛṣṇacarita in the *Harivaṃśa* and Certain *Purāṇas*', *J. Am. Or. Soc.* **61**, 115–127.

____________: (1943), *Krishna. Konkordanz und Kommentar der Motive seines Heldenlebens*, Istanbul Yazilari, No. 17, Istanbul.

Rubinfiine, David L.: (1967), 'Notes on a Theory of Reconstruction', *Brit. J. Med. Psychol.* **40**, 195–206.

Rubinstein, Ben: (1955), 'The Meaning of the Cinderella Story in the Development of a Little Girl', *Am. Imago* **12**, 197–205.

Sachs, H.: (1923), 'Zur Genese der Perversionen', *Int. Z. Psa.* **9**, 172–182.

__________: (1941), 'Psychotherapy and the Pursuit of Happiness', *Am. Imago* **2**, 356–364.

__________: (1948), *Memories of Life and Art,* Cambridge, Sci-Art.

Sachs, Oscar: (1967), 'Distinctions between Fantasy and Reality Elements in Memory and Reconstructions', *Int. J. Psycho-Anal.* **48**, 416–423.

Saduktikarṇāmṛta of Śrīdharadāsa (13th Century): (1965), critical ed., Sures Chandra Banerji (ed.), Calcutta, K. L. Mukhopadhyay.

Sanderson, S. F.: (1973), 'The Cottingley Fairy Photographs: A Reappraisal of the Evidence', *Folklore* **84**, 89–101.

Sandler, Joseph and Joffe, Walter G.: (1965), 'Notes on childhood depression', *Int. J. Psycho-Anal.* **46**, 88–96.

Saradananda, Swami: (1911-1918), *Sri Ramakrishna the Great Naster: Originally Written in Bengali in 5 Vols. (Sri Ramakrishna Līla-prasaṅga),* by Swami Saradananda, a direct disciple of the master, translation by Swamí Jagadananda, Madras, Sri Ramakrishna Math, 1952.

Sarlin, Charles N.: (1962), 'Depersonalization and Derealization', *J, Am. Psychoanal. Assoc.* **10**, 784–804.

Sastri, Rama: (1952), *Pātañjala-Yogasūtra-bhāṣya vivaraṇam of Śaṅkara-Bhagavatpāda,* critical ed., Sri Rama Sastri and S. R. Krishnamurthi Sastri (eds.), Madras, Government Oriental Manuscripts Library.

Sāstrin, Duṇḍirāja: (1931), *Yogasūtras, with the Yogapradīpikā Vivṛtti,* Nyāyācārya Duṇḍirāja Śāstrin (ed.), Kashi Sanskrit Series, No. 85, Benares, Chowkhamba Sanskrit Series Office.

Saul, Leon J. (1938), 'Telepathic Sensitiveness as a Neurotic Symptom', *Psychoanal. Q.* **7**, 329–335.

__________ et al.: (1956), 'On Earliest Memories', *Psychoanal. Q.* **25**, 228–237.

*Schachtel, Ernest G.: (1947), 'On Memory and Childhood Amnesia', *Psychiatry* **10**, 1–26.

Schafer, R.: (1960), 'The Loving and Beloved Superego in Freud's Structural Theory', *Psychoanal. Study Child* **15**, 163–188.

———: (1964), 'The Clinical Analysis of Affects', *J. Am. Psychoanal. Assoc.* **12**, 275–299.

*———: (1956), 'Leonardo and Freud: An Art-Historical Study', *J. Hist. Ideas* **17**, 147–178.

Scharfstein, Ben-Ami: (1973), *Mystical Experience*, Oxford, Basil Blackwell.

Schilder, P.: (1935), *The Image and Appearance of the Human Body*, New York, Int. Univ. Press, 1950.

Schmideberg, Melitta: (1936), 'A Note on Suicide', *Int. J. Psycho-Anal.* **17**, 1-5.

———: (1946), 'On Querulance', *Psychoanal. Q.* **15**, 472–501.

———: (1950), 'Infant Memories and Constructions', *Psychoanal. Q.* **19**, 468–481.

———: (1956), 'Delinquent Acts as Perversions and Fetishes', *Int. J. Psycho-Anal.* **37**, 422–424.

*Schmidt, Richard: (1908), *Fakire und Fakirtum im alten und modernen Indien: Yoga-Lehre und Yoga Praxis*, Berlin, Hermann Barsdorf.

———: (1922), *Beiträge zur Indischen Erotik. Das Liebesleben des Sanskritvolkes*, Berlin, Hermann Barsdorf Verlag.

*Scholem, Gershom: (1957), *Sabbatai Ṣevi: The Mystical Messiah, 1626-1676*, translated by R. J. Zwi Werblowsky, Princeton, Princeton Univ. Press, 1973.

Schreiber, Sanford: (1974), 'A Filmed Fairy Tale as a Screen Memory', *Psychoanal. Study Child* **29**, 389–410.

Schroeder. T.: (1922), 'Prenatal Psychisms and Mystical Pantheisms', *Int. J. Psycho-Anal.* **3**, 445–466.

Schuhl, Pierre-Maxime: (1969), *L'imagination et le merveilleux*, Paris, Flammarion.

Schur, Max: (1953), 'The Ego in Anxiety' in *Drives, Affects, Behaviour*, R. M. Loewenstein (ed.), New York, Int. Univ. Press. pp. 67–103.

———: (1960), 'Phylogenesis and Ontogenesis of Affect- and Structure-Formation and the Phenomenon of Repetition Compulsion', *Int. J. Psycho-Anal.* **41**, 275–287.

———: (1966a), *The Id and the Regulatory Principles of Mental Functioning*, New York, Int. Univ. Press.

*__________: (1966b), 'Some Additional "Day Residues" of "The Specimen Dream of Psychoanalysis" ' in *Psychoanalysis – A General Psychology: Essays in Honor of Heinz Hartmann*, R. M. Loewenstein et al. (eds.), New York, Int. Univ. Press, pp. 45–85.

__________: (1969), 'Affects and Cognition', *Int. J. Psycho-Anal.* **50**, 647–653.

*__________: (1972), *Freud: Living and Dying*, New York, Int. Univ. Press.

Schwarzbaum, Haim: (1968), *Studies in Jewish and World Folklore*, Supplement-Serie zu *Fabula*, Vol. 3, Berlin, Walter de Gruyter and Co.

Segal, Hanna: (1955), 'A Psycho-Analytical Approach to Aesthetics' in *New Directions in Psychoanalysis: The Significance of Infant Conflict in the Pattern of Adult Behavior*, M. Klein et al. (eds.), London, Tavistock Publications, pp. 384–405.

Segal, N. P.: (1961), reporter on 'The Psychoanalytic Theory of the Symbolic Process', *J. Am. Psychoanal. Assoc.* **9**, 146–157.

Seidensticker, E. (translator): (1964), *The Gossamer Years: The Diary of a Noblewoman of Heian Japan*, Tokyo, Charles E. Tuttle.

Sen, Rai Saheb Dineschandra: (1920), *The Bengali Ramayana*, Calcutta, Univ. of Calcutta.

*Senart, E.: (1882), *Essai sur la légende du Buddha, son caractère et ses origines*, 2nd ed., rev., Paris, Ernest Leroux.

__________: (1900), 'Bouddhisme et yoga', *Revue de l'histoire des religions* **41**, 345–364.

__________: (1930), *Chāndogya-Upaniṣad*, Paris, Société d'édition "Les Belles Lettres".

*__________: (1934), *Bṛhad-Āraṇyaka-Upaniṣad*, Paris, Société d'éditions "Les Belles Letters".

Servadio, Emilio: (1958), 'Magic and the Castration-Complex', *Int. J. Psychoanal.* **39**, 147–150.

__________: (1966), 'A Psychodynamic Approach to Yoga Experience', *Int. J. Parapsychol.* **8**, 181–191.

*Seung, Ok-Ryen: (1971), *Psychopédagogie du conte (Essai suivi de seize contes coréens)*, Paris, Éditions Fleurus.

Shafli, Mohammad: (1973), 'Silence in the Service of the Ego: Psychoanalytic Study of Meditation', *Int. J. Psychoanal.* **54**, 431–444.

*Shahidullah, M. (ed. and translator): (1928), *Les chants mystiques de Kaṇha et de Sarāha: Les Dohā-kośa et les Caryā*, Paris, 1928, reprinted, L. Misch (ed.), Library of Congress, 1958.

Shapiro, Meyer: (1950), *Vincent van Gogh,* New York, Harry N. Abrahams.

*Sharpe, Ella Freeman: (1930), 'The Technique of Psycho-analysis. Seven Lectures' in *Collected Papers on Psycho-Analysis.* pp. 9–124. Ed. by M. Brierly. London: The Hogarth Press, 1968.

*____________: (1934-1936), *Dream Analysis,* London, The Hogarth Press, 1961.

____________: (1943), 'Cautionary Tales' in *Collected Papers on Psycho-Analysis,* pp. 170–182.

Shastri, Haraprasad (ed.): (1910), *Saundarananda Kāvya of Ārya Bhadanta Aśvaghoṣa,* Reissued with additions by Chintaharan Chakravarti, Calcutta, Royal Asiatic Society, 1939.

Shastri, Suryakanta: (1950), *The Flood Legend in Sanskrit Literature,* Delhi, S. Chand and Co.

*Shengold, L.: (1963), 'The Parent as Sphinx', *J. Am. Psychoanal.* Assoc. **11**, 416–423.

*____________: (1967), 'The Effects of Overstimulation: Rat People', *Int. J. Psycho-Anal.* **48**, 403–415.

____________: (1978), 'Kaspar Hauser and Soul Murder: A Study of Deprivation', *Int. Rev. Psycho-Anal.* **5**, 457–476.

Shukla, Badarinath: (1970), *Tantrasaṅgrahah,* Vol. 2, Gopinath Kaviraj (ed.), in the *Yogatantragranthamālā,* Vol. 4, B. S. (ed.), Banaras, Varaneyasya Sanskrit Vishvavidyalay.

Siegman, Alfred J. (1954), 'Emotionality: A Hysterical Character Defence', *Psychoanal. Q.* **23**, 339–354.

____________: (1956), 'The Psychological Economy of *Déjà Raconté', Psychoanal. Q.* **25**, 83–86.

Sierksma, F.: (1966), *Tibet's Terrifying Deities: Sex and Aggression in Religious Acculturation,* Rutland, Charles E. Tuttle.

Siggins, Lorraine D.: (1966), 'Mourning: A critical survey of the literature', *Int. J. Psycho-Anal.* **47**, 14–25.

Simmel, E. (1925), 'A Screen Memory *in Statu Nascendi', Int. J. Psycho-Anal.* **6**, 454–457.

*____________: (1948), 'Alcoholism and Addiction', *Psychoanal. Q.* **17**, 6–31.

Singer, Milton (ed.): (1966), *Krishna: Myths, Rites and Attitudes,* Honolulu, East-West Center Press.

Singh, J. A. L. and Zingg, Robert M.: (1939), *Wolf-Children and Feral Man. Contributions of the Univ. of Denver,* New York, Harper and Brothers.

Sinha, T.C.: (1966), 'Development of Psycho-analysis in India', *Int. J. Psycho-Anal.* **47**, 427–439.

*Sirén, Osvald: (1956-1958), *Chinese Painting: Leading Masters and Principles,* 7 Vols., London, Lund, Humphries.

Skinner, John: (1957), 'James M. Barrie, or the Boy who Wouldn't Grow Up', *Am. Imago* **14**, 111–141.

Slap, J. W.: (1966), 'On Sarcasm', *Psychoanal. Q.* **35**, 98–107.

Sloman, Albert E.: (1961), 'La Vida es Sueño by Don Pedro Calderón de la Barca', edited with introduction and notes, Manchester, University of Manchester Press.

Smirnoff, V. N.: (1967), 'Le souvenir-écran', *Bull. Assoc. Psa. Fra.* **2**, 27–62.

Smith, Lillian H. (1953), *The Unreluctant Years: A Critical Approach to Children's Literature,* New York, The Viking Press, 1967.

Snellgrove, David and Richardson, Hugh: (1968), *A Cultural History of Tibet,* New York, Frederick A. Praeger.

Socarides, C. W.: (1971), 'On Disillusionment: The Desire to Remain Disappointed', *Brit. J. Med. Psychol.* **44**, 35–44.

———: (1974), 'The Demonified Mother: A Study of Voyeurism and Sexual Sadism', *Int. Rev. Psycho-Anal.* **1**, 187–195.

——— (ed.): (1977), *The World of Emotions: Clinical Studies of Affects and Their Expression,* New York, Int. Univ. Press.

Solomon, Joseph C.: (1958), 'Fugue in a Four-Year-Old', *Psychoanal. Q.* **27**, 101–103.

Soper, Alexander C.: (1941), 'Early Chinese Landscape Painting', *Art Bulletin* **23**.

Sörensen, S.: (1904), *An Index to the Names in the Mahābhārata,* London, Ernest Benn.

*Soriano, Marc: (1968), *Les contes de Perrault: Culture savante et traditions populaires,* Paris, Gallimard.

Sperling, Melitta: (1950), 'Children's Interpretation and Reaction to the Unconscious of Their Mothers', *Int. J. Psycho-Anal.* **31**, 36–41.

___________: (1963), 'Fetishism in Children', *Psychoanal. Q.* **32**, 374–392.

___________: (1970), 'The Clinical Effects of Parental Neurosis on the Child' in *Parenthood: Its Psychonolgy and Psychopathology,* James E, Anthony and Therese Benedek (eds.), Boston, Little, Brown and Co.

Sperling, O. E.: (1954), 'An Imaginary Companion Representing a Prestage of the Superego', *Psychoanal. Study Child* **9**, 252–258.

*Sperling, Samuel J.: (1953), 'On Denial and the Essential Nature of Defence', *Int. J. Psycho-Anal.* **39**, (1958), 25–38.

Spindler, George D. (ed.): (1978), *The Making of Psychological Anthropology,* Berkeley, Univ. of Calif. Press.

*Spitz, R. (1945), 'Hospitalism: An Inquiry into the Genesis of Psychiatric Conditions in Early Childhood', *Psychoanal. Study Child* **1**, 53–74.

*___________: (1946), 'Anaclitic Depression: An Inquiry into the Genesis of Psychiatric Conditions in Early Childhood, II', *Psychoanal. Study Child* **2** 313–342.

___________: (1946b), 'Hospitalism: A Follow-up Report', *Psychoanal. Study Child* **2**, 113–117.

___________: (1949), 'Autoerotism: Some Empirical Findings and Hypotheses on Three of Its Manifestations in the First Year of Life', *Psychoanal. Study Child* **3/4**, 85–120.

___________: (1950), 'Relevancy of Direct Infant Observation', *Psychoanal. Study Child* **5**, 66–73.

___________: (1951a), 'Enviornment versus Race: Environment as an Etiological Factor in Psychiatric Disturbances in Infancy' in *Psychoanalysis and Culture,* G.B. Wilbur and W. Muensterberger (eds.), New York, Int. Univ. Press, pp. 32–41.

___________: (1951b), 'The Psychogenic Diseases in Infancy: An Attempt at Their Etiologic Classification', *Psychoanal. Study Child* **6**, 255–275.

___________: (1952), 'Authority and Masturbation', *Psychoanal. Q.* **21**, 490–527.

Spitzer, Leo: (1944), *Classical and Christian Ideas of World Harmony: Prolegomena to an Interpretation of the Word 'Stimmung'.* Anna G. Hatcher (ed.), Preface by René Wellek, Baltimore, The Johns Hopkins Press, 1963.

Sprague de Camp, L.: (1954), *Lost Continents: The Atlantis Theme in History, Science, and Literature,* New York, Gnome Press.

Spratt, P.: (1966), *Hindu Culture and Personality: A Psycho-Analytic Study,* Bombay, Manaktalas.

Spring, W. J.: (1939), 'Observations on World-Destruction Fantasies', *Psychoanal. Q.* **8**, 48–56.

Staal, Frits: (1975), *Exploring Mysticism,* London, Penguin.

Stace, W. T.: (1961), *Mysticism and Philosophy,* London, Macmillan.

Stamm, Julian L.: (1962), 'Altered Ego States Allied to Depersonalization', *J. Am. Psychoanal. Assoc.* **10**, 762–783.

Stanford, W. B.: (1954), *The Ulysses Theme: A Study in the Adaptability of a Traditional Hero*, Oxford. Basil Blackwell.

Starbuck, E. D.: (1900), *The Psychology of Religion: An Empirical Study of the Growth of Religious Consciousness,* Preface by William James, London, Walter Scott, 1900.

Starobinski, Jean: (1966), 'The Idea of Nostalgia', *Diogenes* **54**, 81–103.

Starr, William T.: (1971), *Romain Rolland: One Against All: A Biography,* The Hague, Mouton.

*Stauffer, Donald W.: (1930), *English Biography Before 1700,* Cambridge, Harvard Univ. Press.

*Stein, M.: (1965), 'States of Consciousness in the Analytic Situation: Including a Note on the Traumatic Dream' in *Drives, Affects, Behaviour,* Vol. 2., M. Schur (ed.), New York, Int. Univ. Press.

Stein, R. A.: (1962), *La civilization tibétaine,* Paris, Dunod.

__________: (1971), 'Illumination subite ou saisie simultanée: Note sur la terminologie chinoise et tibétaine', *Revue de l'Histoire des Religions* **179**, 3–30.

__________: (1972), *Vie et chants de 'brug-pa kun-legs le Yogin*, traduit du Tibétain et annoté, Paris, G.P. Maisonneuve et Larose.

Stephen, Karin: (1934), 'Introjection and Projection: Guilt and Rage', *Brit. J. Med. Psychol.* **14**, 316–331.

Sterba, R.: (1940), 'Aggression in Rescue Phantasy', *Psychoanal. Q.* **9**, 505–508.

__________ and Sterba, E.: (1954), *Beethoven and his Nephew: A Psycho-Analytic Study of their Relationship,* New York, Pantheon Books.

Stern, Max M.: (1961), 'Blank Hallucinations: Some Remarks about Trauma and Perceptual Disturbances', *Int. J. Psycho-Anal.* **42**, 205–210.

Stevenson, Ian: (1975), *Cases of the Reincarnation Type. Vol. 1 Ten Cases in India,* Charlottesville, Univ. Press of Virginia.

Stewart, Walter A.: (1964), Reporter for Panel on Depersonalization. *J. Am. Psychoanal. Assoc.* **12**, 171–186.

Stoller, R. J.: (1966), 'The Mother's Contribution to Infantile Transvestic Behaviour', *Int. J. Psycho-Anal.* **47**, 384–395.

__________: (1968), *Sex and Gender,* Vol. 1, New York, Science House; Vol. 2. New York, Jason Aronson, 1975.

__________: (1970), 'The Transsexual Boy: Mother's Feminized Phallus', *Brit. J. Med. Psychol.* **43**, 117–128.

__________: (1975), *Perversion: The Erotic Form of Hatred,* New York, Pantheon Books.

Storch, A.: (1922), *The Primitive Archaic Forms of Inner Experiences and Thought in Schizophrenia: A Genetic and Clinical Study of Schizophrenia,* translated by Clara Willard, Nervous and Mental Disease Monograph Series, No. 36, New York, 1924.

Strachey, James: (1934), 'The Nature of the Therapeutic Action of Psychoanalysis', *Int. J. Psycho-Anal.* **15**, 127–159.

Stuart, Duane Reed: (1931), 'Author's Lives as Revealed in Their Works: A Critical Resumé' in *Classical Studies in Honor of John C. Rolfe,* G. D. Hadzsits (ed.), Philadelphia, Univ. of Penn. Press, pp. 285–304.

Sukthankar, Vishnu S.: (1942), The *Āraṇyakaparavan,* Part II, Vol. 4, *Critical Edition of the Mahābhārata,* Poona, Bhandarkar Oriental Reearch Institute.

*__________: 'The Bhṛgus and the Bharata; A Text Historical Study', *Annals of the Bhandarkar Oriental Research Institute* 18: 1–76, reprinted in *Critical Studies in the Mahābhārata,* P. K. Gode (ed.), Poona, V. S. Sukthankar Memorial Edition Committee, Vol. 1, Bombay: Karnatak Pub. House, 1944.

Sullivan, Michael: (1955), 'Notes on Early Chinese Landscape Painting', *Harvard J. Asian Studies* **18**.

__________: (1962), *The Birth of Landscape Painting in China,* London, Routledge and Kegan Paul.

__________: (1974), *The Three Perfections: Chinese Painting, Poetry and Calligraphy,* London, Thames and Hudson.

Suzuki, D.T. and Hokei Idzumi: (1934-1936), The *Gaṇḍavyūhasūtra,* Kyoto, The Sanskrit Buddhist Texts Publication Society.

Svendsen, M.: (1934), 'Children's Imaginary Companions', *Arch. Neur. Psychiat.* **2**, 985–999.

Szasz, Thomas S,: (1958), 'The Role of the Counterphobic Mechanism in Addiction', *J. Am. Psychoanal. Assoc.* **6**, 309–325.

*Tadapatrikar, S. N., 'The Kṛṣṇa Problem', *Annals of the Bhandarkar Oriental Research Institute,* pp. 269–343.

Taṃḍana, R.: (1960), *Rāsapaṃcādhyāyī,* Lucknow, Hindi Sāhitya Bhāṃdāra.

Tarachow, Sidney: (1965), 'Ambiguity and Human Imperfection', *J. Am. Psychoanal. Assoc.* **13**, 85–101.

Thakur, Upendra: (1963), *The History of Suicide in India,* Delhi, Munshi Ram Manoharlal.

*Thomas, E. J.: (1927), *The Life of the Buddha as Legend and History,* London, Kegan and Paul, Trench, Trubner and Co., 1931.

Thompson, Stith and Balys, Jonas: (1958), *The Oral Tales of India,* Indiana Univ. Publication Folklore Series, No. 10, Bloomington, Indiana Univ. Press.

____________ and Roberts, Warren E.: (1960), *Types of Indic Oral Tales: India, Pakistan and Ceylon,* Folklore Fellows Communications, No. 180, Helsinki, Academia Scientiarum Fennica.

Thwaite, M. F.: (1963), *From Primer to Pleasure: An Introduction to the History of Children's Books in England,* London, The Library Association, 1963.

*Timpanaro, Sebastiano: (1974), *The Freudian Slip: Psychoanalysis and Textual Criticism,* translated from the Italian (*Il Lapsus Freudiano,* pub. by La Nuova Italia) by Kate Soper, London, NLB Atlantic Highlands, Humanities Press, 1976.

Tolkien, J. R. R.: (1937), 'On Fairy-Stories' in *Essays Presented to Charles Williams,* Oxford, Oxford Univ. Press, 1947, pp. 38–89, rpt. Grand Rapids, W. B. Erdman's Pub. Co., 1968.

Trevor, M. H.: (1969), *The Ox and his Herdsman: A Chinese Zen Text,* translated from the Tsujimuro-Buchner versions, Tōkyō, The Hokuseidō Press.

Trilling, Lionel: (1945), 'Art and Neurosis, in *The Liberal Imagination.* New York, Viking.

____________: (1964), 'The Fate of Pleasure: Wordsworth to Dostoevsky' in *Literary Views,* C. Camden (ed.), Chicago, Rice Univ. Semicentennial Series.

Truzzo, Marcello: (1972), 'The Occult Revival as Popular Culture: Some Random Observations on the Old and Nouveau Witch', *Soc. Q.* **13**, 16–36.

Tucci, G.: (1956), *To Lhasa and Beyond: Diary of the Expedition to Tibet in the Year 1948*, with an appendix on Tibetan medicine and hygiene by R. Moise, translated by Mario Carelli, Rome, Libreria della Stato.

__________: (1958), *Minor Buddhist Texts. Part II. Bhāvanākrama* of Kamalaśīla: Sanskrit and Tibetan Texts with Introduction and English summary, Serie Orientale Roma, 9, Rome, Is. M. E. O.

__________: (1971), *Minor Buddhist Texts*. Part III, Third *Bhāvanākrama*, Serie Orientale Roma, 43, Rome Is. M. E. O.

Underhill, Evelyn: (1911), *Mysticism*, New York, E. P. Dutton, 1961.

Vahia, N. S.: (1967), 'Psychiatry in India', *Topical Probl. Psychiat. Neurol.* **5**, 85–101.

Vaidya, P. L.: (ed.): (1960), *Gaṇḍavyūhasūtra*, Buddhist Sanskrit Texts, No. 5, Darbhanga, Mithila Institute of Post-Graduate Studies and Research in Sanskrit Learning.

Valenstein, Arthur F.: (1962), 'Affects, Emotional Reliving, and Insight in the Psychoanalytic Process', *Int. J. Psycho-Anal.* **43**, 315–324.

__________: (1973), 'On Attachment to Painful Feelings and the Negative Therapeutic Reaction', *Psychoanal. Study Child* **28**, 365–392.

Van Gulik, R. H.: (1958), *Chinese Pictorial Art as Viewed by the Connoisseur*, Rome.

*__________: (1967), *The Gibbon in China: An Essay on Chinese Animal Lore*, Leiden, E. J. Brill.

Vandendriessche, G.: (1972), 'La relation entre la pulsion et la fonction congitive dans le rêve de la monographie botanique et le souvenir – écran de la scène dans la prairie', *Revue Française de Psychanalyse* **36**, 987–998.

Vandier-Nicolas, Nicole: (1963), *Art et sagesse en Chine: Mi Fou (1051-1101)*, Annales du Musée Guimet, Paris, Presses Universitaires de France.

Vaudeville, Charlotte: (1975), 'The Cowherd-God in Ancient India' in *Pastoralists and Nomads in South Asia*, L. Saadia Leshnik and G. Sontheimer (eds.), Wiesbaden, Otto Harrassowitz, pp. 90–116.

Vidyāsāgara, Jīvānanda: (1901), *Ashtabakra-Samhīta: A Treatise on Vedanta Philosophy by Ashtabakra Muni*, with a full commentary by Pandit Kulapati Shri Jibananda Vidyasagara (ed.), Calcutta, Siddheshwar Press.

Vinge, Louise: (1967), *The Narcissus Theme in Western European Literature Up to the Early 19th Century*, translated from the Swedish by R. Dewsnap et al., Lund, Glurups.

Viṣṇupurāṇa: (1882), Jibanada Vidyasagara (ed.), with the commendary of Śrīdharasvāmī, Calcutta, Saraswati Press, 1882 also: Munilal Gupta (ed.), Gorakhpur, Gitapress, Saṃvat, 1890.

Waelder, Robert: (1930), 'The Principle of Multiple Function', *Psychoanal. Q.* **5**, 45–62.

__________: (1937), 'The Problem of the Genesis of Psychical Conflict in Earliest Infancy', *Int. J. Psycho-Anal.* **18**, 406–473.

__________: (1967), 'Inhibitions, Symptoms and Anxiety: Forty Years Later', *Psychoanal. Q.* **36**, 1–36.

Wahl, C. W.: (1957), 'Suicide as a Magic Act', *Bull. of the Menninger Clinic* **21**, 91–98.

Waldhorn, H. F. and Fine, B. D.: (1974), *Symbolism: Monograph V of the Kris Study Group of the New York Psychoanalytic Institute,* New York, Int. Univ. Press.

Waldschmidt, E.: (1944-1948), *Die Uberlieferung vom Lebensende des Buddha,* Abhandlungen der Akademie der Wissenschaften in Göttingen, Phil.-Hist. Klasse, Dritte Folge, No. 29–30. Göttingen.

Waley, Arthur: (1923), *An Introduction to the Study of Chinese Painting,* London, Ernest Benn.

*__________: (1942), *Monkey by Wu Ch'êng'ên,* translated from the Chinese, London, George Allen and Unwin.

*__________: (1946), *Chinese Poems,* London, Allen and Unwin.

__________: (1955), *The Nine Songs: A Study of Shamanism in Ancient China,* London, Allen and Unwin.

__________: (1956), *Yuan Mei: Eighteenth Century Chinese Poet,* London, George Allen and Unwin.

Walter, H.: (1968), 'Depersonalization and Self-Destruction', *Am. J. Psychoanal. Assoc.* **125**, 399–401.

*Warren, Henry Clarke: (1922), *Buddhism in Translations,* Harvard Oriental Series, Vol. 3, Cambridge, Harvard Univ. Press.

Wangh, Martin: (1954), 'Day Residue in Dream and Myth', *J. Am. Psychoanal. Assoc.* **2**, 446–452.

Wax, M. and Wax, R.: (1963), 'The Notion of Magic', *Current Anthropology* **4**, 495–518.

Weiss, Edoardo: (1935), 'Agoraphobia and Its Relation to Hysterical Attacks and to Trauma', *Int. J. Psycho-Anal.* **16**, 59–83.

____________: (1942a), 'Psychic Defence and the Technique of Analysis', *Int. J. Psycho-Anal.* **23**, 69–80.

*____________: (1942b), 'Emotional Memories and Acting Out', *Psychoanal. Q.* **11**, 477–492.

____________: (1944), 'Clinical Aspects of Depression', *Psychoanal. Q.* **13**, 445–461.

Weiss, Joseph: (1959), 'Intensity as a Character Trait', *Psychoanal. Q.* **28**, 64–72.

Weissman, Philip: (1966), 'The Counterphobic State and Its Objects', *Int. J. Psycho-Anal.* **47**, 486–491.

Wenger, M. A. and Bagchi, B. K.: (1961), 'Studies of Autonomic Functions in Practitioners of Yoga in India', *Behav. Sci.* **6**, 312–323.

Werman, D. S.: (1977), 'Normal and Pathological Nostalgia', *J. Am. Psychoanal. Assoc.* **25**.

____________: (1979), 'Chance, Ambiguity and Psychological-mindedness', *Psychoanal. Q.* **48**, 107–115.

Wermer, H. and Leving, S.: (1967), 'Masturbation Fantasies', *Psychoanal. Study Child* **22**, 315–328.

Whitehead, Harriet: (1974), 'Reasonably Fantastic: Some Perspectives on Scientology Science Fiction and Occultism' in Zaretsky, pp. 547–587.

Whiting, Beatrice B.: (1963), *Six Cultures: Studies of Child Rearing,* New York, John Wiley and Sons.

Widdowson, John: (1973), 'The Witch as a Frightening and Threatening Figure' in *The Witch Figure: Folklore Essays in Honor of K. M. Brigg.* Venetial Newall (ed.), London, Routledge and Kegan Paul.

Wilson, Edmund: (1956), 'Oo, Those Awful Orcs!' in *The Bit Between My Teeth: A Literary Chronicle of 1950-1965,* New York, Farrar Strauss and Giroux, 1965.

*Wilson, H. H.: (1840), *The Vishnu Purāṇa, a System of Hindu Mythology and Tradition,* 5 Vols., Fitzedward Hall (ed.), London, John Murray.

*Winternitz, M.: (1904-1920), *Geschichte der Indischen Literatur,* 3 Vols., Leipzig; English translation: *A History of Indian Literature, 1927-1963,* New Delhi, Motilal Banarsidass.

____________: (1937), Bhāsa and the *Mahābhārata* and Kṛṣṇa plays of the Trivandrum series, *Bull. of the Ramavarma Research Institute (Trichur)* **5**, 1–15.

Wittkower, R.: (1963), *Born Under Saturn,* The Character and Conduct of Artists, London, Weidenfeld and Nicholson, (1967).

Wolfenstein, Martha: (1950), 'Some Variants in Moral Training of Children', *Psychoanal. Study Child* **5**, 310–328.

———: (1966), 'How is Mourning Possible?', *Psychoanal. Study Child* **21**, 93–123.

———: (1969), 'Loss, Rage and Repetition', *Psychoanal. Study Child* **24**, 432–460.

Woodbury, Michael A.: (1966), 'Altered Body-Ego Experience', *J. Am. Psychoanal. Assoc.* **14**, 273–303.

Woods, James Haugton: (1914), *The Yoga System of Patañjali: Or the Ancient Hindu Doctrine of Concentration of Mind (Yogasūtras, Yogabhāṣya,* and Vācaspatimiśra *Tattvaviśāradī),* Harvard Oriental Series, Vol. 17, Cambridge, Harvard Univ. Press, 1927.

Woolf, M.: (1955), 'On Castration Anxiety', *Int. J. Psycho-Anal.* **36**, 95–107.

*Woolner, A. C. and Sarup, L.: (1930-31), *Thirteen Trivandrum Plays,* 3 Vols., London, Oxford Univ. Press.

Yearsley, Mcleod: (1924), *The Folklore of Fairy-Tale,* London, Watts and Co.

Yerkes, Robert M. and Yerkes, Ada W.: (1929), *The Great Apes: A Study of Anthropoid Life,* New Haven, Yale Univ. Press.

**Yogavāsiṣṭhamahārāmāmayaṇa*: (1937), Wāsudev Laxman Śāstrī Panśikar (ed.), 3rd ed., revised by Narayan Ram Acharya, 2 Vols., Bombay, Nirnayasagar Press.

Yoshirō, Imaeda: (1975), 'Documents tibetains de Touen-houang concernant le concile de Tibet', *Journal Asiatique,* 1975, 125–156.

Zaehner, R. C.: (1957), *Mysticism, Sacred and Profane: An Inquiry into Some Varieties of Praeter-natural Experiences,* Oxford, Clarendon Press.

———: (1960), *Hindu and Muslim Mysticism,* London, Univ. of London, Athlone Press.

Zaretsky, Irving I. and Leone, Mark P. (eds.): (1974), *Religious Movements in Contemporary America,* Princeton, Princeton Univ. Press.

Zetzel, E. R.: (1965), 'Depression and the Incapacity to Bear It' in *Drives, Affects, Behaviour,* Vol. 2, M. Schur (ed.), New York, Int. Univ. Press, pp. 243–277.

*Zilboorg, Gregory: (1933), 'Anxiety without Affect', *Psychoanal. Q.* **2**, 48–67.

———: (1938), 'The Sense of Immortality', *Psychoanal. Q.* **7**, 171–199.

———: (1941), 'The Sense of Reality', *Psychoanal. Q.* **10**, 183–210.

———: (1943), 'Fear of Death', *Psychoanal. Q.* **12**, 465–475.

Zimmer, Heinrich: (1942), *Myths and Symbols in Indian Art and Civilization,* Joseph Campbell (ed.) Bollingen Series VI, New York, Pantheon Books, 1963.

INDEX

Index prepared by Alex von Brand

GPSR Compliance

The European Union's (EU) General Product Safety Regulation (GPSR) is a set of rules that requires consumer products to be safe and our obligations to ensure this.

If you have any concerns about our products, you can contact us on ProductSafety@springernature.com

In case Publisher is established outside the EU, the EU authorized representative is:

Springer Nature Customer Service Center GmbH
Europaplatz 3
69115 Heidelberg, Germany

Batch number: 10823959

Printed by Printforce, the Netherlands